W9-DBZ-130

CULTURE

AND

NEGOTIATION

For
Anne, Aurélia, and Elise Faure and
Carol, Sally, David, and Noah Rubin

CULTURE
AND
NEGOTIATION

THE RESOLUTION
OF WATER DISPUTES

edited by

Guy Olivier Faure
Jeffrey Z. Rubin

Sponsored jointly by the
United Nations Educational, Scientific, and Cultural Organization
and the International Institute for Applied Systems Analysis

SAGE Publications
International Educational and Professional Publisher
Newbury Park   London   New Delhi

For information address:

 SAGE Publications, Inc.
2455 Teller Road
Newbury Park, California 91320

SAGE Publications Ltd.
6 Bonhill Street
London EC2A 4PU
United Kingdom

SAGE Publications India Pvt. Ltd.
M-32 Market
Greater Kailash I
New Delhi 110 048 India

Printed in the United States of America

Library of Congress Cataloging-in-Publication Data

Main entry under title:

Culture and negotiation : the resolution of water disputes / edited by
    Guy Olivier Faure, Jeffrey Z. Rubin.
        p.   cm.
    "Sponsored jointly by the United Nations Educational, Scientific, and Cultural Organization and the International Institute for Applied Systems Analysis."
    Includes bibliographical references and index.
    ISBN 0-8039-5370-4 (cl.)   — ISBN 0-8039-5371-2 (pb)
    1. Diplomatic negotiations in international disputes—Cultural aspects. 2. Water rights. I. Faure, Guy. II. Rubin, Jeffrey Z.
JX4473.C85   1993
327.2—dc20   93-27755

93 94 95 96   10 9 8 7 6 5 4 3 2 1

Sage Production Editor: Diane S. Foster

Contents

Foreword

I take pleasure in introducing this study on culture and negotiation, which is the outcome of fruitful cooperation between UNESCO and the International Institute for Applied Systems Analysis (IIASA). UNESCO is grateful to IIASA for having assembled a panel of authors enabling this important and complex subject to be treated from a variety of standpoints.

There is, at the present time, a growing awareness of the pervasive influence of culture on all facets of human existence, not least on a society's choice and pursuit of its development goals. The World Decade for Cultural Development (1988-1997), for which UNESCO is the lead agency, has among its main purposes to promote the incorporation of a cultural dimension into development thinking and to contribute to the affirmation and enrichment of cultural identities. The marked contemporary trend toward globalization heightens the importance of recognizing and nourishing humanity's diverse cultural roots. Reconciling local allegiances with global affinities, fostering a vision of the whole that accommodates the diversity of the parts, is one of the great challenges with which our world is confronted.

This challenge is nowhere greater than in the environmental sphere, where the safeguarding of local interests is inseparable from concern for the planet at large. The obligation to think globally, moreover, cannot be confined to any one sphere: Environmental questions are bound up with a whole series of development issues, including the cultural ends that particular forms of development presuppose. Beyond the specific agreements reached at Rio de Janeiro in 1992, the most significant achievement of the United Nations Conference on Environment and Development was the consecration of a vision of global solidarity linked to an affirmation of the value of cultural diversity.

The Rio summit was itself the demonstration of the importance of negotiation in reconciling human beings to their simultaneously local and global addresses in the universe. The conference, which began with the threat of a North-South confrontation, was able, through sustained discussion, to achieve a fair degree of consensus and to conclude agreements on some vital issues. Such diplomacy clearly will be at a premium in the efforts of the international community to strengthen and extend the Rio agreements in the interests of the health and well-being of the present and future inhabitants of the planet. More generally, the fostering of negotiating skills, cultural understanding, and the spirit of cooperation at all levels of society will be essential if we are to move beyond the conflicts and confrontations of a war culture toward a genuine culture of peace.

The cultural factors bearing on international negotiations are a topic of obvious importance, not least in the environmental field, where so many essential concerns converge and where the need for agreement is so urgent. The strength of this book, it seems to me, is to combine a lucid and comprehensive discussion of issues and concepts with a series of case studies concerning specific rivers and the people who live and produce on their banks and tributaries. The result throws interesting light on the cultural parameters of human agreement and discord, offers useful, practical pointers to the art of negotiation, and highlights some profitable lines of future research.

Culture may, in fact, serve as bridge or barrier. In a world where modern communications are abolishing physical distance, resources are shrinking, population is growing exponentially, and environmental problems are escalating, reflexes of understanding and sharing become an evolutionary necessity. We are challenged to throw off, as Lewis Mumford put it in his *Condition of Man,* "the fatal temptation to worship our dead selves and perpetuate our past mistakes." We must dare to renew ourselves by renewing our vision of our relationship with others and with nature. Our inclination and capacity to negotiate agreements with one another will be a significant indicator of our progress in this regard.

Federico Mayor
Director-General of UNESCO

Preface

What is it that cannot quite be seen but follows us around constantly? And what is it that remains when all else is forgotten, yet is so much a part of our daily lives that we take it for granted? The answer to both questions, of course, is *culture.*

Even as one poses abstract riddles of this sort, the world is becoming a smaller, more interdependent place. New and remarkable forms of communication and transportation technology have made it easier for ideas and individuals to find their way to every corner of the globe. Simultaneously, old political lines of division—witness the collapse of the Berlin Wall in this regard, a symbol of the cold war's demise—have blurred with astonishing speed, even as new multinational economic communities have emerged in their place. To all of this must be added the increasing awareness of the global dangers posed by various threats to our environment.

Each of these factors, alone and in combination, has created greater interdependence among the community of nations than perhaps ever before. Such enhanced interdependence, in turn, has had two inevitable and important effects. First, it has increased the visibility of national culture, while leaving unclear the matter of whether culture in an increasingly inter-dependent world is a more important—or less important—consideration. Thus increasing interdependence might lead to relationships that transcend the bounds of culture, or it might lead the parties concerned to be more sensitive than ever to the differentiating effects of culture. Second, enhanced global interdependence has increased the likelihood that conflict will erupt in our dwindling world. Moreover, if global warfare is perhaps a bit less likely to gain acceptance as the means for settling such conflict, then the instruments of diplomacy and the process of negotiation are perhaps more important than ever.

The intellectual challenge of this project is to hold in one's hands the complex, quicksilver concept of culture while trying to understand some of the many ways it influences the shape and outcome of international negotiation. It goes without saying that culture often *does* have an impact on negotiation, but so do countless other variables and considerations. The question, then, is more what the *distinctive* effect of culture may be, both in creating unexpected opportunities for dispute settlement and in imposing obstacles to agreement.

Culture has too often been used as an excuse to justify negotiation failures; when one has run out of other explanations, there is always the residue of culture to fall back on. All the more reason, therefore, for finding some way of bringing this elusive concept out of the closet of justification and politicization to the intellectual forefront. We have tried to do this in this book by searching for a common context in which culture might be expected to play a prominent role. Needed is an international conflict setting with identifiable characteristics and of sufficient importance that the dimension of culture matters.

Our candidate has turned out to be water resource conflicts, river disputes in particular. Riverine conflicts share a number of attributes, whose effects can be identified and understood. By trying to hold these general attributes as constant as possible, it has been our hope that the often subtle effects of culture would be more likely to gain prominence. In addition to affording this bit of intellectual nicety, the focus on riverine conflict has allowed us to address an area that promises to be of ongoing and practical importance in global economic and environmental development.

When the Editorial Committee of this project first met to discuss the possibility of organizing a book on culture and international negotiation, a lively debate emerged. Some participants believed that culture is an important element in understanding negotiation, while others held to the view that the effects of culture are swamped by a host of situational, contextual constraints. Still others argued that culture does have important effects but that they result not from national or ethnic differences but from the emergence of a group of professional negotiators/diplomats who share a special culture of their own. Finally it was argued that, across the sweep of history, societies have emerged with distinctive political structures and that it is largely these structures that determine what might be called culture. Rather than abandon the project because of such disagreement, we decided to incorporate this intellectual exchange into the pages of the book.

In the book's introductory chapter, Guy Olivier Faure, a French sociologist, and Gunnar Sjöstedt, a Swedish international relations specialist, present an overview of approaches and issues in the study of culture, negotiation, and the interaction between these two key concepts of the book. Part I of the book consists of four chapters designed to stimulate further exchange among those who wish to understand the nature and limits of culture's influence on negotiation. In Chapter 2 American political scientist I. William Zartman takes the part of *agent provocateur,* briefly presenting a skeptic's viewpoint. In Chapter 3 Raymond Cohen, an Israeli international relations specialist and author of a recent volume on culture and conflict, states the case for the importance of culture. Chapter 4, by Winfried Lang, an Austrian diplomat and lawyer by training, argues for the existence in today's world of multinational corporations and international diplomacy of a global culture among professionals. Finally, Russian political scientist Victor Kremenyuk (editor of another volume to come out of the deliberations of the same Editorial Committee [Kremenyuk, 1991]) makes the case in Chapter 5 for a broader, pluralistic view, arguing from a political and historical perspective that the culture that matters is determined not by national or ethnic differences but by the nature of societal functioning.

Part II constitutes the core of the book and consists of a series of case descriptions and analyses of water resource disputes. Authors of these chapters were asked to address the following kinds of questions in their chapters: In what ways did the cultural background of the disputants influence the way negotiations proceeded, the outcomes that resulted, and the disputants' satisfaction with these outcomes? What specific cultural components made a difference? How did culture play a role in the negotiation process? What are some specific illustrations of the contributing role of culture both to the dispute in question and to the ways it was handled? Authors were encouraged to provide as many detailed, context-rich examples of negotiation as possible, on the grounds that such textured accounts provide valuable insight into the role of culture.

Such detailed accounts of negotiation, as told by narrators from diverse perspectives, may differ widely in scope and content. Thus some negotiation accounts may resemble the formal exchanges that most people think of as negotiation. Other accounts, however, may focus on the issues that make it possible for people to come to the negotiating table in the first place or that look beyond the formal process to its implementation. In this book we wish to look at the broad tapestry of negotiation to study its colorful variations at every stage along the way.

We deliberately invited contributions to this core portion of the volume based not on the authors' negotiation expertise or on their understanding of water resource disputes; rather we hoped to find authors who would be sympathetic to the effects of culture and therefore would give it a strong hearing.

In Chapter 6, French sociologist Guy Olivier Faure and American psychologist Jeffery Z. Rubin offer a brief overview of water resource conflicts, their importance, and the shared attributes that tie them together. Chapters 7 through 12 offer a diverse array of case analyses of water resource disputes, written by authors who come from different disciplines and different cultures. Moving (very) roughly from West to East, one continent at a time, these chapters are as follows: Anthropologist and diplomat Francis Deng examines the conflict over the Nile between northern and southern Sudanese in Chapter 7. In Chapter 8 French economist Christophe Dupont analyzes the four-party conflict over the Rhine among Switzerland, Germany, France, and the Netherlands. The Black Sea (the only instance of a nonriverine setting in the book) is examined by Russian historian Vladimir Pisarev in Chapter 9. In Chapter 10 Lebanese social psychologist Randa Slim analyzes the conflict among Turkey, Syria, and Iraq over the Euphrates. The Jordan River conflict, in particular the ongoing dispute between Israel and Jordan, is the focus of Chapter 11; both authors, Miriam Lowi and Jay Rothman, are American political scientists, but both have extensive experience living in other cultures in the Middle East. The final chapter in Part II (Chap. 12), written by American political scientist Kenneth Lieberthal, examines the role of bureaucratic culture in the construction of the Three Gorges Dam on the Yangtze River of China.

Part III turns to the lessons drawn from the intellectual exchange of Part I and the case analyses of Part II. Jeswald Salacuse, an American international lawyer and Dean of the Fletcher School of Law and Diplomacy, builds on his years of experience as both a scholar and a practitioner to develop some of the many lessons for practitioners in Chapter 13. Finally, we have reserved for ourselves the last word, using Chapter 14 to describe some of the lessons to be gleaned from this challenging intellectual exercise for both theory and research on negotiation.

In the truest and, we believe, best sense of the word, the several years' work culminating in the present book has been an intellectual *encounter* among cultures and disciplines. Citizens of nearly a dozen countries have contributed to the book, coming from the disciplines of anthropology, economics, history, international relations, law, political science, psychology, and sociology. The contributors attended meetings at the International Institute for Applied Systems Analysis (IIASA), near Vienna, Austria, on two separate occasions. The intellectual exchange that resulted from these two meetings was a lively one, exactly as we hoped and expected, and we believe that some of this exciting exchange has been captured in the pages of the book.

This book has been written with several audiences in mind. First are practitioners with an interest in international relations, be they in business or diplomacy, among others. As noted at the outset, the world has become a smaller place over the last decade, and the dimension of culture therefore has emerged as a more significant theme than ever, something that practitioners will want to keep in mind. Second are our social scientist colleagues. Whether as students of the nature of culture from a theoretical or a research perspective or as analysts of negotiation in concept or in detail, we believe that social scientists will find aspects of the multidisciplinary and multicultural exchange to be of intellectual value, as will students in graduate and professional programs. Finally are scholars and practitioners interested in water resource disputes, in particular, and international development conflicts, more generally. Although the study of riverine conflict was not chosen as the focus of study in its own right, the collective attention directed to this important class of issues is certain to draw valuable lessons for this audience. In summary, then, we believe that this book will be of interest to a broad array of scholars and practitioners concerned with topics ranging from negotiation to culture to water resources and, most especially, the interconnection among these three topics.

This ambitious project never would have seen the light of day without the assistance of a great many people. First and foremost, we owe a debt of gratitude to our colleagues on the Editorial Committee of the project on Processes of International Negotiation (PIN), housed at IIASA: Victor Kremenyuk, Winfried Lang, Gunnar Sjöstedt, and I. William Zartman. They have assisted us at every step along the way, providing editorial advice and intellectual counsel. Perhaps most important, they have made visible their commitment to the project by kindly agreeing to contribute chapters to the book.

IIASA's Director, Peter de Jánosi, encouraged us to pursue this project from the very beginning, as did his predecessor, Robert Pry; their support ranged from moral encouragement to much needed financial wherewithal. Bertram I. Spector, former Director of the PIN Project, offered us his support throughout the project. Ulrike Neudeck gave unsparingly of her time in preparing the manuscript for publication and assisting us in completing the countless tasks that were involved in this complex, far-flung project.

Wendy Caron edited the manuscript, and Anna Korula and Heather Pabrezis offered necessary support as well.

Finally it is with special pleasure that we acknowledge the generous support of the United Nations Educational, Scientific, and Cultural Organization (UNESCO), whose financial contribution combined with IIASA's own assistance to make this project possible.

Most especially, we owe a unique debt to our wives and children (Anne, Elise, and Aurélia Faure; Carol, Noah, Sally, and David Rubin) for their patience, understanding, challenging perspective, and constant support through every twist and bend of the ceaseless negotiations that accompanied the development of this book.

Guy Olivier Faure
Jeffrey Z. Rubin
Larnaca, Cyprus

1

Culture and Negotiation: An Introduction

GUY OLIVIER FAURE

GUNNAR SJÖSTEDT

Is negotiation an act or process of the moment, or is there meaning behind the words and actions that embodies long-term significance? Much of the research undertaken in the social sciences concerns the meaning that people ascribe to their actions. By understanding the effects of culture on the process of negotiation, we may be able to understand better the negotiation process itself. We believe that the meaning of negotiation cannot be understood fully unless it is interpreted in the cultural context in which it occurs.

Often negotiations are described or modeled as a process entailing rational choice, with little explanatory room for such factors as culture. One purpose of this chapter is to challenge that contention. To be sure, the character of individual processes of negotiation may vary considerably. However, all negotiations have a common characteristic: They put men and women on the stage, thus inevitably introducing culture into the process.

If asked whether they believe that cultural factors are at play in negotiation, most analysts probably would answer affirmatively. Culture does matter. Most likely the same analysts also would acknowledge that cultural differences exist within, as well as across, national borders and between different kinds of groupings of individuals such as tribes and professions. The analytical issue is thus not whether culture is at play, but the degree to which it affects negotiation. Moreover, because different cultures are likely to influence negotiation in dissimilar ways, a negotiation may be regarded, in part, as a confrontation between two or more cultures. How, then, does the "correlation of cultures" affect negotiations?

Although culture is a key concept in this study, this is not a book about culture per se; volumes of theory and research findings already have been published on the subject. Nor is it a book about negotiation most broadly, another topic that has received great attention over the last several decades. Rather the project focuses on the effect of different cultures on the particular form of social interaction and conflict settlement known as negotiation—and this is a topic in great need of attention by scholars and practitioners. A clearer understanding of the consequences of culture for negotiation may help predict, and perhaps improve, both negotiation outcomes and the process along the way. For example, individual actors clearly are constrained both by reality and by their perceptions of this reality. Perceptions, in turn, are determined partly by culture. Furthermore actors organize their negotiating behavior in relation to the feedback they obtain from the other party's actions—feedback that, in turn, is based on culture. To some extent, then, negotiators are prisoners of their culture, which, in turn, acts as a regulator of social interaction. A main objective of this project is to clarify further how culture serves to regulate negotiation, how it affects process, and to what extent it constrains outcomes.

This chapter is designed to serve three purposes: first, to provide the reader with the elements necessary to describe and analyze culture as a social component, while suggesting some operational *problematiques;* second, to introduce briefly an analytical framework for understanding negotiation; and third, to explore some of the many relations between culture and negotiation, the ways the former may influence the latter through the actors, their behavior, and the final outcomes that result.

Culture

Herriot, a 20th-century French writer and politician, has defined culture as what remains when one has forgotten everything. This paradoxical proposition captures one of the most salient properties of culture: the fact that it is not a matter of substance but a way of thinking or acting of which the subject is typically unaware. It remains an academic controversy how this general understanding of culture may be specified further. Anthropologists such as Kroeber and Kluckhohn (1963) have collected more than 160 different definitions of culture. It is beyond the objective of this study to synthesize these various notions of culture into a generally accepted definition, but it is hoped that a number of basic and recurring characteristics of culture can be defined.

Culture is an aggregate product of the processes occurring in human society. It typically consists of such social phenomena as beliefs, ideas, language, customs, rules, and family patterns. Culture also expresses itself in artifacts and physical objects such as paintings or handicraft. This perspective of culture refers to the fact that the people involved in social interaction —for example, in negotiation—need to understand the meaning of their own behavior. People produce symbols, as well as other cultural elements, that create such meaning. As symbols vary from culture to culture, the meaning attributed to negotiation is also likely to differ from nation to nation.

Expressed in general terms, *culture* may be understood as a system of widely accepted beliefs combined with a set of self-justified assumptions. These beliefs and assumptions are transmitted from one generation to the next. They pertain to people and their interaction, the relationship between people and their environment, as well as the way people look upon nature, time, and space. One characteristic of a social group is the culture shared by its members. Within the same social group, however, there may be degrees of sophistication of cultural achievement. Refinements in taste in art or literature, for example, represent a way of developing and influencing culture when exercised collectively. Thus, although in a short-term perspective culture should perhaps best be seen as a kind of structure conditioning human behavior, in a long-term perspective it is a dynamic social phenomenon. The pace of change evidently differs considerably from one culture to the next. Some societies are in a state of transition in which new ideas and life-styles substitute for old ones. In other societies, values and customs prevail that have been dominant for a very long period, sometimes for centuries.

Culture is a complex concept, and no single definition has been acknowledged in the literature. It is possible, however, to offer a working definition of culture, one that will guide the present study: *Culture is a set of shared and enduring meanings, values, and beliefs that characterize national, ethnic, or other groups and orient their behavior.*

Culture in Motion, and Its Problematiques

The beliefs, ideas, and values that constitute the core of culture may influence human behavior in several ways. First, culture orients, or perhaps even directs, judgment and opinion. For instance, culture often embodies the criteria for what is good or bad. Values as a part of culture also represent "the desirable which influences the selection from available modes, means and ends of action" (Kluckhohn, 1951b, p. 395). Hence cultural values may represent an orientation for action by indicating or prescribing socially desirable ends and means. Cultural factors also may influence or determine social action in a much more direct way. Actors may be guided unconsciously by cultural values that help reproduce learned behavior.

Language is another important layer of culture that may help explain or predict how cultural factors influence social action. One function of language is to structure reality and to order experience. Therefore the language of an individual significantly influences his or her perceptions and thinking. Any particular language necessarily interprets events through a unique set of categories. These categories may differ considerably between societies and language groups. For instance, the Eskimo have more than 20 words to differentiate among types of snow, while the Aztecs put snow, ice, and frost under the same broad denomination. European languages divide the spectrum into six basic colors, whereas the Jale of New Guinea recognize only two colors—warm and cold. As a meaningful system of symbols, culture thus fulfills a number of societal functions, one of the most important being communication. Note in this connection that communication is not only a way to interact with others but also a necessary means to transmit culture, to disseminate and refine it.

A French sociologist stated, "This is the role of culture: to answer questions even before they are raised" (Akoun, 1989, p. 31). Culture functions as a substitute for instinct, providing organized answers to external stimuli. For instance, culture is a bearer of social norms that may guide behavior or trigger specific actions in a particular type of situation. But the role of culture goes far beyond this substitutive function because it, at the same time, is both a product and a source. Cultural factors should not be compared to the software in a computer, which functions exactly the same way each time it is used. In each particular situation, culture helps the individual give meaning to reality when confronted with it. At the same time, culture is created and modified by such confrontations.

With regard to interaction and communication, culture may be both an obstacle and a facilitator. It is an obstacle to the extent that cultural stereotypes and differences distort signals and cause misunderstandings. On the one hand, the ultimate effect may be that the perceptions and expectations that two parties have of each other become affected in a negative way. On the other hand, if in the process of settling conflict the two parties perceive cultural similarities between themselves or if they share overarching values, communication and other forms of interaction may be facilitated.

Still another highly important function of culture is to help people build and preserve their own identity. For example, one mechanism producing such as effect occurs when individuals become aware of their cultural identity as the result of regarding themselves as different from others (Blake & Mouton, 1962). Again, social interaction may be affected in various ways. For instance, the individual may become disturbed and perhaps aggressive by discovering his or her identity in a confrontation. Another possibility is that the discovery of the identity strengthens the self-esteem of the individual. This strengthening may, for instance, make it easier for the individual to accept compromises in deals with other parties without being afraid of "losing face."

National cultures presumably affect negotiations in various systematic ways—for instance, by coloring negotiating styles. In a general sense, culture pertains to societies and ethnic groups. What commonly is referred to as *national negotiating style* combines several national influences: culture, history, political system, and position in the world. This perspective, however, leaves an essential research question unanswered: How does one deal with the context-bound character of culture and the assumption that the structure of culture is isomorphic? This question must be answered in any systematic comparison of negotiating styles.

Other kinds of culture than that related to a specific ethnic group may influence negotiating behavior—for instance, corporate or professional cultures. *Corporate culture* can be viewed as a subculture that provides its own meanings, norms of behavior, and symbols. Such a subculture may easily complement the national or ethnic culture but may also contradict it, as when it carries values conflicting with the norms prevalent in the nation or ethnic group concerned. A corporate culture also may retain a transnational quality, shared by people in different countries. *Professional culture* functions in a very similar way and may conflict not only with the ethnic culture but also with the corporate culture, proposing different organizational rationales and sometimes leading to the adoption of opposite strategies. The *family culture,* too, may have its own impact. It is unclear how relatively influential each cultural subsystem is and under what conditions its impact is unleashed. The uncertainty of how particular individuals are likely to behave in a social interaction such as negotiation increases when their cultural subsystems embody conflicting and competing values. Thus there is a need to understand better the complex interplay between culture and subcultures.

Usually it is very difficult to evaluate objectively and precisely the effect that culture or a subculture may have on human behavior. One reason is that culture is rarely the only external influencing factor. In most "real-world situations," it is, no doubt, a cumbersome analytical task to differentiate systematically the effects of culture on human behavior and social interaction from the impact of a host of other background factors, be they incidental (e.g., the personality of key individuals) or structural (e.g., organizational setting). There is more to this problem of distinction than just the practical difficulty of separating different causes and effects. The influence of culture may coincide or interact with the effects caused by other background factors. For instance, cultural impact may be either neutralized or reinforced by social structure.

The French historian Braudel formulated the paradox that "the present explains the past" (1969, p. 239). Similarly individuals performing as negotiators are likely to reveal their values through their behavior. Culture as a system of values supposedly orients the actions of negotiators, imposing on these individuals certain norms of conduct. Cultural factors also influence the way negotiators perceive and understand the situation at hand. Culture even may advise the negotiator about appropriate behavior in the current situation.

It is evidently cumbersome to decode correctly one's own culture, partly because culture is present everywhere. In the words of an old saying: A fish does not know how essential it is for it to live in water until it is taken out of it. At the same time, negotiators are likely to assess foreign cultures through their own cultural lenses. Typical for negotiators characterized by ethnocentrism is a marked tendency to interpret and judge other cultures by their own standards. The effect may be an inclination to belittle or misinterpret the intentions or designs of other parties involved in the negotiations. To the extent that negotiators behave along these lines, they are likely to impede an agreement.

A central research question is: Does the meaning and function of negotiations vary significantly from culture to culture? There is not yet any clear basis for developing a reliable answer to this question. National cultures are difficult to compare systematically. For example, negotiators representing different cultures use the same term to refer to something that in reality is quite different. This usage raises the question of whether negotiations can be understood accurately in terms other than those of the society in which they actually take place. Another closely related line of query concerns whether the Western culturally biased, analytical approach is appropriate for understanding negotiations involving cultures other than those of the Occident. A key question is, hence: Is it meaningful to strive to construct a generally valid behavioral model that, in principle, should be able to explain the performance of all negotiators, regardless of where they come from?

We believe that, consistent with the literature, the search for general models is meaningful and should be pursued. Various approaches to understanding the possible fit between culture and negotiation have been advanced. Sawyer and Guetzkow (1965) developed a model of negotiation accommodating the impact of culture as a set of external background factors. Another notable example is the multidimensional approach designed by Parsons and Shils in their general theory of action (1951, p. 77). Still another example is the value-orientation model developed by Kluckhohn and Strodbeck (1961, p. 12).

With a similar concern, Hofstede (1980) suggested four basic dimensions of culture that may be used to classify the behavior of negotiators. One dimension pertains to the "power distance" between actors. Another concerns the tendency toward uncertainty avoidance that, among other things, deals with stress, stability, and concern for rule enforcement. A third dimension is labeled "individualism" and relates to the relationship between the individual and the collectivity. The fourth dimension, called "masculinity," mainly deals with ambition—the desire to achieve and earn more.

According to Hofstede, the behavior of individual social actors such as negotiators may be classified fruitfully into these categories. Furthermore whole cultures may be characterized with the help of the same indicators. Thus different cultural profiles are discernible. For instance, West Africans and Arabs clearly respect authority and are apt to subordinate themselves to the dictum of the collectivity. In contrast, Swedes and Israelis are much more individualistic and have less concern for formal authority. In principle, it should be possible to construct the cultural image of any country with the help of the Hofstede cultural dimensions.

Negotiation

Culture is one of two key concepts framing this study. The other is negotiation. Basically *negotiation* is a method of conflict settlement. It involves at least two parties but may, in the multilateral case, engage several hundred actors representing governments and governmental or nongovernmental organizations. Typically the purpose of negotiation is to find a formula for the distribution of a contested value or set of values between the negotiating parties. Thus negotiation is a joint decision-making process through which negotiating parties accommodate their conflicting interests into a mutually acceptable settlement.

The profile of particular negotiation processes may vary considerably, depending on the actors involved, the nature of the issue at stake, and the setting of the negotiation. Obviously negotiations between the European Community and the People's Republic of China on trade issues must be quite different from global negotiations on the environment or those designing a postwar settlement. Regardless of these evident differences across different "real-world cases," all negotiations include five key elements: structure, actors, strategy, process, and outcome.

The meaning of these negotiation elements may be illustrated with a metaphor. Consider an Olympic bicycle race. The actor is the individual racer competing with racers not only from other countries but also from his or her own national team. The performance of each racer is constrained or otherwise conditioned by a number of structural factors, such as the technical qualities of one's own bike compared with the other bikes, the terrain, the distance of the race, and weather conditions. To compete, the racer will have to develop a strategy that is competitive relative to those of the racers on other teams but that at the same time takes into account a mixture of competitive and cooperative designs vis-à-vis his or her teammates; eventually only one racer will win the race. The process is the race itself. Finally, and naturally, the outcome reflects the order in which competing racers manage to cross the finish line.

Culture and Negotiation: Interactions and Influences

Recall the working definition of *culture* suggested earlier: a set of shared and enduring meanings, values, and beliefs that characterize national, ethnic, or other groups and orient their behavior. Also recall the basic meaning of *negotiation* as a process of joint decision making in which two or more parties accommodate conflicting interests. Culture may affect negotiation in many ways. One category of such effects derives from the fact that culture conditions how individual actors behave in negotiation. Another category of influence results from the confrontation of diverging cultures in the negotiation process and may impede negotiations by hardening the parties' positions or by causing unnecessary misunderstanding. A third type of effect of a cultural encounter may be described as facilitation. One example is the case when two parties discover they have culturally determined values and concepts that simplify communication between them or elicit superordinate goals providing substantial ground for consensus.

In order to specify the impact of culture, it is useful to distinguish between the basic elements of negotiation: actors, structure, strategy, process, and outcome. Cultural factors relate somewhat differently to each. It is conceivable that a cultural factor or set of factors that influences one dimension of negotiation—say, strategy—has no immediate significant effect on other dimensions—for example, process or structure.

Actors

Cultural factors are linked most clearly to the dimension of negotiation represented by actors. Individuals, groups, or organizations may perform as actors in negotiations. All such actors directly represent a national, ethnic, professional, organizational, or other culture—or usually a combination thereof. Cultural background conditions how the actor perceives issues, other actors, and their intentions. Indeed culture may determine the whole outlook on negotiations. Representatives of some cultures tend to regard negotiation as a power confrontation, whereas others view it as a cooperative venture. Negotiators from some cultures are strongly result oriented: They tend to focus on the outcome and the ways to get there. In other cultures the negotiation process represents significant values that must be defended. In any case, the way negotiators interact with a counterpart, from the most elementary gestures to the most sophisticated rhetoric, will depend largely on their cultural backgrounds.

Ethics are also part of the cultural components that may affect negotiation. Thus negotiators from different cultures may vary in their proclivity to view the opposition at the other side of the table as enemies—representatives of something evil. If the opposition is so considered, it may affect the inclination of a negotiating party to employ dirty negotiation tactics such as bribes, lies, or deception.

Culture sometimes influences who will be the actors in the negotiations. For example, female experts may be recruited easily to some delegations, whereas in other cultures strong cultural barriers may prohibit women from taking part in the process. More generally, culture is likely to influence how negotiation delegations are selected. There are seemingly culture-conditioned concepts of how the distribution of work should be organized in a delegation between professional diplomats and experts, how the hierarchical order should be structured, and how intercourse with other delegations should be conducted. For instance, in a culture emphasizing the value of hierarchy and formal procedures, all communication with other parties in the negotiation should be conducted according to protocol. Contact across ranks is not acceptable; ambassadors should speak only to other ambassadors, and third secretaries should speak only to other third secretaries.

Structure

The structural dimension refers to the enduring external constraints within which negotiations unfold. Typical structural factors include the number of parties involved (two, a few, or many), the number of issues at stake and the way they relate to each other, the distribution of power between negotiating parties, the organizational setting, and the degree of transparency of the negotiations for nonparticipants such as nongovernmental organizations and the media. The impact of structure on other elements of the negotiation is often diffuse and difficult to specify in the analysis but may nevertheless be quite strong. Culture, for instance, tends to legitimize some types of situational power and to disavow others.

Culture may be one of the components of structure. For example, culture may manifest itself as a code of conduct, such as the shared belief of negotiating parties that it is necessary to adhere to rules of secret or open diplomacy. The organizational culture of an international institution is another example of culture as part of the structure of negotiations. Institutions such as the United Nations, the International Monetary Fund and the Organization for Economic Cooperation and Development (OECD) are infused with different organizational cultures that lead the same kinds of issues to sometimes be handled quite differently in each organization.

Strategy

Strategy may be described as the art of devising plans to achieve a goal or set of goals. Therefore a strategy is the result of deliberate calculations that consider the cost-effectiveness of different possible means. Strategic choices, however, are steered by values, some of which are considerably conditioned by culture. The anthropologist Benedict (1934) differentiated a few arch models incorporating different packages of cultural factors. For example, she distinguished an Apollonian culture, characterized by a preference for conflict avoidance, and a Dionysian culture, apt to elicit violent behavior. Representatives of these two cultures are likely to demonstrate different orientations toward the negotiations. For instance, the representatives of some cultures are likely to have an inclination to search for compromises in difficult situations. Others find it natural to strive for consensus, and still others will try to attain victory in the form of the opposing party's virtual surrender.

Culture also may influence the way negotiators envisage how a settlement on an issue should best be reached. Some cultures seem to prefer a deductive approach: The first step is to agree on principles, and later these principles can be applied to particular issues. In other cultures, induction is a more natural strategy: First one deals pragmatically with the concrete problems at hand, and principles are crystallized along the way.

A final example of how culture may influence strategy concerns the way cooperation may be used to promote one's own interests in a negotiation.

In some cultures a pragmatic orientation is permissive or even desirable; such actors will find it easy to join forces with other actors who have common or compatible interests, regardless of who they are. Other actors may prefer to cooperate only with like-minded partners, believing that it is unethical to be part of a coalition consisting of ideological or cultural foes.

Process

Negotiation depends on the communication between the parties involved. The effectiveness of communication may be affected considerably by cross-cultural dissimilarities. To begin with, differences in the style of communication may be important. In some cultures it is natural to try to get the substance of the message across to the other party or parties as fast as possible. In other cultures the appropriate form of the message is an important constraint. The way to approach sensitive issues varies drastically from one culture to another. In some societies the problem is met head on; in other societies people go around in an elusive manner.

Different views among actors of the legitimate and appropriate negotiation tactics and ploys may disrupt the process. For instance, in some cultures humor may be an effective means of facilitating bargaining over sensitive issues. Humor employed as a facilitation device, however, may be counterproductive and impede negotiations because what is a good joke in one culture may be regarded as nonsense or even an insult in other cultures. Bluffing, bribing, and threats may have similar effects. These tactics may be employed as natural elements of the negotiating strategies of some countries but may seriously disturb the process when they are discovered by other actors who consider such negotiation methods to be illegitimate.

Not sticking to one's word or deceiving the other party about a deadline and doing it while knowing that this deadline could not have been met, can be viewed from very different angles. In some cultures being polite is more important than giving the right information. What is called "lying" in some societies may be called "paying respect" in others.

Cross-cultural differences in the understanding of time also may disturb the process of negotiation. In the West time is conceived of as something akin to a commodity in limited supply; just like a good, it can be saved, wasted, controlled, or organized. In contrast, in the Near East time is not a phenomenon characterized by scarcity. As a result, disparate conceptions of time may complicate the important task of respecting the general time frame or the deadlines established for a particular negotiation.

Outcome

Outcome is the function of all of the other dimensions of negotiation:
actors, structure, strategy, and process. Accordingly the impact of culture
on these other elements of negotiation eventually also indirectly influences the outcome. It is also possible to discern a number of more direct
linkages between culture and outcome. For example, different national,
ethnic, and professional cultures contain preferences to the proper form of
the outcome. Thus some cultures not only prefer but also require an agreement in which each word has been assessed carefully. Representatives of
other cultures may be more concerned with the substance of the agreement
and therefore also may be somewhat more willing to accept final texts that
are formulated more loosely.

Culture may influence how different actors interpret and value the
outcome attained in the negotiation. Some actors may view the agreement
reached as a constraint against future action, which it is therefore legitimate
to try circumventing as much as possible. Others may regard the agreement
as a deal between negotiating partners that each party has an obligation to
respect and implement as far as possible. Still other actors may acknowledge the substantive results of the negotiation, while regarding the outcome as an important symbolic manifestation of the good relations between the parties who have entered the agreement.

Fairness is a key concept for any negotiator trying to assess the result
of the process. Behind such a concept one can find different principles of
justice strongly connected with social values. Some actors, for instance,
would favor equality as the basic norm of fairness; others would think that
gains should go according to the contributions brought by each party; others
would prefer to see gains distributed according to the needs of the parties.

Conclusions

This book is about how culture affects negotiation over one particular
kind of issue: water disputes related to rivers and closed seas. An assumption of the project is that unless this relationship is understood properly,
pitfalls will emerge and opportunities will be lost in future negotiations
over the same problem. The distribution of water resources will become
an increasingly sensitive issue in the future. The various possible cou-
plings between culture and negotiation suggested in this chapter will serve
as a general frame of reference for the case studies described in Part II.
This framework, however, should be regarded as tentative and merely
suggestive. The present state of knowledge simply does not permit any

categorical statements to be made regarding the influence of cultural factors on negotiation. In fact, one objective of this project is to elucidate the complex causal linkages between culture and negotiation, on the basis of the conclusions drawn from the case analyses.

The importance of culture as a determinant of the character of negotiations is debatable. That the debate itself is important is reflected in the "confrontation" between the skeptic in Chapter 2 and the advocate in Chapter 3. It is not controversial to claim that, to the extent culture does have an effect on negotiation, this influence varies in form, direction, and effect. All elements of a negotiation may be affected by culture. Culture is usually part of the structure of the negotiation. It influences who the active negotiators are, their behavior, their strategies, and ultimately the very negotiation process itself. Even the outcome may be affected directly by cultural factors. For instance, the bearers of some cultures may be more concerned with symbolic manifestations of victory or defeat than are others. But those influences also may be incidental to a practice and understanding of the basic process.

PART I

INTERNATIONAL NEGOTIATION

Does Culture Make a Difference?

2

A Skeptic's View

I. WILLIAM ZARTMAN

Culture is indeed relevant to the understanding of the negotiation process—every bit as relevant as breakfast and to much the same extent. Like the particular type of breakfast the negotiators ate, culture is cited primarily for its *negative* effects. Yet even the best understanding of any such effect is *tautological,* its measure *vague,* and its role in the process basically *epiphenomenal.* Each of these traits bears further elaboration.

A major claim made by culturalists is that ignoring culture is a principal cause of breakdown of negotiations (Bochner, 1981; Cohen, 1991; Moran & Stripp, 1991; Nicolson, 1954). Thus the only negotiations outcome that culture is purported to explain is failure. But failure in negotiations is already overdetermined: Because failure means conflict (the preexisting condition), there are as many causes of failure as of conflict itself. It is the successful outcomes or the effective negotiations that need explanation so that they can be replicated and conflict can be overcome. No culturalist makes this claim for the subject. Indeed many conclusions of cultural studies give cross-cultural advice, good for all cultures (Binnendijk, 1987, pp. viii-ix; Gulliver, 1979, pp. 64-67).

Nor could the cultural claim be made. To use culture to explain how conflict is overcome through negotiation, analysts would have to show either that a culture contains "pro-negotiating" traits or that two cultures are paired appropriately to conduct negotiations. Culture might include single-party attributes, such as trustworthiness, requirement (the intention of reciprocating concessions), or even a high evaluation of negotiation (Nader & Todd, 1978; Nicolson, 1964, pp. 25ff), or interactional attributes such as matching behavior from both sides (Pruitt, 1981) or an appropriate fit with the other party's culture. But these elements only set up the process; they do not explain it. Culture in these cases becomes an add-on to the basic process. Some excellent studies have been made of the ways particular countries have of conducting negotiations (Armstrong et al., 1979; Blaker, 1977a, 1977b; Dennet & Johnson, 1951; Khuri, 1968; Lall, 1968; Mushakoji, 1968, 1972; Whelan, 1988; Young, 1968), but they deal with the importance and techniques of negotiation. They do not set out a culturally distinct process or relate distinct behavior in a common process to independent cultural traits. Despite suspicions to the contrary (Sawyer & Guetzkow, 1965), serious experimental studies of negotiation document the absence of cultural differentiation in bargaining behavior (Brehmer & Hammond, 1977, p. 91; Rubin & Brown, 1975, pp. 165-166).

Even when treated negatively, culture tends to be defined tautologically. Although conceived of as the determinant of personal behavior, culture is a social phenomenon and so is related to a particular society. But it is never clearly established why the given traits inhere in that society, other than that they are the society's defining traits. African culture is what Africans (or whoever) do, and they do it because they are Africans (or whoever). Exceptions are treated as deviants, Africans who do not act like Africans (or whomever). The approach perpetuates stereotypes and self-proving hypotheses, usually advanced by the opponent who thus forces the other party to behave as the assigned stereotype. Conforming behavior then becomes self-confirming, and nonconforming behavior is out of character and difficult to explain (Snyder & Diesing, 1977, ch. 4, esp. p. 337).

When culture is related to some independent variable, such as frequently used structural concepts, the variable ends up being cultural too; social structure is claimed to determine culture, but social structure is a cultural trait and hence determined by culture, of which it is a part. Thus cultural analysis assumes coherence within difference, discards deviance, and finishes by focusing on incompatible distinctions, such as the clash between "high context" and "low context" cultures (Cohen, 1991). Driven by its assumptions, culture proves the inability of East and West to meet, while negotiation analysis is seeking to explain when and how that meeting can take place. This is not to say that negotiation analysis assumes that all people can meet and negotiate (although some proponents of negotiation do fall into that trap), but that it is the chances and manner of overcoming conflict that is its problematique.

Beyond its tautology, culture is a vague concept, drawing very little agreement among analysts (Janosik, 1987). If culture is the sum of the behavioral traits of a collectivity, an inability to agree conceptually at the appropriate level of collectivity suggests a basic problem with the concept itself. When one talks of a particular culture's negotiating style, it is not clear what is the significant cultural basket. If subnational group traits are dominant, can national traits be significant? And if national traits are significant, can continental traits be important? And if continental traits are important, can one speak of world traits? Specifically, can Third World low context cultures be grouped as a significant collectivity if Arab or Latin American negotiating cultures are viewed as distinct and dominant, or if Egyptians negotiate differently from Syrians or Saudis, or if the real and telling distinction is between Upper Egyptians (as exemplified by Nasser) and Lower Egyptians (such as Sadat)? The question is not merely at which level the dominant trait is to be found, but more significant, because if these levels are not considered to be subcategories of each other, what (or where) is culture?

In this internationalized world, is it not clear that previous national differences prevail any longer, because many have disappeared into a homogenized cosmopolitan culture of international negotiations fostered by the United Nations and other multilateral encounters. This objection is initially empirical rather than conceptual, suggesting that cultural distinctions did exist but do not any longer, at least among practicing diplomats, or, alternatively, that cultural distinctions—or incompatibilities—need to be suspended if agreements are to be negotiated. But more deeply it is also a conceptual question to the extent it suggests that culture is what exists outside of negotiable situations and is absent within.

Finally, and most important, culture is epiphenomenal. Most cultural analyses focus on the way certain people do other things than negotiation (Do not show the soles of your feet, Do not backslap, Do develop a relationship) and the effects these things have on negotiations. An understanding of national idiosyncrasies that can make negotiations smoother and avoid misunderstandings is knowledge that is helpful but scarcely profound or basic to an understanding of the negotiation process itself. Culture is to negotiation what birds flying into engines are to flying airplanes or, at most, what weather is to aerodynamics—practical impediments that need to be taken into account (and avoided) once the basic process is fully understood and implemented. The understanding of the negotiation process is still in its infancy and needs a broader conceptual and consensual analysis on which to rest before a fruitful evaluation of the role of culture can be established.

It may be objected that these criticisms are not directed against the concept of culture per se but against its empirical uncertainty. Like power, class, and quarks, we know that culture exists but are uncertain about its precise definition, its referent group, and other more specific attributes. The preceding discussion, it might be asserted, merely confirms that *the thing* plays a role in negotiation and that what is missing is research on the positive fit of cultures, a large mapping project indicating the extent of dominant cultural collectivities, or an identification of externally—and behavioral-ly—related variations on a common process. Yet if that is "all" that is missing, the concept of *culture* is reduced to a ghost—a shadow without form or substance that is suspected of being present but whose supposed effects can be explained more significantly and directly by something else.

What *is* needed is greater attention to the common process of negotiation so that outcomes can be better understood and better agreements can be built. Despite the variety of ways of thinking creatively about negotiation, only a small number of basic concepts are in this process (Kremenyuk, 1991), defined as the process of bringing divergent positions into a joint decision. The components of the process are limited, comprising divisions, exchanges, and creations of items, played against alternatives and expec-tations. Concessions on the *division* of items are the most commonly conceived course to an agreement because negotiation generally means giving up something to get something. *Exchanges* are achieved by widen-ing the scope of negotiation so that trade-offs are possible, allowing negotia-tion to be conceptualized as a commercial process in which both parties are better off with an agreement. *Creation* widens the scope even further, allowing the parties to bring into being an outcome that was not possible when each acted alone. Each of these three paths is based on a formula or common understanding of the problem, and its solution is based on a shared notion of fairness of justice. Proposals in these processes are compared continually with parties' expectations and alternatives, which give them values other than their intrinsic worth.

From such relatively simple and limited concepts (or others developed through a conceptualization of the negotiation process), a wide variety of analytical and practical methods can be laid out for studying and conduct-ing negotiations. After appropriate concepts of culture have been elaborated, methods can be developed for examining their role within the context of this process. A better understanding of these methods, based on a common process, can lead to better knowledge about the ways agreements are reached and a better conduct of the process of reaching agreements.

Once this understanding is achieved, analysis can return to the cultural question. But to find sound answers, the question must be turned on its head. Instead of asking, How do the Fijians negotiate?—a question that usually allows that author to illustrate preconceived notions about Fijian culture with well-selected examples from negotiation behavior, never asking whether anyone else acts the same way or whether any Fijians act any other way—one must ask, Out of a conceivable range of ways of performing the common process, which one is associated with Fijians (or with subcategories or supercategories of them), and what is it in being Fijian (or whatever) that determines the choice of particular behaviors?

Only by asking the cross-cultural question can one get a cultural answer, paradoxical as that may seem. Such questions include the following as parts of a broad research agenda: At what rates and rhythms, determined by an independent variable, do different groups concede (Jensen, 1983)? Do different groups have different notions about fairness and justice in regard to divisions, exchanges, and creations, which are determined by some external factor (Druckman, Benton, Ali, & Bagur, 1975)? Are there different and independently explained degrees of acceptability and usage of alternatives (e.g., threats, warnings, promises, predictions, bargaining chips, bluffs) (Abu-Nimer, 1993)? Only when we know what negotiations and breakfast are all about will we be able to analyze the role of one on the other.

3

An Advocate's View

RAYMOND COHEN

In this chapter I make the case for the often powerful effects of culture on negotiation. I argue not only that culture affects the negotiating behavior of international actors—clearly it is simply one among many influences—but also that cross-cultural antinomies between the parties may affect the course and outcome of negotiations. The extensive intercultural communication literature (e.g., Fisher, 1988; Gudykunst & Kim, 1984; Singer, 1987) has shown that relationships between cultural strangers involve more than an awkward encounter between contrasting languages, manners, and habits. They also may entail the confrontation of profoundly incompatible, culturally grounded assumptions about the nature of the world, verbal and nonverbal communication, and key aspects of behavior. The issue is not just which hand one eats with or whether showing the soles of one's feet is considered to be seemly. At stake are more momentous matters, such as whether society puts the individual or group first or approaches the resolution of disputes on the basis of abstract justice or social harmony.

Not all cross-cultural contacts, of course, result in dissension. To clarify the point, a distinction has to be drawn between four quite different cross-cultural encounters. First is the compatible interaction between similar or related cultures. Negotiations between states bordering the Rhine, described by Dupont in Chapter 8, would fall into this category. Second is the complementary interaction between dissimilar cultures. Strazar (1981), in a study of the harmonious U.S.-Japanese relationship at the 1951 San Francisco Conference, analyzes such a situation. Third is the noncomplementary interaction of related cultures. In Chapter 10, concerning the Euphrates, Slim touches on the inability of adjacent Arab societies to cooperate. Fourth is the incompatible interaction that may occur between dissimilar cultures divided by history, language, religion, and civilization. A striking example of such a disharmonious relationship in the modern period is that of Israel and Egypt.

When incompatible philosophies of life and codes of communication and behavior come into conflict, serious misunderstandings may arise and the parties fail to synchronize their actions. International negotiation, requiring unencumbered communication, mutual comprehension, and the coordination of a complex series of interrelated moves, provides fertile ground for intercultural dissonance. To illustrate my argument, I review various case studies. I conclude by suggesting ways cultural differences can be overcome or even transformed from hindrances into positive assets for negotiators. Alongside Fisher's (1986) depiction of Model T (traditional) and Model A (alternative) approaches to negotiation, a Model C (culturally sensitive) approach is advocated.

The Nature of Culture

The concept of *culture* was invented by anthropologists as a way of accounting for the remarkable variety of practices, beliefs, and forms of social organization displayed by the different branches of the human race in their communal life. Since Edward Tylor (1871/1958), researchers have argued that the way of life of a collectivity is more than a random and arbitrary set of habits. Rather it is the outward expression of a unifying and consistent vision brought by a particular community to its confrontation with such core issues as the origins of the cosmos, the harsh unpredictability of the natural environment, the nature of society, and humankind's place in the order of things. Human heterogeneity results when alternative answers are proffered to invariant questions.

Three key features of culture are stressed in the anthropology literature: (a) It is a quality not of individuals as such, but of the society of which they are part; (b) it is acquired—through acculturation or socialization—by the individual from that society; and (c) each culture is a unique complex of attributes subsuming every area of social life. In this chapter my definition of culture will follow Kluckhohn's view that culture is fundamentally about information and the projection of significance onto the world (Kluckhohn, 1951a). I see *culture* as an integrated system of basic assumptions, both normative and factual, about the nature of human beings and the social, physical, and metaphysical environment in which they exist. It can be thought of as a set of underlying grammatical rules, a semiology, guiding perception and structuring meaning—in fact, creating reality.

This definition can be clarified by a computer analogy. Humankind can be thought of as displaying a rich selection of physical hardware. We come in a variety of shapes, sizes, and shades. But our capacities and potentialities are astonishingly similar. It is the programming of the human system—the software—that translates potential into actuality. And here the diversity is enormous. Human cultural software is made up of ideas, meanings, conventions, and assumptions. It molds our perceptions, so that where the city dweller sees only sand, the nomad picks up a host of clues about the nature of the terrain, the presence of wildlife, the weather, the availability of pasture, and the presence of other tribes. It structures our ideas, so that one group sees work as the fulfillment of human destiny, while another sees it as a curse. It shapes our actions, defining the rules of interaction for meeting, parting, bestowing hospitality, trading, begging, giving—and negotiating.

The Intercultural Perspective

It is not culture as a one-sided influence on negotiating behavior that concerns us here, but the effect on a bilateral negotiation of cultural contrasts between the parties. Relative, not absolute, values are at stake. Of interest is the chemistry of the combination: What happens when incongruent cultural expectations come into contact and react with each other? A series of useful studies has appeared on the national negotiating styles of various countries (Binnendijk, 1987; Blaker, 1977a, 1977b; Pye, 1982; Smith, 1989). But style, like beauty, is in the eye of the beholder, and these were studies written by Americans, for Americans. From another cultural perspective, the negotiating style of a given state might appear very different. Actors negotiate differently with different partners, and different partners do not necessarily perceive the same traits to be salient.

Because this point is fundamental, it is worth giving a concrete illustration. Consider the perceived effect of cross-national differences on a certain aspect of entry-response behavior—the point at which negotiators decide to respond to an opponent's opening proposal. In a simulation-type, experimental study Janosik (1986) found that, across a range of management-labor scenarios, American and Japanese subjects reacted to the same offers at very different rates. By a difference of as much as 2 to 1, American subjects responded earlier, whereas Japanese subjects tended to prefer to wait for additional information before committing themselves. This experimental observation is corroborated by Blaker's (1977b) historical study of Japan's tactical negotiating style in 20th-century diplomatic negotiations with the Western powers, particularly the United States. He notes such tendencies as "watchful waiting, avoiding early commitment, deferring major concessions until the opponent has compromised" (p. 83).

The possible effect of contrasting Japanese and American initiation behavior may be exemplified in the 1981-1982 air service negotiations between the two countries. Before the talks began, the U.S. delegation developed what it saw as a balanced package that it laid before its Japanese counterparts at the very first round in Honolulu in January 1981. As both the Janosik and Blaker findings predict, the Japanese team probed the U.S. offer without coming up with a counterproposal. It was only in the second round, held in April 1981, that Japan tabled its response, which, in the words of an American participant, satisfied virtually all of Japan's objectives and none of the aims of the United States. Tactically Japan was in a favorable position because it had learned early the minimal concessions the United States was prepared to make without disclosing its own intentions. Having made its best concessions up front, the U.S. delegation found itself at a disadvantage as the negotiations progressed (Kasper, 1988, Sequel A, pp. 4-6). In my judgment this disadvantage translated into a real position of inferiority in the final stages of the negotiation and a worse agreement, from an American point of view, than the objective circumstances warranted.

It might be argued that the Japanese delegation was simply more adept or had been provided with more cunning instructions than the U.S. team. To establish whether this is a single case proving nothing or whether it exemplifies a more general intercultural tendency would require the comparative analysis of a large number of Japanese-U.S. negotiations, at different times, over varying issues, and with changing casts of participants. In the absence of such definitive information (regrettably, a characteristic of the field), my contention would be that, in this instance, relative Japanese caution proved fortuitously more functional than the business-like dispatch of the U.S. delegation. But if we turn from U.S.-Japanese negotiations from an American angle to Sino-Japanese negotiations from a Japanese perspective, a different picture appears. Kazuo, in his study of Chinese negotiating tactics vis-à-vis the Japanese, found that Japanese delegations were quite unable to maintain a wait-and-see attitude in the face of immovable Chinese insistence that the Japanese present their own proposals first (Kazuo, 1979, p. 541). In this particular relationship, then, Japanese negotiators derive no relative benefit from "delayed" initiation. Indeed, relative to their Chinese counterparts, Japanese negotiators might appear to err on the side of haste.

Problems of Intercultural Negotiations: The Literature

A substantial literature, both theoretical and applied, has accrued over about the last 20 years on the many issues associated with intercultural relations (see Stening, 1979). The journal *Culture, Medicine and Psychiatry* has published many fascinating accounts of the problems facing health workers in cross-cultural settings. The *International Journal of Intercultural Relations* is the primary outlet for narrative, experimental, and prescriptive information on the intercultural issues found in such varied fields as social work, education, and management. Finally, international business negotiations have been analyzed particularly widely from an intercultural perspective both in periodicals such as the *Journal of International Business Studies* and in books (e.g., Adler, 1986; Casse & Deol, 1985; Graham, 1985).

Work on the influence of culture on diplomatic negotiation has proceeded alongside the general expansion in intercultural studies. Initial steps were taken by area specialists struck by the deterioration in U.S.-Japanese relations under President Nixon in the early 1970s. Kunihiro (1972) was the first to point out the detrimental effect on diplomacy of incompatible uses of language and nonverbal communication. His study was followed by a Brookings Institution project that examined the consequences of cross-cultural differences on a whole range of historical U.S.-Japanese negotiations (Destler, Sato, Clapp, & Fukuri, 1976, pp. 89-124). Iriye (1979) then set the diplomatic conundrum in a wider civilizational context. Finally, a 1979 conference at the East-West Center in Hawaii produced the wide-ranging book *Cultural Factors in International Relations* (Anand, 1981); the chapters by Kimura, Strazar, and Wang are particularly noteworthy. Taken together, this series of studies presents a convincing portrait of the effect of cultural dissonance on negotiation, all the more convincing for being painted by scholars of both Japanese origin and American origin.

The next step was to provide a theoretical underpinning to the empirical findings. Credit for this must go to Fisher (1980), an anthropologist and former U.S. Foreign Service officer. The more pronounced the cultural gap between the negotiating parties, he argues, the greater the potential for misunderstanding and the more time they will lose talking past each other. Different values, mannerisms, forms of verbal and nonverbal behavior, and notions of status may block confidence and impede communication even before the substance of negotiation is addressed. Culture, he believes, impinges on negotiation itself in four crucial ways: (a) by conditioning one's perception of reality, (b) by blocking out information inconsistent or unfamiliar with culturally grounded assumptions, (c) by projecting meaning onto the other party's words and actions, and (d) by possibly impelling the ethnocentric observer to an incorrect attribution of motive. Fisher goes on to compare American, French, Japanese, and Mexican assumptions about such issues as the nature of the negotiating encounter; the importance of form, hospitality, and protocol; the choice of delegates; decision-making style; national self-image; methods of persuasion; and linguistic conventions. In his 1988 study *Mindsets,* Fisher provides a textbook for the student of culture and diplomacy and sets his thesis within a general context.

Alongside Fisher's pioneering work, a number of other authors have helped consolidate the study of culture and negotiation. Plantey (1982) provides the authoritative insight of a former ambassador to Madagascar, a UN delegate, and an assistant secretary-general of the Western European Union. Calling for a culturalist interpretation of negotiation, Plantey points out that "few nations have the same scale of values, the same idea of society or the same linguistic, cultural or religious heritage" (p. 536). The international negotiator should take this into account. However, "Westerners often wrongly underestimate the foundation of some of their partners' attitudes" (p. 538), giving unnecessary offense and impeding agreement. Coming from the conflict resolution school of thought, the Korzenny and Ting-Toomey volume (1990) and recent articles by Janosik (1987), Black and Avruch (1989), and Avruch and Black (1991) also should be mentioned. Finally, in *Negotiating Across Cultures* (Cohen, 1991), I attempt to marry theory to empirical findings in a comparative study of U.S. diplomacy. From extensive interviews with practitioners and, where possible, primary documents, I demonstrate how cultural differences may impinge on every stage of the negotiating process.

Case Studies

A substantial body of evidence corroborates the culturalist thesis. Let us briefly examine a selection of the material. Strazar (1981) considered the effect of cross-cultural elements in the negotiation of the 1951 San Francisco peace treaty between the United States and Japan. Her conclusion was that an important contribution to the success of the talks was made by the complementarity, in this particular situation, of cultural traits. She observed several congruences, three particularly salient. The first of these derived from the contrasting outlooks on the natural environment inculcated by the two cultures. Briefly, whereas the Japanese *awase* ethos requires humans to adjust themselves to their surroundings, the American *erabi* ethos seeks to tame and manipulate nature. Thus, historically, Japan has displayed an outstanding adaptability toward a changing international situation; the United States has had an optimistic and manipulative ("can do") approach to international problems. In the context of the post-war American occupation of Japan, these characteristics enabled both sides to work together constructively for the rehabilitation of the war-torn country. Counterexamples, such as the outcomes of the Franco-Prussian War of 1870-1971 and World War I, demonstrate that such an easy mutual accommodation should not be taken for granted.

The second element of complementarity derived from the different principles governing the organization of the two societies. Here the hierarchical, or vertical, structure of Japanese society was faced by the egalitarian, or horizontal, structure of American life. This difference meant that, on the one hand, the Japanese were prepared to accept without resentment their subordination to the American occupiers and to defer to their judgment. On the other hand, American willingness to treat the Japanese on an equal status and to draw them into partnership not only laid the groundwork for the peace treaty but also ensured that the Japanese negotiators could express freely their own views. What might have been seen as a dictated peace was transformed into an accord based on full consent.

At a third level, the traditional Japanese concept of *amae* (roughly, the propensity to depend and presume on another's benevolence), a derivative of the interdependence of Japan's intensely group-oriented culture, matched up with American readiness to accept responsibility and leadership— which can be accounted for in terms of the equally characteristic American values of enterprise and individualism. Strazar saw these paradigms reflected in the curious allocation of roles at San Francisco, where Japan played the part of the client and the United States the defending attorney, pleading Japan's case before the other allies.

Kimura (1980), a Japanese Sovietologist, examined the interaction between Soviet and Japanese negotiating tendencies in a study of the fisheries talks held between the two countries in the spring of 1977 in Moscow. He is convinced that it was not just the objective intractability of the issues involved that weighed on negotiation. The clash of culturally conditioned patterns of behavior and thought also complicated and prolonged matters. Whereas cultural differences acted complementarily at San Francisco, they proved antithetical in Moscow.

Like Strazar, Kimura sees Japan as attempting to exploit its relative weakness in the face of a stronger opponent by creating an *amae* relationship with the Soviet Union. However, *amae,* which casts the weaker party in the role of supplicant, presupposes the indulgence of the more powerful partner. What worked with the United States, with its tradition of equity and sympathy for the downtrodden, was not calculated to succeed with a Soviet Union preoccupied with rank, power relationships, and the establishment of its own superiority. To the contrary, true to the time-honored authoritarian ethos of Mother Russia, Soviet negotiators were inclined to hammer home their advantage and conducted, in the eyes of the Japanese press, diplomacy by intimidation. Thus the asymmetry of U.S. and Japanese social organization, which proved so helpfully complementary in 1951, was replaced by the disruptive symmetry of Japanese and Soviet status consciousness in 1977.

As far as the tactics of negotiation are concerned, Kimura argues that, on the whole, the Japanese are skeptical of the value of elaborate ploys and stratagems. It is sufficient, they believe, to convey the justice of their position as accurately as possible for their rival to be convinced. This approach was exemplified fully in the fisheries talks. In the face of a symmetrical Soviet tendency to self-righteousness, it was unlikely to help matters. After all, the spirit of give-and-take, pivotal in the Western tradition of negotiation, assumes that neither partner has a monopoly of truth and justice.

A Swedish perspective on intercultural problems in aid negotiations with Tanzania has been provided by Elgström (1990). In the light of the lopsided, philanthropic nature of the relationship, acute difficulties are hardly to be expected in the course of talks. Cross-cultural antinomies emerge, rather, after agreements have been reached. One fundamental, philosophical gap derives from contrasting attitudes to the very meaning and purpose of aid. For Sweden, foreign aid is intended to set the recipient on the road to sturdy self-reliance; donor responsibility and independence are stressed; and goals and priorities are to be determined, at the very least, on the basis of a mature, mutual exchange between partners in development. In short, Swedes see aid from an individualist, egalitarian perspective. To their frustration and disappointment, Tanzanians, coming from a quite different tradition of community life and patron-client relations, seldom say no, only infrequently raise demands or complaints, and are not apt to come forward with initiatives of their own. Worse yet, aid, rather than promoting proud independence, creates devastating and overwhelming dependence. In contradiction to the West European Marshall Plan experience, enterprise is undermined rather than promoted, and incentives to passivity, not autonomy, are provided.

After mentioning other familiar problems of intercultural communication, Elgström turns to the question of the fulfillment of aid agreements. The key point here is that Sweden, according to Elgström, tends to adopt a rather soft approach. Because of a culturally grounded dislike of confrontation, and an eminently sensible, problem-solving approach to disagreement, Swedish negotiators are very reluctant to introduce proposals containing harsh demands and conditions. Officials from the Swedish aid agency SIDA (presumably aghast at the prospect of their performing a patronizingly supervisory role) are also unwilling to adopt a strict attitude to Tanzanian implementation. However, experience has taught the Swedes not to place too much confidence in the Tanzanians' ability to plan and carry out aid projects, and optimism about the possibility of improving the situation has been dented severely.

Egypt and Israel:
Civilizational Disjunction

A prominent contemporary example of intercultural disharmony is provided by the relationship between Egypt and Israel. Various studies, by participants or based on primary resources, have demonstrated that Egypt and Israel had several opportunities over the years to resolve their conflict (e.g., Cohen, 1990; Ya'acobi, 1989). My own research established four chances before the 1973 war—in 1953, 1954-1955, 1970, and 1971. During each period there were numerous contacts, prenegotiations, and abortive mediation efforts. Early on, both sides recognized that no insuperable conflict of interests was dividing them. Separated by an enormous desert, they could easily afford to live and let live. Sadly, chances were squandered. But for U.S. mediation, it is doubtful whether the post-1973 peace process would have borne fruit. Indeed the 1979 peace treaty and the establishment of diplomatic relations have not solved the inability of the Egyptian and Israeli governments to settle their differences bilaterally. As one "converted" Israeli put it: "Neither understands the other, and everyone talks like a deaf man. Each side thinks it knows what the other is thinking, and they're both wrong" (Fletcher, 1988, p. 5).

The gap between Egyptian and Israeli cultures runs deep and wide. Whereas Egyptian society is a product of millennia of settled village life, Israel is a society of immigrants gathered in from the townships and cities of Eastern Europe and the Arab world. For Egyptians the extended family —the clan—provides a vital and almost inescapable framework for life's activities. Group values reign supreme, defining a subordinate role for the individual and casting leadership in a paternalist mold. A supreme value is assigned to the avoidance of shame, and elaborate codes of hospitality and courtesy have evolved. To preserve face and to defend communal harmony from the ravages of the feud—that inevitable concomitant of segmental lineage—a language of hints and nuances has developed, avoiding embarrassment at all costs and softening disagreement. Conflict is to be masked and evaded as much as possible, but intricate mechanisms of dispute settlement are in place if required. Arabic, the language of the sacred Koran, the unmediated word of God, is cherished for its declamatory, bardic qualities. Islam itself, a great rock of reassurance in a cruel world, teaches reverence for eternal truths, respect for authority—both divine and human—and affinity with the wider community of the faithful.

Jewish culture was formed by very different influences. Instead of attachment to a universal *umma,* Judaism inculcated a sense of separateness, of being picked out by the deity for a special role. Following defeat at the hands of Rome and subsequent dispersion, it was the sacred texts of Judaism (Bible, Mishna, and Talmud) that preserved national identity and attachment to the ancient homeland. Study was regarded highly, literacy a religious duty. Wherever Jews lived, academies of learning were established and habits of rigorous textual analysis were inculcated. To support themselves, the Jews, prohibited from owning land and drawn together to practice their faith, lived an urban existence of artisans and petty traders. Not for them the tranquility of uninterrupted settlement, but memories of a precarious, wandering existence—a long chain of pogroms, persecutions, and expulsions terminating, finally, in the Nazi death camps. Out of the disasters, social experiments, and wrecked empires of the 20th century, a motley collection of idealists, refugees, and survivors gathered to establish somehow an independent state. A clean break was to be made with the past, but much cultural baggage was carried forward: the collective lessons and defense mechanisms of history's victims; a political system, fiercely disputatious and democratic, that has its roots in the communal politics of the *shtetl* (small town); an abrasive society of patriotic individualists, moved not by shame, but by guilt, the internalized dictates of conscience; and a mode of discourse dismissive of the circumlocutions, rituals, and small courtesies of the Orient, preferring, rather, an unadorned, *dugry* (straightforward, blunt) style of speech.

From this civilizational disjunction, a volatile chemistry of intercultural dissonance emerged between Egypt and Israel. Crisis management was gravely undermined by it. Ongoing diplomacy, to this day, is hindered by its effects. Nowhere is it more acutely felt than in prenegotiation contacts and at the negotiating table. During the 1949-1977 period, the clash of two contradictory impulses proved a formidable obstacle to negotiation. On the one side was Egyptian insistence on a prior guarantee of satisfaction from Israel on certain irreducible points of principle such as the land, sovereignty, and rights of the Palestinians. Behind the scenes Egyptians and Israelis might meet. But after military defeat, Egypt, as a quintessentially shame culture, could not run the risk of another public humiliation. On matters of honor, mediation is the conventional mode of conflict resolution. So the cut-and-thrust of a negotiation, let alone the risk of failure, was an unbearable prospect. If Egypt could not persuade Israel to settle for mediation, it had to have an advance assurance that its basic conditions would be met. Israelis, for their part, impatient of the seeming Arab preoccupation with honor, wedded to the adversarial tradition of litigation, and having been ostracized and blackballed for generations, viewed direct negotiations as a sine qua non. Furthermore, in the pragmatic, meticulous, case-by-case tradition of Talmudic literature, they failed to see the virtue in philosophical formulas. Significantly, the 1977 Sadat visit to Jerusalem broke the taboo on meetings in public but did not remove Egyptian inhibitions on direct talks. Within a few weeks, Israelis discovered that the parties were still unable to negotiate without an intermediary. Nor could they overcome, unaided, their dispute over the relative merits of detail versus principles, Egypt needed a generalized declaration of principles; the best it could get was the detailed Camp David framework for peace. Israel resisted to the end, explicitly agreeing to the territories-for-peace formula, and only conceded the phrase "legitimate rights of the Palestinian people" within an entangling thicket of procedural detail. Since 1981 the two states enjoy full diplomatic relations. But the protracted procedural wrangling over Palestinian autonomy, Taba, and broadening the peace process demonstrated that the old antinomies persist.

Actual negotiations have been hindered by linguistic, behavioral, and tactical dissonances. In person Egyptians have shown themselves to be charming and courteous interlocutors. But the surrounding atmosphere for negotiations has been damaged by the effect of Arabic hyperbole on the Israeli ear. (Even a cursory comparison between the Bible and the Koran in translation brings out the striking contrast between the two ancient expressive traditions.) From an Israeli perspective, Egyptian leaders and the Cairo press appear to have striven often for rhetorical effect at the expense of international tranquility. It is difficult for Israeli governments to negotiate against a background of personal (and, regrettably, racial) abuse. More at home with a lower key, less baroque presentation, Hebrew speakers may well take verbal excess at its face value. This factor undermined confidence in Egyptian good faith pre-1956, contributed to the outbreak of the 1967 war, harmed contacts in the winter of 1978 (when semiofficial Egyptian newspapers were replete with virulent denunciations of Israeli Prime Minister Begin), and has continued intermittently to this day.

When it comes to face-to-face contact, roles are reversed. Here the typical Israeli preference for plainspokenness has conflicted with the Egyptian instinct for more emollient, indirect formulations. Time and again, Egyptians have been distressed and offended by blunt remarks, unadorned proposals, or ultimatums. Israeli military officers and political figures are the main culprits here; trained diplomats are less prone to this kind of solecism. An example is Foreign Minister Dayan's tactless suggestion, at his very first meeting with his Egyptian counterpart in November 1977, of a separate peace. Another is Begin's hectoring and patronizing address at the official dinner for an Egyptian delegation in January 1978, after which the Egyptians were withdrawn. Yet another was Defense Minister Arens's demand, following the Ras Burka tragedy, for an immediate apology and a full report within a few days—or else. All such efforts at "straight talking" did more harm than good.

Many important Egyptian *démarches* toward Israel have taken the form of subtle political signals. Such communications avoid the danger of humiliating snubs and come naturally from what Hall (1976) has called a "high context" culture (in which timing, circumstances, and gesture may be more expressive than the actual words). However, they invariably cut little ice with "low context" Israeli governments more at home with carefully drafted legal propositions. In 1953 a barrage of signals from Egypt was not given due weight by Israeli Prime Minister Ben-Gurion. For instance, Ben-Gurion chose to nitpick the contents of a letter from Egyptian leader Nasser, disregarding both the remarkable fact of its dispatch and its official letterhead. Before the 1973 war, Prime Minister Meir similarly squandered opportunities for negotiation contained in albeit indirect Egyptian initiatives. In 1970, Nasser, following behind-the-scenes mediation by President Tito, invited veteran Zionist leader and noted dove Nahum Goldmann to Cairo. Meir refused to accept the invitation on the grounds that she alone would choose Israel's envoy. Again in 1971 she and her government were preoccupied with textual details of President Sadat's February 4 proposal for an interim agreement to reopen the Suez Canal, while overlooking the underlying significance of the proposal itself (Ya'acobi, 1989).

The conduct of Egyptian-Israeli negotiations, particularly on security-related matters, has been marked by the encounter of opposing motifs.

Egypt's opening gambits, from the armistice talks of 1949 onward, usually have left considerable leeway for maneuver. Proposals for interim agreements in 1974 and 1975 called for much deeper Israeli withdrawals than subsequently were agreed to. Egypt's opening proposal at Camp David, including a cheeky claim for war damages, was also demonstrably far from a last word. Israel's reaction has been to question the good faith of its interlocutor. As Israeli President Herzog once patronizingly remarked: "This atmosphere of Middle East market bargaining is rather typical and emphasizes one of the problems which face Israel—or indeed anybody else—in negotiations with the Arab World" (*Jerusalem Post,* 1971). Experience has not blunted the surprise of being faced with what seem like exorbitant demands or helped Israel distinguish the negotiable from the irreducible elements of the Egyptian position. Meanwhile, Israel, preoccupied with the narrowness of its margin of survival and also constrained by a vigilant public opinion, has tended to stake out opening positions leaving relatively little room for subsequent withdrawal.

In the middle and end games of a negotiation, the logic of these rival strategies works itself out. For Israel the dogged rear guard action, the belated and grudging concession eked out to extract the maximum advantage, has corresponded nicely to its sense of vulnerability. Particular emphasis is placed, in the scholastic tradition of Jewish learning, on contractual precision and fine shades of meaning. Enormous effort is invested in shutting off possible loopholes even beyond the point at which diminishing returns set in. In 1979 Israel at first insisted that the peace treaty specify the position of every Egyptian guard post in the Sinai. Egypt, for its part, having left itself greater freedom of action, can afford more self-confident and expansive maneuvering. The different decision-making processes—that of Israel diffuse and irreverent, that of Egypt centralized and deferential—reinforce these respective tendencies. At this stage, faced by Israeli tenacity, pedantry, and delaying tactics, Egyptian negotiators begin to indicate acute signs of discomfort; the psychological costs of an anyway fraught encounter begin to outweigh the benefits; deadlock descends.

One could continue with this narrative, but the point is clear: For more than 40 years, Egyptian-Israeli diplomacy has been gravely impeded by intercultural communication problems and antithetical approaches to negotiation. A clear pattern exists against a backdrop of shifting actors and circumstances. But for U.S. (and in a few instances, UN) mediation, most Egyptian-Israeli negotiations never would have got off the ground at all, notwithstanding a convergence of interests. Once under way, the parties, left to their own devices, soon have lost patience with each other and have begun to doubt each other's good faith. Some aspects of the Egyptian-Israeli relationship are obviously unique. But observing other uneasy associations, such as those between India and China, Australia and Malaysia, Greece and Turkey, the United States and Mexico, one suspects that this pattern of pervasive intercultural dissonance may be less aberrant than it appears at first sight.

Bridging the Culture Gap: Model C

Is there an antidote to the disorder diagnosed above? One answer is already implicit in the Egyptian-Israeli experience: Resort to mediation. The remarkable fact is that, without exception, every major agreement between the two states from 1949 to the present has rested on the constant good offices of a mediator. Among their manifold contributions to dispute settlement, mediators can perform vital intercultural functions. In a confrontation between collectivistic and individualistic cultures, they can protect and, if necessary, save the face of the honor-conscious party; they can smooth the friction between adversarial and conciliatory ethoses of conflict resolution; they can ease the linguistic strain between high and low context communicators. Above all, they can act as cultural interpreters, explaining the parties to each other.

Some or all of these functions can be shown to have been performed by empathetic mediators such as Bunche and Kissinger. More than that, when these functions were not performed or were performed inadequately, the result was failure. Samuel Lewis, United States ambassador to Israel from 1977 to 1985, is convinced that the Egyptian-Israeli autonomy talks broke down because the United States unwisely insisted that the two sides negotiate face-to-face. Rug merchants might haggle this way, but when it came to matters of honor in the Middle East, parties to a dispute did not make concessions in each other's presence. A more successful example of cross-cultural perspicacity can be taken from an earlier period: In July 1977, when President Sadat sought a political gesture to win the confidence of the new Begin government, he turned to the United States ambassador for advice. Ambassador Eilts's idea struck the perfect intercultural note of reconciliation: the return with full military honors of the recently discovered bodies of 19 Israeli soldiers killed in the 1973 war. To bring a body to rest in consecrated ground is an important Jewish religious injunction with powerful emotional overtones for the state of Israel.

Lewis's warning and Eilts's inspiration suggest the necessary qualities and qualifications of what I propose to call Model C, culturally-sensitive actors, whether mediators or negotiators. First, these individuals are aware of the gamut of cultural differences and do not naively assume that "underneath we are all pretty much the same." Second, they perceive the potency of religious and other cultural resonances. Third, Model C actors grasp that Western rationality is based on culture-bound values and assumptions. Finally, they do not take for granted that an expedient (such as face-to-face negotiation) that works for one culture necessarily works for another.

In recent years many negotiation theorists have concluded that in an interdependent world in which armed conflict is increasingly unacceptable, states must learn to surmount the cramped, competitive, win-lose, traditional philosophy of negotiation. At best this approach can do no more than produce compromise, the distribution of existing goods. In its place, it is suggested, a win-win, alternative philosophy should be fostered. Based on joint problem-solving and nonconfrontational methods, this approach looks beyond narrow definitions of self-interest and a static resource base to seek innovative, integrative solutions.

Win-win presents a more edifying prospect than win-lose. However, Model A, as opposed to Model T (as Fisher, 1986, calls it), makes certain presuppositions that may be ethnocentric. Joint problem solving assumes the ability of actors to establish an egalitarian working partnership, to engage in a sustained and unmediated exchange of ideas, to detach the immediate issue from the overall relationship, and to separate the subjective—emotional, personal, ethnic—from the objective aspects of the matter. In the light of what has been said so far, these assumptions can hardly be taken as given. Societies that place a high premium on intangibles such as status, honor, face, hierarchy, personalism in relationships, and ethnic or religious identity may find it difficult to engage in joint problem solving. Difficulties faced by Swedish SIDA officials in Tanzania illustrate this point.

Model C negotiators recognize diversity and eschew universal panaceas—ready-made recipes for success. To the contrary, they prepare for their task, first, by achieving self-awareness of the hidden assumptions they themselves bring to the negotiating table. Before entering a negotiation, they immerse themselves in their partners' culture and history, not just the issue at hand. Ideally they will know the target language. Only after all of this will they feel in a position to design a negotiating strategy adapted to the individual cultural expectations and needs of their interlocutors.

Conclusion

The historical record provides compelling evidence of the disruptive effects of intercultural incompatibility. A range of possible outcomes may be discerned. Dissonance may contribute to the failure of negotiations.

The Egyptian-Israeli case strikingly demonstrates this gloomy eventuality. It may produce a less than efficient outcome. Examples can be found in the U.S.-Japanese relationship. It may disrupt the wider relationship. The Soviet-Japanese fisheries negotiation is a case in point. What is particularly significant in the Swedish-Tanzanian and Egyptian-Israeli cases is that antinomies recurred over long periods of time even though context and participants changed. In other words, an underlying, relational incompatibility, rather than transient factors, was at work.

Some theorists have tended to minimize the effect of intercultural factors on the grounds that diplomats and experts share common assumptions—indeed belong to an international culture. The evidence presented here suggests that this theory is only partially valid. In the Egyptian-Israeli dispute, the ethnocentric views of political leaders, parliamentarians, and army officers usually drowned out the voices of professional diplomats. In Soviet-Japanese and Swedish-Tanzanian negotiations, technical experts also were seen to be subject to cultural dissonances. Doubtless in long-running negotiations over highly specialized topics such as the law of the sea, arms control, and trade, supercultural attitudes are fostered among participants. But it is surely dangerous to take this encouraging development for granted.

Disharmonies in negotiation, then, derive from profound philosophical and methodological incompatibilities, not just from superficial, stylistic differences or momentary misunderstandings. In negotiations across cultures, a disinterested definition of the problem and an optimal solution derived from universal principles are not always attainable. This is no cause for pessimism. It does mean that improvements in negotiating outcomes cannot be derived just from perfecting the techniques and tactics of the negotiating process. On the other hand, it also follows that increased attention to cross-cultural skills cultivation of the Model C negotiator may pay handsome dividends.

4

A Professional's View

WINFRIED LANG

National Versus Professional Cultures

A broad working definition of culture is suggested by the *New Encyclopedia Britannica:*

> Culture, the integrated pattern of human knowledge, belief and behavior. Culture thus defined consists of language, ideas, beliefs, customs, taboos, codes, institutions, tools, techniques, works of art, rituals, ceremonies and other related components; and the development of culture depends upon man's capacity to learn and to transmit knowledge to succeeding generations. (1990, Vol. 3, p. 784)

This comprehensive definition, which amounts to an impressive though probably incomplete list of component parts, has one major advantage: It does not restrict culture to a specific ethnic phenomenon. It not only applies to so-called national cultures shared by people that have a specific ethnic or national background but also covers what Faure and Sjöstedt in

Chapter 1 call "subcultures," such as organizational culture, professional culture, and corporate culture.

If one examines linkages between culture and negotiation—in particular, inter*national* negotiation—one is tempted to regard culture exclusively as *national* culture.

Recent developments, such as European integration, should remind us that, at least in parallel to the national cultures of Europe, a broader *regional culture* cutting across traditional boundaries is about to emerge. The delegates negotiating on behalf of the European Community are, as far as their negotiating styles and perceptions are concerned, influenced not only by their respective national cultures but also by a new composite culture proper to the Community.

As the features of a common European culture are about to emerge—the consequence of centuries of a common history—one should not neglect the various regional cultures that exist below the level of nation-states, cultures that sometimes reflect the specific identity of an ethnic minority. Culture above and below the state level has its political significance.

With some justification the linkage between culture and negotiation has been called by Zartman and Berman (1982, p. 224) a "most troublesome question," especially in the context of international negotiation research. These authors also refer to the existence of an *international diplomatic culture* that socializes its members into similar behavior (p. 226). Furthermore they qualify elements such as language, cultural connotations, social rules, and taboos as peripheral to the understanding of the basic negotiating process (p. 227).

The existence of a "common professional culture of diplomacy" also has been recognized by Glenn, Witmeyer, and Stevenson (1977, p. 59); however, they are unable to determine exactly the extent and direction of the modifications brought into national negotiating cultures by the more transnational negotiating practice. They try to assign specific negotiating styles (factual-inductive, axiomatic-deductive, intuitive-affective) to specific delegations (U.S., Soviet, Arab), an endeavor that has been criticized by practitioners who attended the United Nations Institute for Training and Research (UNITAR) seminar in Geneva in 1980.

Hofstede (1989) stresses the important impact that culture has on national negotiating styles but acknowledges that persons involved in international negotiations have developed a "professional negotiation culture." This professional culture is more superficial than the national cultures because it consists of well-understood symbols and common habits, rather than shared values. Instead of accepting the existence of a general professional culture of negotiators, Hofstede assigns to each type of negotiator (e.g., diplomats, bureaucrats, business people, lawyers, engineers) a professional culture of its own. In a nutshell, "Negotiations are easier with people from other countries sharing the same professional culture than with those who do not" (p. 194).

To some extent this view could be related to the view of Poortinga and Hendriks (1989, p. 203). These researchers describe negotiators as "expatriates." Despite a proverbial grain of truth, this view represents an overall erroneous perception because it neglects inter alia the fact that practically no negotiator is only a negotiator or mainly a negotiator for most of his or her life. Furthermore this view does not take into account one recent development: Fewer international negotiations are carried out by diplomats residing abroad; more international agreements are negotiated by experts coming from the respective capitals.

In the almost classic treatise on international negotiations, Iklé (1987) expresses the opinion that cultural traditions may find some reflection in negotiation methods. This view is qualified, however, by the following remark: "But usually they [cultural traditions] are not pervasive enough to produce a distinctly recognizable negotiation style. More important are the differences in government structure determining the domestic constraints under which each negotiator must operate" (p. 225). This general statement is followed by an impressionistic comparison of negotiating skills in the East and the West. Now, as the political and ideological separation of East and West is about to disappear—and the assimilation of government structures (parliamentary democracy) is about to take place—one may expect a trend toward a more unified negotiating culture cutting across the old divide between capitalism and communism.

It comes as no surprise that the comprehensive investigation into the cross-cultural dimension of international negotiation (Fisher, 1979) practically neglects professional negotiating culture and its transnational character. This neglect can be explained by the main purpose of this study—namely, to identify the national differences that future career diplomats are likely to be confronted with.

Cultural differences certainly have an impact on North-South negotiations, especially those related to development projects. A handbook addressed to Third World negotiators (Sunshine, 1990, pp. 25-90) gives ample advice on how to negotiate with counterparts from the United States and Japan, on how to react most efficiently to the negotiating styles of these two major donor nations. Despite its focus on national cultural differences, this handbook recognizes the importance of professional cultures: "Many professions have a distinct and distinctive culture, which largely transcends national borders; exactly like ethnic cultures, a profession embraces cultural values (basic beliefs, norms and customs) and adopts a cultural perspective (habits, assumptions and selective perceptions)" (p. 81).

Such professional culture is traced back to professional schools, where students are exposed to a standard method of scholarship, are encouraged to master and apply a standardized analytical approach, and so on. Although fully recognizing the role of professional cultures, this handbook does not hesitate to introduce one major caveat—namely, "that the commonalities of professional cultures will invariably be tempered by differences in the professional's national, sectoral and institutional cultures" (p. 82). This handbook concludes its treatment of professional cultures by defining the profiles of some professional cultures (engineers, lawyers, economists, and politicians; see Table 4.1).

These views, and probably a number of others, confirm that a large body of opinion exists, according to which the role of culture in international negotiations is not restricted to the impact of national cultures. Professional cultures also play a certain role. It even may be assumed that national and professional cultures compete with each other as far as their respective influence on international negotiations and the perceptions and style of negotiators is concerned.

Two important questions remain unanswered: Do professional cultures facilitate the progress of international negotiations? Do national cultures impede the progress of international negotiations?

Factors Curtailing the Role of Culture

In this section I try to shed some light on several issues raised in the previous section and on questions raised elsewhere in studies of the role of culture in international negotiations. Many years of personal involvement in such negotiations facilitate this task.

The chances of assessing the relative importance of the culture factor in international negotiations in a meaningful and reliable way are slim. *Culture* is an extremely broad concept. This broad scope does not facilitate research that goes beyond merely collecting personal impressions. One has to acknowledge that most personal accounts of past negotiating experience will differ in respect of the culture concept from that of other witnesses. In view of those highly personal interpretations of the term *culture,* it is difficult to arrive at a clear conclusion of which elements of a negotiation (actors, structure, strategies, process, outcome) are likely to be influenced by culture. Views already differ on the following questions: Are definitions of terms such as *compromise* or *truth* shared by the representatives of various cultures? Do collective long-standing memories have a stronger impact on negotiating behavior than the exposure of negotiators to recent problems?

TABLE 4.1 Profiles of Some Professional Cultures

Indices	Engineers	Lawyers	Economists	Politicians
Cultural Values				
Believe in:	The laws of physics	Statutory laws	The laws of economics	The law of survival
Have respect for:	Technology, computations, materials, designs	Authority, precedent, the "sanctity of contract," rules in general	Theories and statistical data	Patrons, parties, and partisan loyalty
Cultural Perspective				
See themselves as:	Builders and problem solvers	Defenders of justice, partisan advocates	Planners and policy advisers	Defenders of the public interest; mediators, ultimate decisionmakers
Express themselves through:	Numbers and works	Technical words and documents	Money	Approvals and directives
Suspicious of:	Timely project implementation and worker performance	Parties' good intentions and pledges	Sociopolitical variables	Rival bureaucrats and ambitious subordinates
Negotiating Style				
Team role(s):	Leader or technical specialist	Leader, spokesperson, technical adviser, or excluded	Leader of financial adviser	Leader
Negotiating focus:	Technical specifications	Parties' rights and duties	Costs, prices, payments	Satisfying superiors, avoiding criticism
Future concern:	Project implementation	Conflict resolutions	Cash-flow risks	Project completion
Communication style:	Precise and quantitative	Precise and logical, but perhaps argumentative	Technical and conservative	Cautious and self-protective

No experienced negotiator will dismiss the role of the personality factor in negotiations, be they national or international. No experienced negotiator will deny that the national background of a negotiator has a certain impact on his or her perceptions, styles, and other aspects in international negotiations. Thus culture as an important element of this background of the negotiator may play some role. The negotiator should, however, avoid interpreting actions according to the vague concept of *culture* if they cannot otherwise be explained by concrete facts. No experienced negotiator will reject the idea that for him- or herself each negotiation was a personal experience in which many traits of the respective person determined, to some extent, his or her behavior. Culture is certainly a factor in determining the self-perception of the negotiator; culture is, to some extent, a yardstick for evaluating the performance of a negotiator and for evaluating the outcome of a negotiation.

Despite some highly personal features of international negotiations, one should not lose sight of an important consideration: Negotiators, as a rule, do not act on their own behalf; they act on behalf of those who issue instructions. They receive instructions from some higher authority, if they are involved in intergovernmental negotiations; they receive instructions from the top management of their company, if they are involved in business negotiations. The stringency of these instructions and their implementation may vary according to different cultures, as considerations of leadership and hierarchy may differ from one national culture to another (impact on structure). The human factor and, accordingly, the culture factor certainly do have a direct impact on the negotiating process to the extent that instructions leave some leeway to the negotiator. There may exist some kind of built-in margin of maneuver, when the higher authority leaves it to the negotiator to decide certain issues at a lower level. Thus the role of culture in international negotiation is somewhat mitigated by instructions that follow mainly considerations of political or economic interest. As instructions reflect also the respective bargaining power and the relative weight of the parties involved, they also may be considered as part of the framework within which the personality factor (including culture) exerts its influence.

As previously stated, the question of which culture (national or professional) plays the leading role in international negotiation remains unanswered. Scientists, military officers, lawyers, engineers, and other professionals who attend a negotiating conference and belong to different national delegations speak a common language specific to their profession. In most instances, however, these experts are fully aware that, despite their special know-how and other commonalities, they are expected to represent and defend national positions contained in their respective instructions.

This expectation may well be the origin of some tensions between the national interest given in the respective instructions and the respective scientific or other expert opinion perceived in the light of specific knowledge acquired over the years. This expectation does not prevent negotiators from having almost no problem in understanding their counterparts in other delegations. This relationship with their counterparts in other delegations may be termed "compatibility" and/or "complementarity." It even may be, especially in the context of multilateral negotiations, that these experts are convened in subgroups to treat subsidiary technical (nonpolitical) issues, the solutions of which they are more likely to achieve in the light of their professional knowledge (Lang, 1991, p. 350).

Thus, in conferences devoted to treaty making, the final polishing of the texts usually is left to drafting committees mainly composed of lawyers; in the French language, this is called *toilette juridique*.

The following cases illustrate the role played by experts in international negotiations. When dealing with chemical or biological weapons, it goes without saying that experts in these sectors have a major say; they may act in subgroups specializing in most intricate matters of chemical science, biosciences, and other sciences (Lang, 1989b, p. 200). During negotiations on the protection of the ozone layer, a specialized group of scientists agreed on the ozone-depleting capacity of certain substances that had to be included in a scheme of control measures (e.g., reductions, freeze); this technical agreement was a precondition to be met before real restrictions could be negotiated at the political level. Other examples of experts' involvement in international negotiations may be quoted to corroborate the view that many negotiations are subject to growing specialization, which, in turn, enhances the importance of professional cultures for international relations in general.

The availability of experts in negotiations depends, to some extent, on the size of the respective delegation. Thus smaller delegations, especially from the Third World, are at a disadvantage whenever specialized knowledge is required to influence negotiations. To overcome this drawback, some of these delegations tend to overemphasize political issues, which they may master more easily. As far as the size of delegations is concerned, it should be added that a large delegation also may be a liability to the extent that leadership and coordination may not always be sufficiently available within the delegation.

As the growing complexity and specialization of international negotiations somehow restrict the role of the human factor and thus the impact of national cultures on the negotiating process, one should not neglect the fact that a specific *negotiation culture* is likely to become part of modern international relations. Important elements of this culture include (a) a sense of accommodation (at least somewhat stronger than the sense of confrontation), (b) awareness of the need for efficient and reliable communication, (c) the importance attached to flexibility and creativity, (d) willingness to go beyond traditional constraints of a national character, and (e) readiness to give higher priority to dispute prevention than to dispute settlement. This negotiation culture is constrained, however, by national interests imposed by the respective government on its negotiators by means of more or less stringent instructions.

This type of negotiation culture mainly emerged from two developments: (a) the growing interdependence of nations and issues and (b) the decreasing role of military force. It may well be that this negotiation culture is to benefit from various professional cultures cutting across traditional lines of thinking and behavior anchored in the national background of various negotiators.

Multilateral negotiations (conferences), where more than two national delegations meet, are likely to be less affected by national cultures determining the behavior of individual negotiators than bilateral negotiations, where the clash of national interests may be intensified by a confrontation of national cultures (e.g., perceptions and negotiating style). Because multilateral negotiations are becoming more frequent and more important than bilateral negotiations, they also contribute to this broad, emerging negotiation culture.

Multilateral negotiations tend to be even less affected by national cultures if they are embedded in the framework of an international organization, which by its very nature is supposed to act above and beyond narrow national limits. Nonnational actors, such as presiding officers or the chief executives of such organizations, are likely to contribute to the decreasing impact of national cultures on negotiations (Lang, 1989a, pp. 32-40). However, as regional or other groups have become important actors in multilateral negotiations, it may well be that national cultures are about to be replaced by group cultures, which in some instances could coincide with the national culture of the respective group leader.

While assuming that a plurality of professional cultures affects the actual behavior of the members of a delegation involved in international negotiations, one should not neglect the complexity of each of these professional cultures. For example, the professional culture of lawyers takes into account various elements: national differences in legal training, differences between common law and civil law traditions (the role of case law compared with the role of codified law), purely administrative experience and court experience, degree of familiarity with international law as a body of very specific rules and procedures, and relative dependence on or independence of the political authority issuing instructions. Nevertheless, despite possible variations within the professional culture of lawyers, who are part of different national delegations, they tend to speak a common language and are likely to be masters of largely identical concepts. This characteristic may mitigate barriers and obstacles rooted in national interest or national character (culture). It does not guarantee, however, a smooth course of negotiations, because legal questions usually represent only a minor part of the overall negotiating situation.

Similar impacts of professional culture may result from other participants (engineers, military officers, scientists, economists), who, when taken together, may exert considerable influence cutting across traditional positions of national origin.

Conclusion

The question, Does culture make a difference? cannot receive a simple and final answer. National cultures compete with professional cultures. Culture has some influence on international negotiations to the extent that the human factor plays a role. This human factor, however, is conditioned by two elements: instructions received from the competent authorities, and the growing complexity of international negotiations. Whereas the former element tends to decrease the role of the human factor, the latter, due to the need for specialization and the inclusion of experts in delegations, enhances the role of the human factor. These experts do, however, represent their professional culture at least as much as they represent their national culture.

5

A Pluralistic Viewpoint

VICTOR A. KREMENYUK

There are two extreme views on the interrelation between culture and negotiation. One perspective assumes that negotiation is an integral part of culture, where culture is regarded as a quality of civilization, the ability of people to live together through a certain code of conduct and communication. In this context negotiation may be regarded as a manifestation of culture because it embodies a certain code of conduct that is oriented toward noncoercive, civilized ways of solving disputes.

The other viewpoint regards culture and negotiation as two very separate notions that are far removed from each other. According to this view, *culture* is a broad concept describing basic things in human mentality and behavior such as language, tradition, ideology, approaches, and style. *Negotiation,* in turn, is a part of human activity connected with problem solving. It is oriented toward peaceful, nonviolent means of dispute resolution and, in this sense, is a much more cultured area of activity than the use of force; still there remains little direct connection between culture and negotiation.

In this chapter I offer an integrated picture of the interaction between culture and negotiation. In this sense it is necessary to emphasize that although these two views may seem irreconcilable, there can be no doubt that culture does have an impact on negotiation. The pertinent questions then become, In which ways does negotiation reflect culture? and, To what degree does culture affect negotiation?

Performance of Culture in Negotiation

Presentation of positions, type and composition of proposals, choice of negotiating strategy, bargaining, exchange of concessions, preparedness for compromise—these and other stages of negotiation acquire certain cultural characteristics, and these stages, in turn, are perceived by the other sides according to their cultural characteristics. This perception usually is translated into the so-called *negotiating culture* of an individual negotiator, which is a blend of civilizational, ethnic or national, and professional experiences magnified by the individual's cultural background. The most generalizing context in which culture is used in the study of negotiation, as well as in other areas of human activity, is when *culture* is treated as a synonym of or a substitute for *civilization*. It incorporates the most common, most unspecified, but quite distinctive aspects of the human behavior connected to the deepest roots of human background, type of thinking, education and training, cultural orientation, and so on. The notion of culture is used extensively also in negotiation. Culture is connected directly to the language, ethnic origin, political ideology or system, and place of birth of the negotiator. Here terms like *American, Soviet, French, German,* and *Japanese* are used extensively in the literature (Binnendijk, 1987).

The next dimension of culture is closer to what can be denominated as *professional culture.* This notion is centered on different areas of human activity where a special code of conduct due to occupational characteristics is worked out, implicitly or explicitly, and unites people of different national or ethnic origins in a special world of their professions: merchant marine, navy, aviation, communications, science, creative arts, diplomacy, and so on. Here, too, some voluntary definitions have been used that denominate bureaucratic or technocratic, artistic or scientific, and other similar cultures.

These three notions of culture very often are accompanied by the definition that determines the personal conduct of a negotiator—his or her education, manner, style, and communicability. Some writers would add other categories, such as organizational culture, to the list of cultures (Hofstede, 1989).

These factors have a definite impact on the negotiating style and the general conduct of negotiators, the type and nature of negotiated solutions, both when domestic negotiation is carried out and when cross-cultural contact takes place at the negotiation proper. On each occasion culture is important because it contributes to the way the parties approach each other and the issue they address.

The influence of culture on domestic negotiation is similar to the nation's decision-making process, which usually is based on the political system. The cultural factor here plays an important role in the decision-makers' analysis of the situation, in the type of options suggested, and in the explanation and propaganda of the position accepted. The cultural factor in this case has more of an introverting role, playing one of the components of the domestic setting of a negotiating party.

During cross-cultural negotiations, different cultural approaches are evident and can be compared. Negotiators have different approaches, styles, and manners that can be attributed not only to differences in positions or solutions but also to discrepancies in the whole vision of the situation that can be traced back to cultural heritage. This fact acquires even more importance because it usually overlaps with political and bargaining differences.

So the influence of the cultural factor on the process of negotiation is quite visible and important. It actually plays a role, first, in a certain framework in which positions are formulated and spelled out, and, second, in a certain setting in which these positions are put together and compared. In this respect it is also important to understand how this performance of the culture is conveyed into the process of negotiation.

The most important actors in any process of international negotiation are the negotiator at the table and the decisionmaker at home. Of these two actors, the negotiator has the more important role because it is his or her skill, intellect, knowledge, and abilities that are used to attain the decision-maker's goals. The cultural factor usually is conveyed through the personality of the negotiator.

Impact of the Negotiating Culture

The *civilizational impact* of this negotiating culture is revealed in the negotiator's general approach. Usually all people negotiate, domestically or internationally. Life within a civilization inevitably leads individuals, communities, and nations to find solutions to a disputed problem through nonviolent means. But where cultural background really makes a difference is in the way negotiation is treated by those who participate. Two distinctly different approaches are identified here: one regards negotiation as a secondary part of a relationship based on the balance of power—where military or economic power is the basic means of conflict resolution; the other considers negotiation to be a substitute for power, cherishes negotiation as such, and prefers any negotiated solution to coercion (Schelling, 1960).

This impact on negotiating culture may or may not be associated with a certain religion, tradition, or type of social system. Some traditions and social systems are obsessed with power and are based on the belief that the most reliable solutions are those achieved through force.

The *ethnic* or *national impact* on the negotiating culture can be identified as a host of characteristics tied to the type of decision-making procedure in a particular country and the general relationship between the negotiator and his or her superiors at home, together with national styles of behavior and thinking. Some authors writing about national styles of behavior tend to overemphasize the importance of this factor in understanding negotiating behavior (McDonald, 1984); others, more justifiably, try to trace the influence of national cultural factors to their closeness to the decision-making systems, including such elements as dominant ideology and type of leadership (*Soviet Diplomacy,* 1979). The eventual impact of this cultural factor on the negotiating culture of the negotiator is disclosed in his or her action, openness, readiness for a compromise, flexibility, and communicability.

The impact of *professional culture* on the conduct of negotiators is one of the primary elements that attests to the whole relationship between culture and negotiation. Professional culture usually is formed by the negotiator's education and personal experience and is revealed in such qualities as knowledge of the process and procedures, awareness of past precedents, acquaintance with colleagues from other delegations, and knowledge of the other delegations' language, religion, ideological orientation, or national background. There have been periods in diplomatic history when these qualities were simply indispensable, when professional culture was regarded as necessary as appropriate clothes. This regard was especially relevant for diplomacy of the 18th and 19th centuries, when the French diplomatic culture, along with the French language, was regarded as the only possible means of communication among negotiators and on which the whole negotiating culture was based.

Finally, there is the importance of the negotiator's *personal cultural background.* Level of education; personal qualities such as honesty, dignity, and loyalty; and adherence to basic human values and principles of civilized conduct—each of these plays an important role in the process of negotiation and in communication during this process. These qualities create an appropriate climate during negotiation, a sense of intimacy between negotiators, and the possibility of thinking in terms of joint interest.

Introversive Negotiating Culture

When culture, as described above, is merged with negotiation, two distinctive types of negotiating culture can be identified. The first of these can be found in the conduct of a negotiator who tends to create as much mystery as possible around his or her behavior, strategy, goals, and even interests. This is the type of narrow-minded, closed, secretive person whose whole negotiating performance is that of a mere agent of his or her government, acting as a mouthpiece for the decisionmaker back home and even emphasizing rigidity and intractability because of his or her role as a speaker for the government. Usually this type of negotiating culture is centered on highly formal, inflexible positions that may change only after long and exhausting bargaining, with unpredictable outcomes. This type of negotiating culture can be called *introversive.*

Sometimes an introversive negotiating culture can be used as a negotiating style intentionally, to obtain maximum results, as a tool to wrench as many concessions as possible from the other side. But when it can be traced in the conduct of the negotiator as some permanent feature, then it can be assessed as a blend of the negotiator's civilization, national or ethnic background, professional training, and personal conduct. In this case one even may predict the way such a negotiator will handle the business of "getting to yes" in his or her behavior: initial rigidity, reluctance to communicate except during the formal exchanges, long delays between separate stages of compromise (because in such negotiating culture the extent of power given to negotiators is quite limited), high level of hesitation before a yes is given to the other side's proposal, and emphasis on intragroup talks within one's own delegation, rather than talks across the table.

If we try to identify such a negotiating culture with established or typical patterns of behavior, it can be seen that introversive negotiating culture is usually characteristic of negotiators from closed, politically rigid societies with authoritarian or totalitarian political decision-making systems. These negotiators usually are trained to be the sheer executors of their superiors' instructions, without any deviation, improvisation, or self-initiated decisions. Historically this type of negotiator comes from closed societies (China, Japan, the Ottoman Empire, medieval Russia), where negotiators were oriented toward obedience and following the established rules of conduct, rather than openness and curiosity toward the outside world. In the case of negotiation, these people look for opportunities from the other side's proposals.

This type of negotiating culture may be efficient when negotiation is regarded as a ritual, a long-standing confrontation through nonmilitary means, rather than a process of joint decision making. In this case the negotiator who associates him- or herself with the confrontational style oriented toward "over-sitting" a counterpart may be better suited to the task than any other type of negotiator. But when confronted with other types of negotiators, he or she probably will be regarded as untrustworthy, unreliable, personally irresponsible, and, because of the constraints imposed by cultural background, incapable of striking a favorable deal.

As an example of such negotiations, one may recall U.S. Secretary of State Vance's talks with his Soviet counterpart in March 1977. Vance brought to Moscow a package of proposals that could have advanced results on the Strategic Arms Limitation Talks (SALT) Treaty, but he was rebuffed by Soviet negotiators who could not be flexible enough to abrogate the Vladivostok arrangements reached by President Ford and Secretary Brezhnev in 1974 (Carter, 1983).

Extroversive Negotiating Culture

The distinctive characteristics of the extroversive negotiating culture are (a) reasonable openness of the decision-making process, including interactions with the negotiator; (b) emphasis on informal exchanges during the negotiations and on the availability of different options (each can serve as a basis of agreement); (c) flexibility; and (d) avoidance of hard bargaining. This culture basically is oriented toward negotiation as a universal tool of problem solving. It prefers to regard negotiation as part of a broad process of communication among nations that parallels the development of trade and commerce and the flow of people, goods, services, and ideas. Nations are thus interdependent, creating a relationship in which negotiation becomes not only a universal tool of problem solving but also a modus vivendi.

This culture has its origins in ancient times, when societies built their fortunes on the exchange of goods and services and therefore were interested in the art of negotiation. In the Middle Ages this tradition was continued and developed by other trading nations and city-states such as the Hanseatic League, Italian city-states, and Dutch cities. In modern times the extroversive negotiating culture is associated with the functioning of democratic societies. Based on Rousseau's idea of the "contrat social," these societies incorporate the idea of negotiation into business, politics, consumption, personal relationships (e.g., marriage contracts), labor relations, and many other areas. In these societies the idea of negotiation has been extended into international relations and is regarded as part of a huge, long-term, multilateral process of building a world order based on ideas of a human global community.

The extroversive negotiating culture has developed a profound set of negotiating rules and regulations. It is no surprise that current negotiation practice has been influenced heavily by the work and writings of Western specialists on negotiation; Western society, after all, has moved toward the development of a global community based not so much on national power and affluence, but more on the notions of mutual benefit, joint interest, and a search for opportunity. This type of negotiating culture relies for its effectiveness on working out acceptable options, the inclusion of as many parties to negotiation as possible (legislative bodies, mass media, interest groups), and the active use and manipulation of information. In contrast, the introversive counterpart relies on rigid adherence to a single desirable solution, secrecy, and the concentration of decision-making power in the hands of executive bodies. The extroversive negotiating culture transforms negotiation from a one-shot, government-to-government, highly formalized deal into a larger process that includes a wide variety of negotiating approaches, actors, and forums. It is a whole new world of problem solving.

Conclusion

Over the last several years, relationships between former adversaries have improved dramatically as disputants have come to share such basic principles as adherence to common values, goals, common interest, and joint problem solving. This shift also has resulted in the introduction of some new elements into the culture of negotiation. Adversarial relations have been supplanted by partnership relations, joint decision making has increased while positional bargaining has decreased, and discussions have been carried out in a setting that facilitates achievement of positive results. At the same time, cultural differences persist. Despite all of the measures taken to smooth adversarial rhetoric and to find a sound basis for joint decisions, one still can come across problems arising from the negotiators' different cultural backgrounds.

As the world community enters a new stage of development, oriented toward world order and domination by international law, negotiation may well acquire a new standing as the only suitable substitute for coercion and violence. The importance of negotiation is certain to increase, leading to the creation of a large and loose *system of negotiations*. If this should happen, it will be necessary to work out some guiding principles to facilitate the conduct of these negotiations. Among the most important of these principles will likely be the requirement of a *universal negotiating culture.* Included in the new negotiating culture will have to be a universal *code of conduct,* including some shared approaches to training and education, the conduct of prenegotiation, and the implementation of negotiation in a mutually acceptable and beneficial manner. A cultural approach may well play an important role in achieving each of these larger and emerging purposes.

PART II

CASES AND ANALYSES

6

Water Resources:
Some Introductory Observations

JEFFREY Z. RUBIN

GUY OLIVIER FAURE

This is not a book about water resources. Nor is it a book about conflict and negotiation over water, a topic that deservedly has received a great deal of attention among scholars over the last decade or so. Rather this book addresses the way conflict over water resources—and the way such conflict is settled or resolved—is affected by the dimension of *culture*.

The term *culture* tends to be used as an all-purpose and therefore largely meaningless explanation of the things that one cannot readily explain in other ways. When all else fails, when there remains some bit of unaccounted variability in the data, resort to the explanation of culture. Culture *may* have important consequences for negotiation, of course, but it is often difficult to bring such consequences to the fore. The effects of culture on negotiation are rather subtle, easily masked by a host of situational constraints and opportunities. To make these effects more robust, it may be necessary to find some arena in which conflict is especially likely to arise—and is therefore likely to drag along on its waistcoats the effects of culture.

For this reason we have chosen to focus on the class of conflicts that arise over water resources. As observed earlier, this topic already has been the focus of considerable research. One of the most ambitious examinations of water resource disputes was conducted at IIASA in 1986 at the Workshop on the Management of International River Basin Conflicts. Particularly noteworthy were the contributions to this workshop by Babbitt and McDonald (1986), Kovacs (1986), Loucks and Salewicz (1986), Murphy (1986), Solanes (1986), and Vlachos (1986a).[1] Interestingly, in his summary of key findings to emerge from the 1986 IIASA workshop, Vlachos (1986c) lists a number of factors that were seen as important in describing and analyzing the nature, extent, and duration of transboundary water conflicts, but culture is not among them. A close reading of these findings reveals that culture was indeed an important consideration at work in each of the findings reported. Much has been written about culture, it appears, without acknowledgment of the existence and importance of this dimension.

Water has been part of the human experience from the very beginning; and for just that long it also has been the inspiration for hope, poetic vision, deep despair—and jarring conflict. Wherever water exists, there also exists the raison d'être for conflict between and within nations. The problem may be too much water, as when riparian floods have created human tragedies (e.g., Bangladesh), leading to conflict over the distribution and priority of humanitarian assistance. Even more frequent are the problems causes by scarcity of water resources (witness the conflicts over access to and uses of the Nile or the Euphrates) or the presence of the wrong kind of water ("Water, water, everywhere, nor any drop to drink," wrote Samuel Taylor Coleridge in *The Rime of the Ancient Mariner*).

Precisely because rivers have been around from the very beginning —indeed have helped make it possible for there to *be* a beginning to civilization—they are part of almost every culture's collective memory, its historical sense of itself, and the focus of its grandest national aspirations. As captured by Richard Wagner, the Rhine has been a magical, wondrous place in the mythology of Germany, even as the Nile, Euphrates, Yangtze, and Jordan are symbolic of life itself. Adding increasing complexity to the powerful symbolic meaning of water is the fact that different nations have regarded the same body of water in very different ways. For the Germans the Rhine may have mystical powers, but for the Dutch it is a waterway—often a polluted one—that must be navigated to get from start to destination. The Jordan may mean something very different to the Jews (with their several thousand year history of reliance on its modest flow for survival, agriculture, culture, and religion) and to modern Jordanians who also abut its waters but may have a more utilitarian vision.

Adding even further complexity to all of this is the fact that one's orientation toward the symbolic meaning of a river may be related to where one happens to sit along its banks. Those who sit upstream may be more inclined to focus on a river's utilitarian functions than those who happen to be farther downstream; witness the differing views of the Euphrates in this regard, by Turks, Syrians, and Iraqis. More generally, the fact that rivers are directional, flowing from upstream to down, means (in principle, at least) that the upstream nation can do whatever it wishes with the waterway: pollute it, divert it, and so forth. The downstream nation can do relatively little—or so it appears at first glance—to influence the behavior of its more powerful neighbor. Rivers thus elicit asymmetry, and such asymmetry may bring cultural considerations to the fore.

If rivers have directionality, they also have laterality: Rivers all have sides, or banks. This simple attribute has important consequences because it makes abundantly clear that the nations on either side of a dividing waterway are interdependent; what one side does affects the other. If "streams" elicit asymmetry, "edges" elicit symmetry. The problem of pollution in the Black Sea, the Gulf of Aqaba, the Mediterranean, or the Rhine is a problem that all abutters share in, contribute to, and can help rectify; although riparian abutters may act as if pollution of their shared resource is a local problem, rivers flow into lakes and seas—transforming seemingly regional issues into matters of global interdependence. Although problems are shared, however, conflicting principles may well emerge for deciding whose problem it is and what to do about it. Should the boundary of a river (and therefore control and responsibility) be determined by some imaginary line running down the middle (a midchannel boundary) or by the river's bends and contours? The existence of competing international principles (see Chap. 10 by Slim on the Euphrates in this regard) only exacerbates riparian conflicts—making likely the emergence of cultural considerations.

Whether riparian nations sit across from one another, upstream or down, conflicts are certain to arise over the multiplicity of uses to which the resource is put. Fishing, shipping, waste disposal, generation of electrical power, drinking, irrigation, recreation, and washing are but a few of the many uses to which rivers are subjected. And among other things, conflicts over use may be driven by cultural forces, as when one nation has religious traditions that call for washing or burial in the holy waters of a river, while downstream another nation relies on that very body of water for drinking. Or it may be that a technologically developed nation relies on a river for industrial production, while its more agrarian neighbors depend on the river for farming uses that are rendered impossible once the water has been polluted. For some nations the availability of water is a matter of sheer survival, while for others it is matter of quality of life; such differences may have powerful cultural origins that warrant examination in this book.

In some sense, water is like mineral resources—regarded by nations as part of their national patrimony. Unlike mineral resources, however, it is unclear who owns the water. Snow is the responsibility and property of the country on whose land it happens to lie; but once the snow melts to flow downhill as water, ownership becomes uncertain and problems arise.[2] Who owns the bucket of water that an individual citizen of some country happens to scoop from a stream? The upstream nation? The nation within whose boundaries the bucket happens to lie? Indeed, is water any more the property of any one nation than the air that happens to lie within its national boundaries? Under such conditions of uncertainty, it should not be surprising that the often subtle effects of culture are likely to assume increasing importance.

Vlachos (1986b) has estimated that nearly 40% of the world's population lives in river basins shared by *more than two* nations; if two is company and three a crowd, then it is evident that there exist all too many opportunities for conflict among the world's riparian nations. Adding further tension is the stark reality that because the world's population can be expected to double during the next several decades, the demand on water resources is certain to increase dramatically. Whatever conflicts already have pivoted on the scarcity of water surely will intensify to feverish pitch as the very survival of nations is affected by the distribution of water around the globe.

In the last analysis, it is fair to observe that conflicts over water resources arise not only because of the resources themselves (e.g., their abundance, scarcity) but also because of the users of these resources. The users, inevitably, are people with differing national histories, religions, styles of managing conflict, and orientations toward life itself. It is here, then, that culture may prove to be a powerful orchestrator of the way water resource disputes are understood and resolved.

Notes

1. Of special value is a selected bibliography of papers and books on transboundary river basin conflicts, prepared by Vlachos (1986b) for the IIASA conference. More recently, Scudder (1990) has presented a worthwhile report on the political costs of river basin development. Also, a research workshop on the topic of water resources and international conflict was held at University College, University of Toronto, June 15-16, 1991.

2. Although we may conjecture that the Himalayan snows are the property of Nepal and Tibet, what of the waters that flow from these countries to join with other rivers to form the Ganges—a river that floods its banks and kills thousands of people in Bangladesh?

7

Northern and Southern Sudan:
The Nile

FRANCIS M. DENG

The Jonglei Canal project is a case of culturally determined identities in a process involving several levels, from local to international. The project aims at digging a canal from the tiny village of Jonglei on the Bahr al-Zeraf River to the confluence of the White Nile and the Sobat, a distance of 260 km within the southern Sudan (see Figure 7.1). The canal is supposed to retrieve the water that flows into the spongelike Sudd region—100,000 km^2 of swampy land, where the water stagnates and dissipates through transpiration and evaporation. The retrieved water is to be channeled to Egypt and the northern Sudan, where agricultural needs for water are escalating with population growth.

The project, from its inception, has been associated closely with the problems of the north-south dualistic, Arab-African, Muslim-Christian-Animist Sudan, which eventually resulted in a 17-year civil war that made the implementation of the project impossible. Although resumed after the war, the digging of the canal was halted again by another war. The project

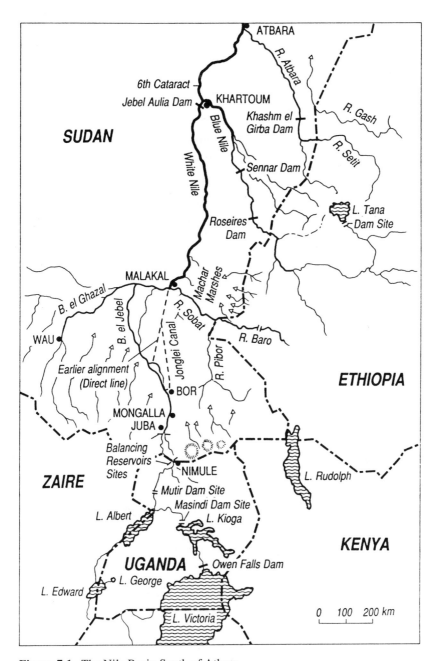

Figure 7.1. The Nile Basin South of Atbara

is now fully embroiled in the conflict, and any prospects for its resumption in the future must be seen within the framework of an overall settlement to the conflict in which the south is contesting the national identity of the north.

Broadly defined in Chapter 1 as "a set of shared and enduring meanings, values, and beliefs that characterize national, ethnic, or other groups and orient their behavior," *culture* has been central to the negotiation process over the Jonglei Canal project. The identities of the actors, including their values and perspectives, were culturally determined. The structural context was one of a conflict over the shaping and sharing of power, wealth, services, and development opportunities. The strategies that the parties used in negotiating the project were, in essence, a combination of fighting the identity war in a different framework and a process of resource allocation between the main factions in the conflict. The outcome was a trade-off between making the water of the Nile available to the northern Sudan and Egypt and allocating resources for development in the south with appropriate sensitivity to the local environment.

A River That Unites and Divides

The Jonglei Canal project touched a sensitive nerve in the relations between the north and the south precisely because it concerned the water of a river that has been a source of life and comfort for its riverine people, has provided them with a natural communication system, but also has brought adversaries into confrontation and conflict. The legends of the Nile fuse the spiritual world with that of humans to externalize the episodes of history. As Ali Mohamed (1984) has noted:

> The Nile represents a long-rooted symbol of might in African literature as well as a means of livelihood. Religious ceremonies have been intimately associated with this symbol to the extent of making the river a God in ancient Egypt named "Habi." The poetry and symbolism of the riparian states are still full of references to the Nile in one way or another. Irrigation and the generation of hydro-electric power came to be classified as the foremost use of the river for securing livelihood everywhere in a predominant agricultural economy. (p. 2)

But the message from the Nile is mixed. A poem by Bereket Habte Selassie exalting the Nile includes the following verses:

> Majestic wanderer!
> Speak, I implore you,
> Tell us the story—
> the millennial story
>
> Of mighty deeds
> and devious words
> that made and
> unmade history . . .
>
> *(Beshir, 1984,*
> *frontispiece)*

Among the peoples of the south, mythology carries an even more ambivalent message about the Nile. Some of these myths speak of creation as having taken place in the river, from which people then crawled. There are stories of spiritual heroes begotten by their mothers with the blessings of river spirits and without human male agency (for the legends of Ayuel Longar, a cultural hero with these attributes, see Lienhardt, 1961).

A myth from the Ngok Dinka concerns the tragic sacrifice of a girl, Achai, to the river spirits by her father, Jok, to redeem the tribes. A rational interpretation of the myth suggests a bitter experience with slavery now cloaked with a more soothing legend of spiritualism. However, this is an interpretation that even the educated members of the clan do not take well, as it destroys the cultural value of the event.

According to the story Jok (whose epithet "Athurkok" meant the one who broke through the way, the founder of the leading clan that bears his name, Pa-Jok), emerged from the byre of creation with the sacred spears that God had given him as symbols of his spiritual powers to bless or curse, to give or take life. As the tribe searched for better land for their cattle, Jok asked Longar, his junior partner in the leadership, to lead in the front while he remained in the back to guard against the evil spirits that were feared to attack from the rear. When the people came to a point on the Nile where they wanted to cross, their way was blocked by powers in the river. Longar and the rest of the people stopped and waited for Jok. The story was narrated by an elder, Acueng Deng, in a tape-recorded interview:

When people came to a standstill, Jok was called to the front. He came and said, "What is the matter?" Longar said, "The earth has baffled me. There is nowhere to cross." Jok said, "And what will become of the people then?" Longar said, "It is for you to see!" Jok said, "Very well; then go to the back. I will let them cross." Jok then took his daughter [Achai] and called all his people, "All those with copper bracelets, give them to me." He collected copper bracelets, and bracelets, and bracelets. Then he decorated the girl. People said, "Jok, what do you intend to do with a live human being?" He said, "I shall offer her to the river so that the people can cross. She is the canoe in which the people will paddle across." People protested. They said the child should be spared. But Jok proceeded ahead with the child. "She alone? Is she equal to this entire people of my grandfather? He took her into the river, and as he was walking deeper and deeper, he was singing hymns and praying. As he walked, the river behind him dried up and continued to dry up. By the time he reached the center of the river, the child was taken from him by the powers of the river and submerged under the water. . . . Suddenly, as she disappeared, the whole river went down and dried up. Then the people followed him and he continued to lead them holding his spears, the same spears which are still used today on oath-taking. (Deng, 1978, pp. 104-105)

To the members of the clan that has retained the leadership to this day, Achai is still remembered and revered as "The Girl in the River," a spiritual power to whom cattle and other material goods are consecrated and dedicated and to whom annual thanksgiving offerings are made in the river. Indeed they refer to the Nile and its tributaries as "The River of Achai." Before people cross a river, they must make a symbolic gesture of offering or prayer to Achai to ensure their safety. Women are prohibited from crossing at night, presumably because of the dangers of darkness and the awesome memories from the tragedy of Achai. Indeed the memory of Achai still evokes mixed sentiments of pride in the self-sacrifice of a valued member of the family for the good of the community, combined with a sense of awe still associated with the river.

The river not only is seen as a source of danger but also is portrayed often in oral literature as an avenue to safety. There are many folktales in which a jealous, childless stepmother wanting to deprive a rival wife of her child without killing the child, or a mother protecting her own baby from the treachery of others, places a newborn baby into a gourd and puts it into the river to float away to safety, to be rescued and raised by adoptive benevolent parents, eventually returning to its people as a beneficent hero, a local version of the story of Moses. Unlike a localized resource, the Nile defies spatial limitations, precisely why it unites and divides at the same time. Each of those involved in the unity and the division exerts a selective memory on the historic events to perpetuate its own dynamics.

Even the Bible has been an important lens for interpreting contemporary hostilities, not between the Israelis and the Egyptians, but between the people of the southern and northern Sudan. The Biblical verse that has been cited most in the southern Sudanese context is the prophecy in Chapter 18 of Isaiah, in which he speaks of God's judgment and ultimate blessing or redemption. This chapter has been quoted by scholars as evidence of the Nilotic link with the Biblical tradition. It also is cited as evidence of historical association between the Nilotic world and the Middle East. But there is a popular and increasing tendency for the people of the South to see it a prophetic statement of both their tragedy and their ultimate salvation and glory. Because of the message in Isaiah, particularly the disparity of the content depending on the version of the Bible quoted, it is capable of varied interpretations, from doom to triumph. Casual Western visitors to the south who are more overwhelmed by the tragedy of the people see only a pessimistic prophecy in the verse and do not understand how it can be a source of inspiration, hope, and determination for the southerners.

A closer look at the variations of the message may indicate why both perspectives are justified. The American Standard Version of the Bible, which was a revision of the King James Version and which agrees with the earlier versions of the Hebrew text, states:

> Ah, land of whirring wings which is beyond the river of Ethiopia; which sends ambassadors by the Nile, in vessels of papyrus upon the waters! Go you swift messengers, to a nation tall and smooth, to a people feared near and far, a nation mighty and conquering, whose land the rivers divide.

For those who saw the Nilotics more as victims of the mightier waves of invasions from the north, this description was confusing, which presumably explains the translation in the King James version:

> Woe to the land shadowing with wings, which is beyond the ruins of Ethiopia: that sendeth ambassadors by the sea, even in vessels of bulrushes upon the water, saying, Go ye swift messengers, to a nation scattered and peeled, to a people terrible from their beginning hitherto; a nation matted out and trodden down, whose land the rivers have spoiled. (*King James Bible,* Isaiah, chap. 18, verses 1-2)

For the Nilotics, then, the river is not just water or the material resources it embodies. Even in such practical activities as fishing, which is carefully regulated and seasonally timed, certain rituals first must be conducted and offerings made to the river. The river is also the land on which it flows and all of the environmental factors associated with it. The people are devoted to cattle not only as a resource but also as a divine gift from God; therefore the river is associated not only with water but also with pastures for the herds. According to the myths of creation, the Dinka chose the cow in preference to the thing called "What," which God had offered as an alternative. According to Loth Adija:

God asked man, "Which one shall I give you, black man; there is the cow and the thing called 'What,' which of the two would you like?" The man said, "I do not want 'What.' " Then God said, "But 'What' is better than the cow!" The man said, "No." God said, "If you like the cow, you had better taste its milk first before you choose it finally." The man squeezed some milk into his hand, tasted it, and said, "Let us have the milk and never see 'What.' " (Deng, 1978, p. 7)

"What" could be associated conceptually with curiosity and the search for scientific knowledge and inventiveness. The Dinka concept of *knowledge* emphasizes social norms and cultural continuity, rather than scientific and technical knowledge: hence the rationalization of Dinka scientific and technical backwardness in comparison with Europeans and Arabs.

Because the people who would be affected most by the Jonglei Canal are the Nilotes, particularly the Dinka and the Nuer, both culturally devoted to cattle, the feared impact of the canal on the people, the livestock, and the way of life were equally prejudicial to the project in the eyes of the SPLA warriors:

> Our cattle were left to die
> And our people were left to die;
> It is cattle which sustain our hearts
> In our land called the Sudan.

(from an unpublished story)

For the Nilotics, negotiating the water of the Nile is, therefore, more than a matter of practical distribution of resources. Of course, the Nile is the water, the fish, the vegetation, the wildlife, the birds, and all that the river provides or attracts to sustain life in an interdependent environment. But it is more: It is the romantic scenery of the majestic river flowing defiantly against the physical and ecological odds of mountains and deserts; it is the magnificent view of the rising and setting sun sending its golden rays across the vast terrain to settle and sparkle on the glimmering surface of the gently meandering Nile, snaking its way to the Mediterranean Sea. But it is also mythology, the legacy of generations of ancestors, a shrine that brings together the male and female strands of ancestral continuity into legendary streams; it is culture; it is identity.

Background of the Conflict

The north-south conflict in the Sudan has deep historical roots. While the north was undergoing Arabization and Islamization, mostly through the Egyptian connection, the south remained isolated, protected by natural barriers and the resistance of the Nilotic warrior tribes, primarily Dinka, Nuer, and Shilluk. This isolation was punctuated, however, with the violent incursions by waves of adventurous invaders from the north in search of slaves, ivory, and gold. The Nile was their link with their victims and their eventual redeemers.

Aggression from the north peaked during the mid-19th century when a semblance of administrative control by the Turko-Egyptian rule of 1821-1885 enabled slave hunters and traders to recruit and deploy local armies for the purpose. Turko-Egyptian administration's attempts at stopping the slave trade only made it more organized and adventurous. It also won Mohamed Ahmed, the self-declared Mahdi, the support of the slave traders for his revolution that ousted the Turko-Egyptian rule in 1885.

The British, who jointly with the Egyptians reconquered the Sudan in 1898, administered the two parts of the country as separate and unequal entities. The north received more economic, social, and cultural development along Arab-Islamic lines and was the first to become politically conscious and to spearhead the nationalist movement in collaboration with Egypt. In the name of protection from the north, the south was "closed" to outside influences and was preserved in its natural milieu, modified only by the activities of the Christian missionaries, whose task it was to introduce Christianity and the rudiments of Western civilization, reflected in basic education and medical services. Whether the country eventually would be united or partitioned, with the south becoming a part of Uganda or Kenya or an independent state, was left unresolved until the dawn of independence.

In 1947, only 9 years before independence, the British, under pressure from the north and Egypt, decided abruptly to reverse their separatist policy and to evolve the country toward independence as a unitary state. From that time on, relations between the north and the south were set on a turbulent course. The fears of the south increasingly intensified. In August 1955, only 4 months before independence, violence erupted and rapidly spread as a result of widely shared fear that independence was going to mean a change of masters—from the British to the Arabs—and could entail the return of the slave trade. The mutineers eventually were persuaded to lay down their arms by the outgoing British governor general, who promised justice. When the northern parties also pledged to give serious consideration to the southern call for a federal system of government, the country united behind the declaration of independence on January 1, 1956.

It soon became evident, however, that the north was not intent on honoring the pledge for a federal constitution but, quite the contrary, sought to impose Arabization and Islamization on the south in an attempt at achieving national unity through uniformity. There was even a serious call for the adoption of an Islamic constitution.[1] In response, hostilities were reactivated under the leadership of the Southern Sudan Liberation Movement (SSLM), better known as Anya-Nya, the name of its military wing, whose objective was the secession of the south and the establishment of an independent state.[2] In 1972, however, the movement agreed with the military government of Jaafar Mohamed Nimeiri on a compromise solution, the Addis Ababa agreement, that granted the south regional autonomy.[3]

Nimeiri's unilateral abrogation of the Addis Ababa agreement—by dividing the south into three regions with reduced constitutional powers and then, in alliance with the Muslim Brotherhood, imposing the so-called September (Islamic) Laws—led to the resumption of hostilities in 1983 by the Sudan People's Liberation Movement (SPLM) and its military wing, the Sudan People's Liberation Army (SPLA). The declared objective of the SPLM/SPLA is not the secession or the autonomy of the south, but rather the creation of a new Sudan, united and free of racial, religious, cultural, or gender discrimination.

In 1985, 2 years after hostilities resumed, Nimeiri was overthrown by a popular uprising. A transitional government coaxed the country back to parliamentary democracy within a year, but military rule returned on June 30, 1989, in a coup led by previously unknown middle-ranking officers proclaiming a "Revolution of National Salvation," which became even more rigorous in imposing Shari'a and the Islamic agenda.

Identities of the Actors

The north-south dichotomy in the Sudan often is described in racial, cultural, and religious terms: The north is perceived as Arab and Islamic, while the south is more indigenously African in culture and religious beliefs, with an educated class that is mostly Christian.

Although the labels of Arab Muslim north and the African Christian and Animist south have been used as guidelines in conceptualizing the identity map of the Sudan, they tend to oversimplify what is, in effect, a more complex situation that has led the country into what is virtually an identity crisis.

Crisis of National Identity

Northerners who define themselves as Arabs are, in effect, the result of mixing of Arab and African elements and the populations of certain areas in the north, notably the Fur of Darfur in the west, the Nuba of southern Kordofan, and the Beja in the east, who, though Muslims, are conspicuously non-Arab. *Arabism* is thus a loosely defined, fluid, and flexible concept, which now is being postulated as a model for national assimilation, the idea being to foster unity through uniformity. But because of the dominance of the Arab-Islamic north and its assimilationist orientation, the southern identity has largely been one of resistance to northern domination and threat of assimilation. With the SPLM/SPLA demanding the creation of a new democratic and secular Sudan, southern identity of resistance is becoming more positively self-assertive in the contest for the national identity.

Although both sides claim to be accommodating in their postulated model of national identity, the contest is conceptualized in terms that are mutually exclusive or discriminatory, the sharp dichotomy being between Arabism and Africanism and between Islamic theocracy and secularism.

Determinants of Identity

Among the objective indicators of ethnic identity usually identified in anthropological literature are that the group (a) is largely biologically self-perpetuating; (b) shares fundamental cultural values, realized in overt unity in cultural forms; (c) makes up a field of communication and interaction; and (d) has a membership that identifies itself, and is identified by others, as constituting a category distinguishable from other categories of the same order (Barth, 1969).

Writing on the Sudan, Kasfir (1990) comments on the balance of both the subjective and objective factors in determining identity. After observing that individuals usually have multiple identities from which to choose, he adds that the choice "depends on the particular situation, not merely on the individual's preference" (p. 340). Kasfir concludes that "though objective ethnic characteristics (race, language, culture, place of birth) usually provide the possible limits, subjective perception of either the identities or the identified—whether objectively accurate or not—may turn out to be decisive for the social situation" (p. 366).

The racial anomalies of northern identity, the identity crisis implicit in the pluralism of the nation-state, and the racial overtones of the Arab attitude toward the more Negroid Africans, particularly in the south, all combine to make the cultural concept of *Arabism* particularly appealing to northern Sudanese politicians, intellectuals, and even scholars. In his statement to the 1965 Round Table Conference on the problem of the south, the then Prime Minister, Sirr El Khatim El Khalifa, observed:

> Gentlemen, Arabism, which is a basic attribute of the majority of the population of this country and of many African countries besides, is not a racial concept which unites the members of a certain racial group. It is a linguistic, cultural and nonracial link that binds together numerous races, black, white

and brown. Had Arabism been anything else but this, most modern Arabs, whether African or Asian, including the entire population of the Northern Sudan, would cease to be "Arab" at all. (Beshir, 1968)

This politically motivated perspective, however, tends to conceal the sentiments of genetic heritage implied in the northern Sudanese overemphasis on the importance of Arab genealogies, traced back to Arabia (e.g., Sanderson & Sanderson, 1981, p. 8). It indeed could be argued that the more doubtful the Arab identity in those who claim to be Arabs, the more the need to assert it with emphasis.

Southerners see no distinction between the subjective sentiments of Arabism and the objective indicators of racial identification among the northerners. In a tape-recorded interview, Ambrose Riny Thiik, a former judge of the Sudanese Court of Appeal, sees the differences between the north and the south in racial terms, defined subjectively, even if unsupported by factual evidence:

The problem is in the mind, is it not? Physically, there are no great differences. Yes, you will find very dark Arabs. But it is not a question of skin pigmentation or appearance. It is a question of what they are hung up with: In their mentality, they are Arabs; in their mentality, they are superior; in their mind, you the black, the African, is *abd* (slave) and it remains to be so no matter what achievement you have accomplished. The feeling among the blacks that this is unacceptable is expressing itself in terms of warfare and the rest of it. . . . I agree that there is no great physical difference; skin color is not that big a thing, but the thing is that in the mind.

The Sudanese poet Salah Ahmed Ibrahim, however, has a message to his fellow Sudanese in a poem, addressed to a fictitious southerner by the name of Malwal, dramatizing Arab-African mixing that the north underwent through historical assimilation (Deng, 1973, pp. 69-70):

Malwal, before you deny me
Listen to my story of the South and the North
The story of enmity and brotherhood from ancient times
The Arab, the carrier of the whip, the driver of the camels . . .
Descended on the valleys of the Sudan like Summer rains
With the book and the ways of the Prophet . . .
Carrying his ambitions and his plates
And two dates and his ancestral tree . . .
A reality blossomed in the womb of every slave mother of a free man
The progeny of the seeds of your Arab ancestors
Among them were the Fur and the Funj

And all those who are charcoal *black*
A reality as large as the elephant and like the crocodile
And like the high mountains of Kassala . . .
He lies who says in the Sudan
That I am pure
That my ancestry is not tinted
He is truly a liar . . .

From these accounts, it is clear that, in the perceptions of the Sudanese, the divisive identity factors in the Sudan have to be both racial and cultural and that the explanation lies in a broad, inclusive understanding of culture as defined in this book, especially because there is not much visible evidence of racial differences between Sudanese Arabs or Africans, despite strong racial sentiments that dichotomize them. Indeed the tenuousness of northern claims to Arabism in itself underscores the role of culture in cultivating self-perceptions, so that even biological or racial claims are ultimately culture bound. Culture becomes an overarching social engineer that molds perspectives on identity, even on racial bases.

This overarching emphasis on culture indicates that, from all visible evidence, it is culture rather than race that divides the people of the Sudan and that whatever racial self-perception individuals or groups might attribute to their claims of a distinctive identity as Arabs or Africans cannot be supported by hard evidence, except as a product of social engineering. On the other hand, the Arab-Islamic and African-Christian dichotomy implies some fundamental structural differences in the value-institutional systems that should be considered seriously.

Structure of Conflicting Values

The Jonglei Canal project negotiations have been influenced profoundly by the structure of conflicting identities between the north and the south. Two principal factors need to be highlighted as pertinent to the conflict situation and the political process of the negotiations over the canal project. One of these, a cause and a consequence, is the cloak of moral and spiritual values. The other is the way the very concept of negotiation is perceived in the light of these conflicting value systems.

Moral and Spiritual Values

Religion appears to have assumed a central place in the north-south conflict because it was precisely through Islamization that the evolution, confrontation, and eventual conflict of identities occurred. Religious perspectives and the moral and spiritual principles that they engender are, therefore, among the factors that both distinguish the people and nourish a mutual sense of prejudice and scorn.

Islamization in the Sudan was predicated on the inherent assumption of the superiority of the Muslims and the inferiority of the non-Muslims, especially the African "heathens" who were regarded as legitimate targets of raids and enslavement. What northerners fail to realize even now is that the people of the south practice traditional religions with deep-rooted moral and spiritual values. They also fail to realize the degree to which these values have combined with the adoption of Christianity to give the south a strong counterforce against the northern objective of Islamization. In both the north and the south, religion is perceived as an integral ingredient of the composite identities exclusively claiming the soul of the nation.

El-Affendi (1991), a northern Sudanese scholar, observed:

> It was the citadel of Islamic culture that stood as a guarantee against the submersion of Sudan in the jungles of the heathen (and he might have added primitive Black) Africa, the source of magazines and books that were the intelligentsia's link with the world beyond, the cradle of the nationalist movement and its heroes. (p. 35)

The assumed superiority of Islam and of the Muslims over all others and things is carried to an astonishing degree from the perspective of this day and age.

The objective of all of the main political forces in the north and in particular the Muslim Brothers, the Ikhwan, has indeed been to redeem their heathen folk in the south whom the concept of the modern nation-state had turned into potential "brethren." As an inside source intimates:

> For Ikhwan, the South was perceived as a distant, vaguely symbolic place. Like the rest of the educated, Ikhwan only saw in the South the alienated, lost brother, who had to be retrieved through the spread of Islam, the Arabic language and better communications. This perception did not reckon with developments in the South, especially the rise of a church-educated elite whose self-perception was not that of oppressed victims of colonialism but of belonging to Western culture, which created them and shaped their perceptions in this very act of "oppression."

Little do northerners, including the enlightened, realize the depth of religiosity among the people of the south in accordance with their traditional beliefs, about which volumes have been written.

The literature on Nilotic religions shows that they largely aim at the well-being of humans in a living society, rather than at individual survival after death. They do have a notion of continued physical existence in the underground world of the dead and a spiritual linkage of that world with that of the living and the powers above, but their concepts in this respect are rather nebulous and, despite the similarities in other respects, tend to differ from the Heaven and Hell concepts popularly associated with Christianity and Islam. The focus of their concept of immortality is on this world, through procreation and agnatic lineage continuation, which lead to ancestral veneration, almost culminating in worship. In the words of British anthropologist Lienhardt (1961, p. 26), "Dinka fear to die without male issue, in whom the survival of their names—the only kind of immortality they know—will be assured."

An important aspect of Nilotic religion that may differ from both Christianity and Islam is that God is perceived and approached through a structural relationship that links the living with their dead, particularly the ancestors and the clan spirits or deities. Nilotic religion, therefore, is segmented in a manner reflective of their segmentary lineage system, which is autonomous to the level of the family and, ultimately, of the individual. This segmentation allows for maximum religious freedom. In contrast, both Christianity and Islam, though Sufism lies somewhere between, are highly centralized.

But autonomous as Nilotic religions are, unification and diversification of experience in the widening direction ultimately embrace the whole of humankind and the environment. Contrary to the Islamic views associated with *tawhid,* in which man is placed above all, including the environment, to the Nilotics man is part and parcel of the cosmic whole. Chief Thon Wai indicated Nilotic sensitivity to the interdependence of the cosmic totality when he appraised President Nimeiri's achievement in ending the civil war between the south and the north:

> He has brought people together. Even the goat and the sheep and the fish in the river have seen what Jaafar Nimeiri has done. What he has done has brought peace to the dog, to the goat, to the sheep, and even to the fish in the river. Nimeiri's work has brought life to all these creatures. This word is a word of truth and life. (Deng, 1978, p. 62)

And in another context, Chief Thon, referring to the universality of the human worth, said: "Even the creatures we call lions are humans. Those creatures we say eat people were born as part of this living world." Chief Makuei Bilkuei expressed a similar view when he advocated an all-embracing concept of national unity:

Our blood, the blood of the black skin, was one. It is the government which has taken harmony away, because black skin was one with our hyenas, with our leopards, with our elephants, with our buffaloes; we were all one skin. We are one people. . . . We should all combine the people, the animals, the birds that fly we are all one. . . . Let us all unite. . . . Even the animals that eat people, even the people who keep the black magic that we do not like, let's embrace them all and be one people. (Deng, 1978, p. 62)

Conceiving of the south-north problem as rooted in the ethnocentrism of northerners and their underestimation of southerners, Chief Thon Wai spoke words that are relevant to Dinka theology: "Even the tree which cannot speak has the nature of a human being. . . to God . . . who created it. Do not despise it; it is a human being" (Deng, 1978, p. 64).

Negotiation on Conflicting Values

A pertinent aspect of the conflicting value systems in north-south relations is the way negotiation is measured by the yardstick of moral and spiritual values. If negotiation is perceived as a game of wits in which the outcome depends on cleverness, rather than on the discovery of the truth and a fair allocation of rights based on that truth, it is hard to conceive of it in the context of the Nilotic scheme of values. Indeed there is no equivalent concept in the Dinka language.

Some anecdotes may help clarify the point. The Ngok Dinka chose to remain under the administration of Kordofan in the north instead of joining the south because their leaders wanted to play a bridging role on the north-south borders, to ensure cooperation with the Arabs, and to secure the protection of their people by the central government. Among those who were most committed to this strategic position was the late paramount chief of the Ngok Dinka, Chief Deng Majok. After the Addis Ababa accord, the Ngok Dinka began to demand joining the south. In a meeting between chiefs and elders from Abyei, the position that Chief Deng Majok had taken was brought to their attention. Chief Pagwot Deng argued that Deng Majok's position had been a clever ploy to protect his people under adverse circumstances. If a lasting settlement had now been reached between north and south, there was no longer any need to hold to that cleverness. In his words, addressing the author:

When your father refused [to join the South], he was being clever. . . . It was just a clever way of doing things. He would say this to the Northerners and tell the Southerners this. . . . He said, "I will remain between the South and the North. If an Arab takes something from the Southerner or the Southerner takes something from the Arab, I will tell my brothers to return each other's property. . . . I am a man on the borders." That was how your father refused . . . . Your father was not refusing to join the South; his was cleverness to protect his people.

Now that . . . the South has received its freedom, why should we remain in the words of cleverness? (Deng, 1980, pp. 24-25)

Of course, life itself is a process of daily negotiations in many small, different ways, but in a situation of open or pronounced conflict, the Nilotic mode of resolution implies a third party mediation. But mediation is more than a neutral search for the truth, however conceived, for the mediator cannot be successful unless he or she can persuade the parties to see and accept the truth. Indeed the Dinka word for mediation is *luk,* which means "persuasion." Lienhardt (1963) wrote the following about Nilotic procedure of settling disputes:

I suppose anyone would agree that one of the most decisive marks of a society we should call in a spiritual sense "civilized" is a highly-developed sense and practice of justice, and here the Nilotics, with their intense respect for the personal independence and dignity of themselves and others, may be superior to societies more civilized in the material sense. . . . The Dinka and the Nuer are a warlike people; and have never been slow to assert their rights as they see them by physical force. Yet, if one sees Dinka trying to resolve a dispute, according to their own customary law, there is often a reasonableness and a gentleness in their demeanor, a courtesy and a quietness in the speech of those elder men superior in status and wisdom, an attempt to get at the whole truth of the situation before them. (p. 828)

It is in this area of the moral and spiritual values that the Nilotics are particularly condescending to the northern Sudanese. The history of animosity between the two parts of the country and the series of promises made and broken or never intended to be met in the first place have left the south with a deep sense of mistrust of northerners as morally corrupt, and they see this corruption as racially and culturally inherent.

The history of north-south relations has indeed been one of promises made and dishonored. The low and high points in the relationship can be correlated directly to agreements and their breach. There are times when agreements promised in a mutually acceptable framework are accepted, and times when the agreements are dishonored: the north attempts to impose its Islamic Arab vision on the whole country, and the south falls back on its violent resistance.

As a result of this historical evidence, even after the highly acclaimed Addis Ababa agreement of 1972, southerners in general and the more experienced tribal chiefs in particular remained skeptical of the long-term prospects of the Addis Ababa accord because of their mistrust of the northerners.

Chief Makuei Bilkuei advised the southerners to take the Addis Ababa accord with cautious reservations: "The Arab said, 'You South, let us unite.' Is that not what the Arab said? If you accept, you open one eye and close the other eye. . . . Let one eye speak with the Arab and let the other eye remain closed" (Deng, 1980, p. 79).

Chief Stephan Thougkol was even more emphatic that the Addis Ababa accord was merely a pragmatic, self-interested concession from the north that did not resolve the real issues dividing the two sets of people. In other words, it was a superficial, clever ploy not based on acceptance of the deeper truths. To him, the conflict continued:

> When they found that the thing was . . . difficult . . . and that it was also killing some of them, they introduced other policies. But the war is going on. We cannot say we are relatives. The war is still on. There is no relationship. . . . Respect towards people is missing. Our chiefs don't have a salary that is respectable. We are still being insulted. Some people still call us slaves. Some of us are still actually slaves. . . . We cannot marry among them. They take our girls and turn them into prostitutes, and when they have made them prostitutes, they send them back. They are still controlling our economy: they are the people who own the shops; and all the money is still in their hands. (Deng, 1980, p. 130)

If, as experience seems to show, negotiation for the south is identifying the truth with the help of mediators, agreeing on the basis of that truth, and holding to it, but for the north it is a game of wits in which one aims at carrying the day in a tactical maneuver that alters with the changing climate, then there is no common moral ground from which to talk. This indeed is the crisis of north-south relations and possibly one of the crucial factors in the cross-purpose manner in which the Jonglei Canal project negotiations transpired.

An Oversight in the Strategy

From the time the Jonglei Canal project first was conceived to the time it was finalized and given the green light for implementation, fundamental changes had taken place in the Sudan as a whole and the southern Sudan in particular. The point of view of the south, which had not figured in earlier discussions of the project, now loomed large in a compensational bid to bridge the historical gap. In essence, that was the beginning of the "negotiation process."

Genesis of the Project

Although the equations of power and related interests and agendas have shifted over the decades to the point where the Jonglei Canal project has become primarily an issue of domestic concern between the central government and the south, the main objective of the initial idea was to provide water for Egypt.[4]

Once the reconquest was accomplished, Lord Cromer, the British consul-general in Cairo, who was the virtual ruler of Egypt and the Sudan, made it clear that he considered the Nile water to be the most important aspect of the reconquest. Within months of the reconquest, Cromer sent Sir William Garstin, under-secretary of state for the Egyptian Ministry of Public Works, an engineer, and a hydrologist, up the Nile to observe the river firsthand and to report on its behavior. Garstin returned to recommend the clearance of a passage through the Sudd region to make navigation possible in both the Bahr al-Jabal and Bahr al-Zeraf rivers, whose channels he found to be completely impassable. He also suggested the digging of a canal in a straight line cutting through the Sudd region from Jonglei on the Bahr al-Zeraf to the confluence of the Sobat River and the White Nile, just south of Malakal. That was the germ of the Jonglei Canal project.[5]

After a series of intermediate considerations, Egypt once again reactivated the project in 1946 by proposing the Equatorial Nile project with provisions for a reservoir and a dam in the great lakes of East Africa. But the circle of concerned parties now included Uganda, which feared that needed land would be inundated by the proposed rise in the height of Lake Albert. The environmental interests of the southern Sudanese also would be harmed by an even greater flood in the Sudd region that would interfere with the dry season pastures for the livestock and fish. The project was deemed risky for the livelihood of the Nilotic people.[6] But Egypt's paramount need for water had to be considered too.

The Jonglei Committee of 1946-1948 and the Jonglei Investigation Team of 1946-1954 were formed to study the situation and to seek ways of harmonizing the conflicting interests. While the Committee laid the groundwork, the most comprehensive multidisciplinary study was conducted by the Jonglei Investigation Team, led by Howell, an anthropologist with considerable experience as administrator in the southern Sudan. The team focused on the economic and social consequences of the proposed Jonglei Canal on the people of the area and on exploring possible remedies. It also explored natural alternatives to the various schemes and remedies and the costs involved.

The task of the team was geared toward exploring remedies for any damage that might affect the people of the Nile valley in both the southern Sudan and East Africa. According to El-Sammani (1988), "The recommendations of the Jonglei Investigation Team only catered to the maintenance of the status quo of the population of the area" (pp. 411-412). The team did not recommend any program for social and economic development because of the remoteness of the area, the high cost of transportation, the financial risks involved in any plans for agricultural development, and the danger such a development would pose to the sustainability of traditional livelihood (El-Sammani, 1988).

Changes in Egypt that brought to power Mohamed Naguib and Jamal Abdel Nassir accelerated Sudan's march to independence but also interrupted progress on the Jonglei Canal project. Sudan and Egypt, however, agreed to undertake at some future date conservation projects in the Sudan that would increase the Nile's yield to be shared equally between the two countries. A Permanent Joint Technical Commission for the Nile Waters, made up of an equal number of members from both countries (but without southern Sudanese representation), was established and charged with the tasks of initiating, implementing, and administering conservation projects.

The civil war raged during the 1950s and the 1960s; it was not until peace returned to the southern Sudan following the Addis Ababa agreement that the Permanent Joint Technical Commission proposed to the two countries the resumption of the Jonglei Canal project. Egypt and the Sudan, as represented by the central government, agreed to proceed with the project. Unwittingly the project fell into the web of the north-south conflict—the strategic gap.

The Project in the North-South Context

News of the agreement between the Sudan and Egypt to resume the Jonglei Canal project was brought to the attention of the regional government by two central government ministers early in 1974. Alier (1990) recalls the event:

> Two central government ministers flew to Juba for consultation with me, in my capacity as President of the High Executive Council, Southern Region. Yahya Abdel Magid, Minister of Irrigation and Wadie Habashie, Minister of Agriculture, said it had become necessary to execute the Jonglei Canal Project. They gave several reasons for reaching that conclusion: agricultural development was being vertically and horizontally expanded to meet needs for a fast

growing population of the country, for agro-industrial processing; there was talk then of Sudan's obligation to provide bread for the Arab world and Egypt needed additional water sources for essential agricultural expansion and power output. Yahya and Wadie said that irrigation expansion in the Sudan would need more water and the Sudan's current share of water would not be enough to irrigate new fields by 1985. It was thus vital to get new sources of Nile yield. The Jonglei Canal Project was the answer. They then unfolded opportunities which the project would provide for the people of the area. (p. 197)

The country had fought a civil war for 17 years, the gist of which was a struggle by the people of the south to be recognized as a distinct cultural entity that should exercise effective control over its own affairs and resources. And it had been barely 2 years since the war had ended, so deep-rooted suspicions still lingered; therefore, to decide on such an important project that was to be fully within the regional borders without prior consultation with the regional government, except as a matter of information, was to risk provocation. Alier uses the word *consultation,* but this was evidently after the fact. As Mawut (1986), a southern Sudanese scholar, observed, "Discussions on the canal project started in the early 1970s between the Sudan Government and the Egyptian Government and in 1974 the two Governments agreed to jointly finance the operations" (p. 69). It is apparent from Alier's account that the regional government had not been in the picture and was being briefed for the first time.

The Political Process of Involvement

The Jonglei Canal project was never formally negotiated between the central government (the north) and the regional government (the south). What transpired was a spontaneous reaction in the south, triggered by the collective memory of the history of relations between the north and the south, a deep-rooted animosity, and a chronic suspicion justified by experience. Because the political environment in the north and, in particular, the attitude of the president in the wake of the Addis Ababa agreement was favorable, southern reaction was met with an understanding and responsive hearing at the center. But the process was by no means harmonious.

Bridging the Gap

"Cool," mild mannered, and predisposed to cooperation with the central government, Alier geared the reaction of his cabinet toward acceptance of the project with low-key suggestions for revisions favorable to the people of the south and sensitive to the environment. A special meeting of the high executive council was convened for an exchange of views with the central government ministers. Among the issues discussed of particular interest to the south were those relating to opportunities for socioeconomic development that might result from the project. An all-weather road was to be constructed along the canal to link Malakal and Juba, reducing the normal steamer time by half. The distance from Kosti to Juba by steamer would be reduced by 300 km. In addition, the whole area would be linked by a river and road transportation system that could be used year round. Above all, this comprehensive development of the area, which the south could not otherwise afford, would be financed by the central government and Egypt. In Alier's words, "Yahya and Wadie had put a persuasive case of multiple socioeconomic development for not only Egypt and the Northern Sudan, but for the South" (Alier, 1990, p. 198).

The rest of the discussion was pragmatic and largely cooperative on both sides. Identity issues had been overridden in favor of pragmatic development considerations by the leadership of the south. Once that strategic shift had been made, the next question was whether the south would get a good deal or would once again be shortchanged by the north. According to Alier's own testimony:

> The High Executive Council debated at great length with the central government Ministers. Three crucial issues were raised. One was the quality of road proposed. The Council wanted a good road, with a firm base and tarmac surface, able to cope with the expected volume of traffic along the canal. The second was how the project was to be executed; what means would be used for digging it. The third was about the amount of land that would emerge in the Sudd area as a result of the diversion of some of the water to the canal. (Alier, 1990, pp. 198-199)

One is struck immediately by the modesty of the reservations implied in the questions: the quality of the road promised, the mechanism for execution, and the land that would be retrieved from the swamps of the Sudd. To the extent that Alier's personality was dominant, this negotiating technique was characteristic. More astonishing is the initial response of the ministers to these minimal reservations, again based on the evidence of Alier: "The response of Yahya and Wadie about the quality of the road was not reassuring. However, when they realized there was unconcealed skepticism about their own proposal, they changed and offered a road project which approximated to the Council's suggested specifications" (Alier, 1990, p. 199).

Alier suddenly provides a far more sophisticated agenda behind these seemingly simple and almost simplistic questions. Referring to the giant bucket wheel to be used for excavation, he noted:

> The point being made here was to allay fears of the possible danger of bringing a large number of foreign labor force into an area that had just been relieved of a war situation, especially a labor force from countries that were not initially supportive of the Southern autonomy. When it was proposed in 1925 and again in 1938, the project was to be executed using foreign labor, probably from Egypt. (Alier, 1990, pp. 198-199)

The question of the amount of land that would be retrieved by the project reflected Alier's own interest in and advocacy of the project, which were based on the arguments that there was excess water in the Sudd region that could do with some reduction and that the amount the canal would drain was insignificant compared to the hazards of the current high water levels and the prospects of further floods. Alier (1990, p. 199) recalls the floods that resulted from heavy rains during the 3-year period from 1961 to 1964 in central Africa that devastated the Jonglei region, destroying trees, flooding valuable land, and killing millions of livestock and wildlife.

For Alier, then, the project was a godsend: It gave the south an opportunity of a leap beyond the peace accord into development, and it promised not only redemption from the devastation of the 1960s floods but also a bright future into modernity. And that was essentially the focus of his cabinet's discussion with the two ministers from Khartoum. But as developments eventually would show, it was not so much what the ministers revealed or what Alier and his cabinet negotiated that would make the critical difference, but the popular reaction to the project and the way Alier pragmatically played a role on both sides—the central government and the southern public—to bridge the north-south gap.

The ministers from the central government and the regional government agreed to proceed with the project on the understanding that it would be reviewed in the light of the points raised in the discussion. One suggestion that came out of the meeting was the establishment of a national body to review the project from time to time, make suggestions, and oversee development in the project area with financing from the central government and Egypt. That was the origin of the National Council for the Development of the Jonglei Canal Area and the Jonglei Executive Organ, which was to be its executive arm.

To keep the event low-key, this highly important project was announced in a press release, rather than in a statement by the president—either of the republic or of the region—to the public.

The Crisis of Rejection

When news of the resumption of the canal project was announced so casually, a spontaneous opposition erupted that unraveled the depth of suspicion and animosity that had been lingering despite the Addis Ababa accord. Massive demonstrations by students began in Juba, where two school-children were killed by the police, and spread to other towns in the south.

Critics of the project began to see the leadership of the southern region as more aligned with Khartoum than with the interests of their people, a judgment that, needless to say, unfairly misconstrued Abel's tact for submissiveness. "The slogan was that the land [the south had] fought for was now given up for sale to the Egyptians by those who had now found places in the government" (Collins [1985, pp. 319-320] quoting Hilary Legali).[7]

As pointed out earlier, despite the Addis Ababa agreement, the south still nursed deep grievances against both the north and Egypt, the former for obvious historical reasons, and the latter for initially not supporting the settlement. As Alier (1990) observed:

> North-South relations had been uneasy in the past and though reconciliation had been reached since 1972 and a great deal of goodwill was fostered, these were marred by frustrations in the South due to failed expectations in economic progress. . . . This state of affairs was blamed on the central government as much as it was also blamed on the regional government. Jonglei Canal demonstrations were outward manifestations of the government's declining credibility. As for Egyptian-Southern Sudan relations, Egypt had not been initially supportive of the Addis Ababa Agreement. . . . For these reasons alone, allowing Egypt and Northern Sudan to benefit from the water saved from the Sudd was resented in the South. Why should a country unsympathetic to a peace settlement benefit by it, some caustically asked. (p. 203)

The demonstrators demanded that the head of the regional government should address them to explain the situation, but Alier refused to do so on the grounds that it was "rather awkward for the government to be seen to carry out the orders of the school children" (Alier, 1990, p. 200).

Collins, on the other hand, implies that despite the briefing of the central ministers, the regional government was not fully in the picture to be able to deliver a credible explanation, which would mean that Alier needed time to gather adequate information to be able to make a convincing statement. In Collins's words, "Abel Alier and his ministers were helpless, having no information about the Jonglei Canal other than gossip with which to refute the allegations which only made the latter seem more plausible" (Collins,

1990, p. 320). Howell and his co-editors corroborate Collins's observation by stating:

> The decision to construct the canal was made in 1974, apparently without reference to the people through whose homelands it would pass, which thus sparked off anxiety and unfavorable reaction among Southern Sudanese sensitive to the right to manage their own affairs after 17 years of civil war which had ended only two year before. (Howell, Lock, & Cobb, 1988, p. 48)

Turning the Crisis Into Opportunity

Quite apart from his predisposition to cooperate with the central government, Alier was convinced that the Addis Ababa agreement had changed things and that the Jonglei Canal offered an opportunity for both the north and Egypt to demonstrate their goodwill by supporting the development of the south. He made his case in an address to the regional assembly and the public.

Alier not only played down the negatives of the project but also highlighted the benefits the south would receive. In his view the project was beneficial both to the people of the canal area and to the south generally. It would, of course, benefit Egypt and the northern Sudan, which was why they planned to dig the canal and provide technical and financial support for it in the first place. In terms of water sharing, although some of the water that spilled annually over the banks of the Bahr al-Jabal and Bahr al-Zeraf to the low floodplains of the Sudd would be channeled through the canal, it was only part of the water. The project would, in fact, result in the reclamation of some land that had been submerged since the flood of the 1960s. Grazing lands that had been lost during those years would re-emerge. Fishing opportunities in the canal would be improved and increased. No Egyptian troops or peasants would be brought to the south, nor were any coming to the Sudan. The project would benefit the south by fulfilling part of the government's objective to launch socioeconomic development in the region. The south needed that development and the benefits of modern social progress, but that could not be attained without mobilization of adequate financial and technical resources, which the south obviously could not provide alone. Nor could the central government give such a project priority unless other regions of the country also stood to benefit. The Jonglei Canal project was a means of bringing to the people of the area development opportunities that would not otherwise be available, had it not been for the external interests involved. The cooperation between the region and the downstream users of the Nile water was a matter of give-and-take. Egypt and the central government in Khartoum wanted some of the water, which the south had in excess, in exchange for financial and technical resources, which the south needed.

Alier went on to explain that a National Council for the Development Projects of Jonglei Canal Area, with an executive organ, would be created to plan and review proposals for the socioeconomic development of the area and to execute programs based on such plans. The council's powers were to be wide enough to enable it to review the entire project, and its membership would include southerners. Alier criticized the perception of the south as a human zoo, stressing that the time had come to move along the path of modernization. The critical question was, Would this be to the benefit or the detriment of the area? In his government's view, the balance was substantially beneficial to the area. As the government was committed to a policy of socioeconomic development of the south, it was prepared in its resolve to translate this policy into plans and programs, "and it would lead, and if need be, drive people along that path even if they might not be willing to go along"[8] (Alier, 1990, p. 204).

Judging from Alier's own account, the policy statement achieved its objective. Whether Alier had cleared his statement with the president or not, and in all probability he had, the moves of the central government conformed remarkably with his perspective. As one observer remarked:

> Both the regional and central governments reacted to the Juba riots with extraordinary speed. An impressive array of leaders from the [ruling] Sudan Socialist Union, accompanied by Southern Sudanese students from Khartoum University and engineers from the Ministry of Irrigation, were flown at once to Juba to explain the facts about the canal to the uninformed and somewhat mystified members of Abel Alier's government who promptly formed three committees from members of the High Executive Council and the Regional Assembly to tour the provinces . . . to try to dismiss the rampant rumors and emphasize the benefits of the canal to the Southern Sudanese. (Collins, 1990, p. 321)

Nimeiri acted promptly to establish by presidential decree the National Council for the Development Projects of the Jonglei Canal Area under the chairmanship of the vice-president of the republic and the president of the High Executive Council, Abel Alier, with the membership of the central ministers of irrigation, finance, agriculture, and planning. Included also were members of the regional and national assemblies from the canal area and regional ministers of finance, agriculture, health, education, wildlife conservation, and rural development.

The Unintended Outcome

The resignation of Yahya Abdel Magid (minister of irrigation) signified the originally unintended outcome of the process and the difference the southerners were able to make once they got involved in the project. Alier's discreet leadership and input effectively benefitted the south without being visible to his southern constituency. As one observer noted, although Jonglei was initially Egyptian in conception, "in the process of implementing the project, its shape has been substantially altered by Sudanese opinion directly influenced by Southern politics" (El-Sammani, 1988, p. 409). The explanation given to the National Council on Jonglei for the belated but significant changes that the southern Sudanese proposed and pushed through after the 1974 initial agreement to proceed with the project was this: "We did not know of these additional benefits in 1974 because we did not have the knowledge to decide otherwise. Now we have the knowledge for a better decision and we should take it" (El-Sammani, 1988, p. 417).

Wisdom in Hindsight

The progress that has been made since the shift from the original project brought about by the southern input, particularly after the demonstrations, has highlighted the shortcomings of the original conception of the canal, even with the modifications of the Jonglei Investigation Team. Howell et al. (1988) stated:

> The Jonglei Investigation Team are often condemned as "negative," meaning that they secured only at maintaining unchanged as far as was possible the physical conditions upon which the subsistence economy of the time could continue, and took no account of economic development potential in a progressive sense. The team was not called upon to do so; indeed, they were specifically discouraged from consideration of development possibilities. (p. 43)

It is obvious that the role of the south under Alier's leadership was never to challenge the decision to proceed with implementation of the canal project, but rather to ameliorate its negative impact on the region and to seize on it as an opportunity for generating development in the region.

What needs to be stressed are the dynamics of the interactive perspectives of the various actors and how they influenced the evolution and conceptualization of the project. The north-south conflict that is culturally rooted provided the setting. The regional government not only was amenable to the central government's desire to see the plan for the project proceed but also found in it an opportunity for generating development in the south. The popular opposition to the project in the south presented both an obstacle and another opportunity for persuading both the north and Egypt to consider further the interests and concerns of the southerners. This opposition, in turn, reinforced the negotiating position of the regional government to demand more for the south from the project.

The Egyptian Connection

In the wake of demonstrations in the south, Egypt was reticent about the implementation of the project, presumably needing time to understand the reasons for and significance of the opposition from the south. It took Alier, carrying a letter from Nimeiri and accompanied by Magid, then still the minister of irrigation, to persuade El Sadat to give the green light for the implementation of the project. It is particularly interesting that El Sadat manipulated his supposed origin in the Sudan to build bridges with the south. According to Alier (1990):

> President Sadat met us and after he read the letter he began to chat fondly about his roots in the Sudan, especially the Southern Sudan. I was told later that this was a familiar theme. Sadat's mother is reported to have been a Sudanese; she was sometimes said to be from the Western Sudan, sometimes from the Central Sudan and yet at other times from the Southern Sudan, all depending on to whom he was speaking. After these short exchanges of diplomatic pleasantries in the luxurious surroundings of the President's comfortable villa in Alexandria, he instructed his Minister of Sudan Affairs, Dr. Ahmed Badran, to start the ball rolling. Sadat appeared to demonstrate keenness about the project, but it was also clear that the Egyptians had somehow put on an appearance of lack of zeal for it. At least they seemed to have decided to treat the matter as very low key. The demonstrations in the South had shaken them. They were no longer sure about the security of the Jonglei canal and its smooth execution. But they eventually came in and work started. (p. 206)

The construction of the canal was undertaken in 1978 by a French consortium, Compagnie de Constructions Internationales (CCI), whose involvement emanated from the fact that it possessed the German-made bucket wheel, the largest mechanical excavation tool in the world, which would shorten considerably the time it otherwise would take to dig the canal by alternative techniques. But that involvement only sharpened the cultural dilemmas of development, which won the central stage by default.

The Development Dilemma

At the time the implementation of the Jonglei Canal project began, the development of the south was a major concern. Certainly Alier's role was pivotal to the acceptance of the project by the south and in using southern resistance to win northern support for the development of the south. A southern Sudanese scholar and a critic of the Jonglei Canal wrote about Alier in unmitigated terms:

> One thing that people do not miss coming across when talking about the Jonglei Canal is the name of Abel Alier. A staunch supporter of the digging of the canal, Abel's personal support for the project ultimately tilted the balance in favor of the digging. While opposition to the canal mounted in the Southern Sudan, the Regional Government under him hung toughly to its commitment to support the project. Mr. Alier, who himself comes from the Sudd region, strongly believes that the project is being done for the interest of the Sudanese people, particularly Southern Sudanese. With this strong conviction, and as he was the final authority in the Southern Sudan when the debate on the Jonglei Canal was on, he effectively silenced opposition to the canal digging by having some of the vocal opponents arrested, or forced to flee the country for a self-imposed exile in a neighboring state. Abel's total commitment to the execution of the project sometimes gives one the impression that he has discovered an alternative route to paradise through the construction of the Jonglei Canal.
>
> Reacting to popular opposition to the project in the 1970s, he made it known that the Government was prepared to use force, if the situation demanded that, in order to proceed with the execution of the canal. Taking opposition to the project as people's refusal to be developed, Vice President Alier warned: "If we have to drive our people to paradise with sticks, we shall do so." And faithful to his words, he indirectly used the stick to discharge his sacred mission on earth by sending a student demonstrator to his grave through the hands of police. (Mawut, 1986, p. 57)

It is not clear what "path" to development Alier envisaged, but his words are indicative of the infamous top-down approach to development. The Jonglei Canal project indeed typifies the classic perception of development as a transfer of resources, scientific know-how, and technical expertise from the north (regionally and globally), in which the local populations are recipients rather than the generators of their own progress from within. The envisaged development projects did not materialize as promised for a number of reasons, the obvious one being the war syndrome, but an independent flaw has to be attributed to the external orientation of the development approach.

Eyes on the Development Sky

By the time work commenced, the southern expectations of the canal had risen considerably with open-ended prospects for further growth. As one southern critic stated:

> In the propaganda stage of the project, all the good things one could imagine for a happy life were promised; modern model villages in the Canal area well-equipped with the basic human needs: clean drinking water, schools, health facilities, agricultural projects, and recreational centers, facilities that are not even available in the average Sudanese town. For the supporters of the Jonglei Canal, the Sudan has at last found the key to the solution of her major socio-economic problems. . . . However, all those attractions about the Jonglei Canal failed to win unanimous support for the project in the southern Sudan. (Mawut, 1986, p. 50)

The people who would be affected by the canal project are the Nilotics, mostly the Dinka, the Nuer, and the Shilluk, who have been reported by anthropologists as conservative and resistant to development and to change in general. Their response to the challenges of modernization has recently demonstrated a surprising ability to adapt to changing conditions. Howell et al. (1988) observed:

> It is something of a paradox that these Nilotes are frequently regarded as conservative pastoralists, deeply resistant to change. Such a view is misleading, because Nilotic society is by no means unchanging. The recent history of Nilotic involvement in Sudanese politics, for example, bears testimony to their vigorous participation in both national and regional economic and political issues. (p. 248)

External Orientation of Development

Nevertheless this bursting energy has been largely a response to external stimuli and has tended to be directed toward emulating outside symbols of development, rather than toward generating an internal process of self-enhancement. This direction has been a source of profound social disruption.

Development in the south was generated by two principal agents of change, both external. One was education, which, at least initially, was spearheaded by Christian missionaries and aimed primarily at proselytization of the faith. The other was the search for employment opportunities, mostly in urban areas and far from the local community. In both cases, development symbolized something foreign to the local population, to be received or sought from foreign sources without whose indulgence there can be no progress.

It must be remembered that, traditionally, the Nilotic society was a self-contained system in which basic human needs were met in a sustainable way. With their cattle wealth, a fertile soil, an environment abounding with game and other food products, and rivers teaming with fish, the Nilotics believed themselves to be blessed and a source of envy by others. Their value system, although stratifying people according to descent, age, and gender, accommodated everyone through compensational devices that included ritualized, culturally legitimated rebelliousness within the system. The world beyond, mostly represented by Arab slave raiders, was a hostile and morally depraved one that did not provide appealing models to be emulated. Even in religious terms, the Nilotics saw no one with a faith superior to theirs.

The notion of endeavoring to elevate society or individuals to an as yet unrealized higher and better level of existence through a process called "development" was clearly foreign to the Nilotics. The spiritual leader is expected, not to lead his community to a higher state, but to maintain unity, harmony, and functional prosperity or to make adjustments to restore them when something goes wrong. But spiritual leaders are not solely responsible for the well-being of society. The individual member of the community, too, must endeavor to achieve it, and to this end, education among the Nilotics is both informative (in the transmission of facts) and morally prescriptive. Individual and societal goals, even to the optimum degree, were considered to be part of experience, achievable, and, at one time or another, actually achieved.

The Nilotics have come to accept their technological inferiority in the modern context as divinely ordained, but they continue to feel strikingly ambivalent about the so-called advantages of the allegedly superior world represented by the urban context to which they now have access. This feeling is especially true following independence and the abrogation of colonial policies aimed at fostering development within the tribal context and along traditional lines. On the one hand, the current ambivalence recognizes that the modern context offers them opportunities that did not exist before. On the other hand, urban labor is viewed as imposing on a person conditions of indignity considered to be repugnant to traditional pride and sense of worth.

The picture that emerges is a complex amalgamation of tradition and modernization in a process that was geared primarily toward "development." Mutual cross-cultural accommodation went side by side with contradictions and unwitting disregard, if not disrespect, of each other's values and institutions. The Christian missionaries took the traditional religious beliefs and practices for granted, while the Dinka pragmatically and selectively benefitted from Christian educational and medical services, which they at first resisted but eventually learned to appreciate. Although the converted youth embraced Christianity with zeal, their elders accepted the conversion of their children as a tolerable component of the more significant benefits that were resulting from the missionary work in the area. But the process of modernization caught on out of the cultural context in a manner that disoriented the people and in disparate ways that tore the society apart, disaffiliating individuals from their families and communities in a fashion strikingly contrasting with their tradition.

Contrasting Models to Development

Nilotic responses to the development crisis they have experienced reveal two contrasting models. The first, which is in line with traditional experience, is a postulate reflecting a process of change within the existing social order, with the generational dynamics of progress through a process of adaptation to changing circumstances and the new challenges they present. The second is the operative model that tends to exclude the people and their value-institutional system as outmoded and irrelevant to the challenge of development.

This model implies an approach that fundamentally undermines the preexisting values, institutions, and proven ways of pursuing the objectives of life. Instead of seeing these as vital and indispensable to the resourcefulness and productivity of the people, they are dismissed as outmoded and antithetic to progress. This rejection inevitably fosters a lack of self-confidence, helplessness, and dependency on the outside world, even for the basics of life in their own environment. It is the lack of knowledge about local cultures and the consequential failure to appreciate their potentials for political and economic development that have aggravated the impoverishment of the modern nation-state in Africa. It has been the principal cause of the failure to tap and release the energies of the Africans, elites, and masses alike to make a sustainable contribution to the development process.

"Negotiation" in Cultural Perspective

Two personalities emerge as the pivotal "actors" managing the "structure" of conflict and developing "strategies" that were tactically complementary or supportive through a political "process" dominated by an ambivalent phase of precarious conflict resolution to produce an "outcome" that was like an organ transplant that risked rejection and failure. These two actors are Nimeiri and Alier.

Following the abortive communist coup of 1971, his popular endorsement as the first elected president of the republic and his successful negotiation of the Addis Ababa accord, Nimeiri was regarded not just as a head of state but also as a powerful and popular leader with a high-level motivation to make the agreement with the south work. Alier had been a close ally in Nimeiri's most significant accomplishment—ending the war in the south. For the same reason, his own political assets were predicated on that achievement. He was also highly motivated not to alienate the president from whom he derived his own power.

The two needed each other and were required to cooperate. But to what extent did they represent the two factions, north and south? Did their attitudes, values, and images represent their northern and southern constituencies? The answer is a relative yes and no, which would explain both the political crises associated with the project in the south and the relative success in resolving them.

Politically, a good case can be made to the effect that they did represent the north and the south to an effective degree. The cultural dimension is, of course, more complex and nebulous. Individuals are the products of the acculturation process that goes back to the earliest years of life and throughout the process of education, both formal and informal. The influence of life on the individual operating within a given cultural context is another source of personality molding. Naturally the degree to which individuals will reflect the salient characteristics of their cultural group is dynamic and too varied to be gauged.

If we take Nimeiri, the mere fact that he had successively changed political colors to win the approval and cooperation of virtually all of the significant constituencies in the north indicates that he, at least in part, shared their objectives and values. If the consistent northern approach to the south had been to make promises to win the cooperation of the south, but which either were not intended to be honored or were subsequently violated, then Nimeiri as a cultural personality represented the north. In fact, he did this in two classic ways: concluding agreements that were not intended to be honored, and dishonoring concluded agreements.

For an example of concluding agreements that were not intended to be honored, there is no better source than Nimeiri himself. During the discussions of a technical committee that was considering the application of regional autonomy throughout the country, building on the experience of the south, Nimeiri made a startling but revealing confession. In response to fears that autonomy might lead to separatist tendencies and risk the eventual disintegration of the nation, he swore to tell the truth in front of God and said that when he initially had accepted the arrangement for the south, he had entertained similar fears and had planned the agreement only as a temporary means of persuading the rebels to surrender their arms. His intention was to tear up the agreement within 2 or 3 years. To his surprise, regional autonomy had worked so well in the south that he now wanted to apply it to the whole country. Fears of separatism resulting from autonomy were, therefore, unjustified. In making that positive point, Nimeiri alluded to the negative northern Sudanese pattern of using agreements with the south as clever ploys aimed more at undermining the cause of the south than at finding lasting solutions.

With respect to dishonoring agreements by unilaterally abrogating the Addis Ababa agreement, Nimeiri also appeared to conform to a northern pattern that Alier had in mind when he subtitled his book *Too Many Agreements Dishonored.*

As for Alier himself, the first remarkable fact about him is his name, which in Dinka means "coolness." The second is that he is known for coolness of temperament and style of cultivation or communication. It is worth recalling in this context that a chief among the Dinka is a spiritual leader whose words are believed to express divine enlightenment and wisdom and to form the point of consensus and reconciliation. To reconcile people, the chief should be a model of purity, righteousness, and patience. In Dinka terms he should be "a man with a cool heart," not hot-tempered or impatient.

If Alier was given that name because the elders had these attributes in mind, and if he was brought up with these attributes as goals toward which he should be geared, then he certainly embodies those cultural values. But whether he was acculturated consciously toward those values, his personality certainly coincides with those attributes. And he brought them into full use both in the way he negotiated the Addis Ababa agreement and in the skillful way he shaped the political dialogue on the Jonglei Canal project, eventually reshaping it to cater to the development objectives of the local people.

The only tone in Alier's entire demeanor that sounded out of character was when he told the regional assembly that he would drive people with sticks through the path of socioeconomic development if need be. But here he was clearly on the defensive not only against the patronizing past policies of preserving the "primitive" cultures but also because the weakness of his government's position for not having been involved in shaping the project had been exposed; he had to appear "tough." In this context it is revealing that he was initially reluctant to address the protestors allegedly because he thought it "rather awkward for the government to be seen to

8

Switzerland, France, Germany, the Netherlands: The Rhine

CHRISTOPHE DUPONT

For several decades the riparian countries of the Rhine River—a major river in Europe—have been involved in negotiations. These negotiations have focused on protecting the Rhine from pollution, especially since the 1950s, when an intergovernmental commission—the International Commission for the Protection of the Rhine Against Pollution (ICPR)—was set up.

These negotiations provide a valuable experience of interest to theoreticians and practitioners. They may be analyzed from many angles. The topic of this chapter is their relevance to the issue of culture and negotiation. In the first section, I summarize the essential background data (see also Dupont, 1993). In the second section, I identify the cultural components in the negotiations. In the third section, I examine the impact of cultural factors on these negotiations.

Background

The rationale behind negotiations between the countries through which the Rhine River flows has been—among other problems such as transportation—the increasing threat of widespread pollution, the consequences of which have had a bearing on the multiple uses of the river water: drinking water, purified water for industry and agriculture, fishing, and leisure. The area comprises four countries (from upstream to downstream): Switzerland, Germany, France, and the Netherlands. Partly for historical reasons Luxembourg, and for institutional reasons the European Community, also have been involved.[1] In 1950 these countries set up the ICPR, which became an intergovernmental organization in 1963. Since then, these actors have conducted several negotiations, the outcomes being the signing and ratification of conventions (the Bonn Convention in 1976 and 1983), declarations of intent, an action program (1987), and more recently (1991), the Rhine Salt Convention.

History and Geography

The negotiations on the Rhine, as they have been organized and have developed in recent decades, cannot be detached from the geographical and historical background.

The Rhine has played an important role in Western Europe. Today it is a border between two main riparian countries, France and Germany (see Figure 8.1), but this has not always been the case. Politically and geographically this area could be regarded as the "Rhine basin." German is spoken in this area. The French territory was extended gradually to the left bank of the Rhine in the 17th and 18th centuries. Having been part of the German Empire after the 1870 Franco-German war, Alsace-Lorraine was regained by France in 1918 after World War I. The Rhine negotiations in the late 19th century were limited in scope. One series of negotiations focused on the need to organize maritime transportation on the river; they resulted in the creation of the Central Commission on Navigation on the Rhine. A second series of negotiations dealt with fishing protection (especially salmon); they resulted in the Berlin Treaty. These negotiations were conducted typically by traditional diplomacy.

Pollution first became a concern just after World War II. The Netherlands was particularly worried by chloride pollution due to potash mining at the site of the Potash Mines of Alsace (MDPA). The Dutch government, through diplomatic channels, suggested that the Commission on Navigation study the problem. But the commission thought it could not handle

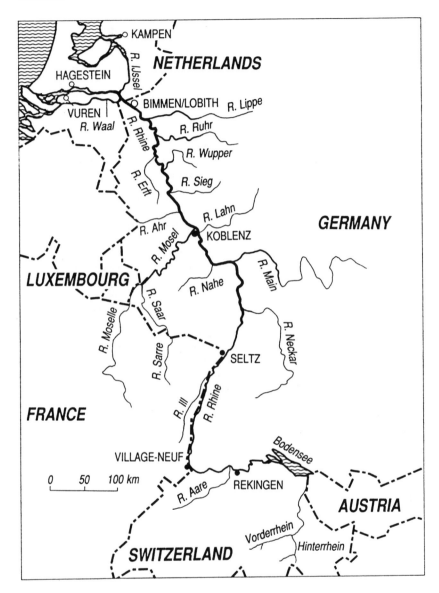

Figure 8.1. The Rhine Basin

the issue. To address the issue, a conference was held in Basel in 1950. This was the starting point of negotiations on pollution. This conference led to the setting up of the ICPR (which received official status as an

TABLE 8.1   ICPR Negotiations on the Rhine and the ICPR (1950-1989)

Date	Event
1950	ICPR set up.
1963 (Apr. 4)	ICPR receives official status as an intergovernmental organization. Signing of the Bern Convention.
1972	First ministerial conference. Decision made to tackle chloride pollution problem (potash mines in Alsace, France).
1973	A proposal to stock salt residues permanently on French soil is rejected by France, which proposes instead alternative solutions to be studied. The ICPR countries agree to conduct more studies.
1976	EEC—as an entity—is made a contracting party of the commission.
1976 (Dec. 3)	The Bonn Convention on chemical pollution in the Rhine and on the chloride problem is signed. For the latter, France agrees to a two-phase program with time limits and partial joint financing.
1977-1983	Strong tensions are due to France lagging in ratifying convention (temporary recall of Dutch ambassador from France in 1979).
1983	Tensions ease. France ratifies convention, which is modified (Apr./May 1983).
1983-1986	Negotiations take place on measures both to reduce chemical pollution and to agree on a mutually accepted solution to the chloride problem.
1986 (Nov. 1)	Sandoz accident occurs. Round of negotiations follows immediately.*
1986 (Dec. 11)	French Declaration of Intent on chloride problem.
1987 (Jan. 1)	French program (1st phase) starts with aim to reduce inputs by 20 kg/sec.
1987 (Oct. 1)	Decision is made to devise an action plan for the Rhine to deal with the various aspects of pollution (toxic substances, accidents, thermic aspects, joint information). The aim is to solve the problem by the year 2000.
1988 (Oct. 11)	Important ministerial conference is held on the action plan and the chloride issue.
1989-1991	Negotiations continue to refine and start implementation of the action plan and the chloride programs.

NOTE: *Toxic substances were released into the Rhine after an accident at the Sandoz chemical factory near Bâle, Switzerland, in November 1986. These substances could not be controlled immediately, which led to pollution downstream over several hundreds of miles.

intergovernmental body in 1963) and to the gradual enlargement of the negotiations that now deal not only with chlorides but also with many other issues. The banks of the Rhine are lined with chemical industries, intensive agriculture, a dense population (hence the problem of municipal waste), and nuclear sites.

An Overview of the Rhine Negotiations

Table 8.1 presents a summary of the Rhine negotiations and their institutional context. It identifies the scope of action covered by the negotiations.

The Dimensions of the Negotiations

In this section I follow the approach described in *International Negotiation: Analysis, Approaches, Issues* (Kremenyuk, 1991) and provide a summary of the actors, structure, strategies, process, and outcomes of the Rhine negotiations. (Further details are available in Dupont, 1993.)

Actors

Principally there are the six national members of the ICPR and the ICPR itself; these actors negotiate in delegations. For a full understanding of the negotiations, it is necessary to consider the forces behind the delegations' behavior and decisions. This is a complex situation, as these forces stem from different ministries and their operating administrations, various agencies, local authorities, private industry, and pressure groups. The ICPR is a coordinating agency; the decision-making power (based on consensus) is in the hands of the governments.[2] Traditional (mainly bilateral) diplomacy and working groups of experts (under the aegis of the ICPR) have an important role, especially in prenegotiations. Occasionally other organizations (e.g., the OECD, the UNEC, the Intergovernmental Commission of the North Sea) have had a role in some of the negotiations.

Structure

The issues include many problems, such as the causes of pollution, the responsibilities involved, the technical measures to tackle it, the sharing of costs, and time schedules. Two issues have long been prominent: (a) chlorides produced by the potash mines in Alsace (France) and (b) toxic substances from municipal waste and industrial factories. More recently, such issues as security (following the Sandoz accident in 1986), pollution from nonpoint sources, and protection of the environment of the Rhine have come to the fore.

Among the constraints that determine the negotiators' positions are the strong political and economic stakes underlying many of these issues. Thus the future of the potash mines and the related consequences for employment and regional development, as well as the cost of corrective measures, have constrained the French position on the chloride issue, whereas the damages and inconveniences caused by this situation, mainly borne by the downstream state (the Netherlands), have constrained the Dutch position.

Apart from the multiplicity and complexity of issues and the corresponding opposite perceptions and interests (elements favoring competitive behavior), other elements of the negotiation structure include the historical, as well as the institutional, context (elements favoring cooperative behaviors). The actual negotiations essentially take place in a "multilateral diplomacy" setting supplemented by traditional diplomacy and meetings of experts organized by the ICPR into numerous working groups. The concluding phase of the more important negotiations take place either in one of the member countries or in Koblenz, the headquarters of ICPR. High-ranking ministers or national officials attend these conferences.

Strategies

Because of the issue structure, the actors' strategies have not been uniform. The most concerned state, the Netherlands, generally has adopted a strategy of pressure aimed at producing concrete and time-sanctioned agreements, giving priority to effective and rapid implementation. Another strategy adopted by the Netherlands includes elements of flexibility to facilitate the attainment of consensus. A third strategy is characterized by the search for alliances mainly on an issue basis. Illustrations of each of these strategies are:

> The recall of the Dutch ambassador from France (1979)
>
> The acceptance of a revision of the Bonn Convention (1983) and the willingness to share costs
>
> The occasional alignment with France on certain issues related to the action program (1988-1989)

French and German strategies were at times similar and at other times very different. The strategies were similar when the aim was to reach agreements based on broad lines of policy giving national entities or administrations some leeway in the implementation of the measures. Both countries were also in agreement when the entire problem was considered. But whereas Germany insisted on a permanent, stringent, and accelerated program on chloride elimination, France was more concerned with temporary, pragmatic, and gradual solutions while insisting on the need to regard other toxic discharges as important as chlorides. Hence France and Germany did align themselves at times but were members of different groupings at other times. "Coalition" reshuffling was essentially tactical.

Swiss strategies were characterized by a marked change following the November 1986 Sandoz accident. Switzerland's main concern until that dramatic event was to prevent encroachments on its sovereignty and "neutrality." As the most upstream state, its delegation was the least involved and acted more as a somewhat distant and moderate mediator. Sandoz produced a shock, and the Swiss attitude changed; it became more active and willing to participate fully in the process.

Luxembourg's strategies were in line with the principal interest of the country, which was focused on fishing needs; thus the Luxembourg delegation's activity was linked mainly to this issue. The EC delegation closely monitored the process to ensure conformity between its own environmental program (mandatory to all EC members) and the decision of the member countries of the ICPR. Finally, ICPR's strategies appeared to be designed to make salient the collective needs of the actors and to give full weight to technical data and factors. The strategy—developing on a low-profile basis—was to be perceived as a machinery facilitating joint goodwill and the reconciliation, mainly on technical grounds, between diverging national interests.

Process

The process of negotiation relating to the Rhine has been characterized by the contrast between the discontinuous mechanism of decision making (materializing at ministerial conferences) and the recurrent activities of the ICPR. The ICPR has developed networks of working groups and meetings where technical national experts help identify the problem, search for reconciliation of opposite positions, and look for viable alternatives (Dupont, 1993). Their work—preceded by internal discussions at various levels in each country—then is embodied in semiofficial "positions" that generally travel through bilateral or multilateral channels before being placed on the agenda of the ICPR, which the commission generally proposes to the conference. This complicated, yet smooth, time-polished process explains the generally cooperative climate (which should not, however, obscure the reality of hard-bargaining episodes that are as much a part of the process). Perhaps this particular mix of cooperative diplomacy and hard bargaining on critical issues is the most salient feature of the Rhine negotiations, and it can be explained, at least partly, by the cultural dimension.

Outcomes

The usual outcome of the Rhine negotiation is either the signing (and subsequent ratification) of binding agreements or conventions or political agreements such as the rather extensive action plan signed in October 1987. In September 1991 the Rhine Salt Treaty (adjusted version) was signed by the riparian states. The agreements call for definite measures and/or commitments to deal with pollution aspects, to determine financing requirements and modalities, to set target dates, and to organize implementation mechanisms. The ICPR has seen its scope of activity increased in the process as it is delegated to intervene directly in certain aspects of the plan.

This type of outcome is the result of a lengthy process that has taken several years to develop. A basic factor has been the implicit joint decision to negotiate, with the goal of reaching a formal agreement only after an issue has sufficiently "matured" following successive rounds of encounters as described above.

An Analytical Perspective:
Identification of the Main Factors
in the Negotiations

The Rhine negotiations have been influenced by a number of factors. Trying to isolate them inevitably involves the risk of some "reductionism" and possibly the danger of oversimplification. The approach used in this chapter, however, is deliberately analytical. Factors first are identified and then are studied from the perspective of their combined influence on the negotiation pattern. Because of the focus of this book, an effort is made to separate culturally linked factors from all others. This is the source of the second type of methodological limitations because, on the one hand, the boundaries between the two categories are not always precise (e.g., they depend on the definition given to *culture*) and, on the other hand, interactions are not at the center of the analysis.

Regarding definition, *culture* is meant in this chapter to represent "a set of shared and enduring meanings, values, and beliefs that characterize national, ethnic, or other groups and orient their behavior" (Faure & Sjöstedt, Chap. 1). *Behavior* has a somewhat broad meaning because it includes "practices . . . and forms of social organization" (Cohen, Chap. 3). It does include "institutions," as in the *New Encyclopedia Britannica*'s definition referred to by Lang in Chapter 4, but it does not include the "political game" as such or the institutional form of the negotiations (their structure).

Ten factors have been identified: Five are considered to be culture based; the remaining five are variables or factors that, although not necessarily immune from cultural influences (culture-free), may be viewed in terms of their own specificity in relation to the negotiation pattern that could be observed. These culture-based factors are:[3]

- Homogeneity (H): The degree to which negotiators ("delegations") share geographical, historical, and social organizational pattern dimensions

- Emotions (E): The intrinsic emotional value and the "mystique" imbedded in the issues at stake
- Environment and Ecology (EE): The attitude toward environment and ecological norms and values
- Socio-Political (institutional) structures (SP): Included is a variety of rules and practices, such as decision-making mechanisms and the attitudes toward limitations to sovereignty
- Negotiating Styles (NSL): Includes language

The other factors are:

- Interests and stakes (I): Seen essentially from an economic viewpoint in a broad sense (i.e., not only economic costs and benefits but also such factors as social effects)
- Distribution Pattern (DP): The cause and consequence of damages
- Technical dimensions (T): Technical problems
- Political opportunism (Po): Includes other related policies
- Institutional factor (IDN): The setup and design of the negotiations themselves

Homogeneity

The actors who were (and are currently) involved in the Rhine negotiations are from a group of countries that shares many cultural characteristics: a common (though often turbulent) historical heritage, close geographical and communication links, and a great familiarity in fundamental norms and values (despite strong differences in national subcultures). Above all, the recent effort toward integration (or association, in the case of Switzerland) undoubtedly has been a major factor in defining the climate of the negotiations. Because of the growing feeling of continental unity, European negotiators tend to interact in a more confident and casual way.

A rather convincing demonstration of this situation is made in a recent sociological research (Mermet, 1991). One result of the study is a matrix showing the degree of confidence among average Europeans (Mermet, 1991, p. 276). The indices of confidence relationship are shown to rank very high (or high) among the four countries (France, Germany, Luxembourg, and the Netherlands) that are both included in my survey and involved in the Rhine negotiations. (Switzerland is not included in the survey.) The matrix also shows that the countries are part of a hardcore group with a high degree of confidence in each other. Thus one may infer that this confidence factor, built on new and revised perceptions of each other, has helped negotiators carry out negotiations in a more constructive way than otherwise would have prevailed (however, this was obviously not sufficient to prevent occasional frictions and misunderstandings among the parties, but rather served as a general background factor).

Emotions: "Mystique" and "Reification"

If the issue clearly were to find ways to reduce the amount of pollution in the Rhine—basically a socioeconomic, technical agenda—one would have to bear in mind that delegations, apart from their economic interests, have not approached the problem exclusively in these terms. Below the surface but still influencing behaviors were the emotions raised by a subtle, implicit, almost subconscious relationship to the river itself.

For Germany, in particular, the Rhine not only is a political-economic issue but also is viscerally linked to its history, literature, and music. Perhaps Wagner's dramatization of the river in his famous operatic *Tetralogy* is the most tangible evidence of the mystique that the Rhine generates in the German culture. In fact, a kind of reification fuses in a complex relationship of dreams and reality, past and present, emotions and facts.

By comparison the French feeling toward the Rhine has long been influenced by strategic considerations (derived, in part, from memories connected with wars and territorial rivalry). More recently, however, this subconscious feeling has given way to a more positive view symbolized by the claim to have Strasbourg recognized as one of the headquarters of the European Community as a result of French-German reconciliation. The emotional attachment is certainly keener for France's other large rivers, notably the Seine, a subject, for instance, of many popular songs and works of fiction.

The Dutch cultural attitude toward the Rhine is different: The Rhine is of key importance in its geography (the delta), and its impact looms very large in the socioeconomic structures. The Netherlands depends a lot on quality water for many, not only industrial, uses. Hence the country has a pragmatic, result-oriented view colored by economic constraints and realities.

The Swiss culture often has been described as showing a strong attachment for the mountains and the lakes. As far as water is concerned, the lakes, more than the Rhine, are imbedded in their collective consciousness.

The fifth country involved in the negotiations—Luxembourg—sees the Rhine as a river into which its own river (the Moselle) flows and where social activities (e.g., leisure and fishing) can conveniently take place.

How can such cultural components have influenced negotiations? Obviously not in a direct, explicit way. But one can suspect that the very way negotiators have approached negotiations has been influenced by these emotional factors and their symbolic dimension. Furthermore a link exists between this general factor and the more direct influences exerted by more specific factors such as the pressures of the media and the role played by environmental sensitiveness.

Environment and Ecological Norms and Values

The increasing pollution of the Rhine until the late 1970s caused considerable damage to the environment. Pressures were put on the ecological balance, as evidenced by the disappearance of certain traditional species in and along the river. It is worthwhile to note that a logo sometimes used in ICPR publications shows the picture of a salmon, a species that, it is hoped, will reappear in the Rhine by the end of the century once the measures in the action plan have sufficiently cleaned up the river.

The member countries involved in the negotiations, though agreeing on the need for improving the environmental and ecological situations, have not shown, at least until recently, the same degree of concern and sensitivity on this issue. This disparity can be inferred from the differing strength of the ecological/green parties and associations in the various countries. Germany, for instance, has had for a few decades strong, active, and influential groups that have forced their way into the existing political structures. France, on the other hand, has not exhibited the same pattern, though a notable change has taken place in recent years (the government now includes a Ministry of Environment, and recent political surveys indicate a sharp increase in voting intentions in favor of the two main ecological parties).

It must be emphasized that, for all countries, the importance of the environment has been intensified since the Sandoz accident in 1986.

Socio-Political (Institutional) Structures

Negotiations on the Rhine have involved multiple actors located at different levels of the administrative and governmental structures.

Decision-making mechanisms are thus complex and, because they operate differently in the various member countries, these differences affect the negotiations. The crucial point is the relationship between local authorities and central bodies. The delineation of responsibilities, the power balance, the role and weight of the actors at the periphery (who are those most involved in the practical issues), and the initiatives allocated to deal with the problems have shaped the behavior of negotiators. Negotiation strategies have been influenced by these differing decision-making systems. Thus the existence of the Länder in Germany, the complex relationship between central and local agencies in France, and the distribution of decision power between several entities in the Netherlands or Switzerland have had a direct bearing on issue formulation, priorities, and flexibility.

Another factor that should be taken into consideration is the strength of the underlying economic and social philosophies of the various states. Although they all share an economic system based on a free-market economy, they do not appear to give that concept exactly the same importance; relatively minor differences do exist regarding, for instance, the weight to be given to social factors and nonmarket forces. Related to this aspect is the degree to which the countries define their attitude toward sovereignty and the limitations they ascribe to decision rules formulated or edited outside the national sphere. As regards the Rhine, the Netherlands have pushed for more power to be given to the intergovernmental structure (ICPR), whereas Switzerland has shown (especially before Sandoz) a reluctance to give up its right to edict rules applying to its own territory. France (and to a lesser extent, Germany) has been closer to Switzerland than to the Netherlands on this issue. Altogether, however, the trend has been gradually to grant ICPR a broader scope of activity and authority.

Negotiating Styles and Language

Delegates generally admit that there are observed national negotiating styles (see, for instance, Fisher, 1980; Posses, 1978; Weiss & Stripp, 1985b). Although there are several reasons for adhering to that proposition, it is also true that caution is needed when applying it to specific negotiations and/or negotiators. Apart from the danger of stereotypes, one may point to such factors as the gradual emergence of an international culture among professionals and career diplomats—in particular, the closeness that results from enduring interpersonal relationships, the importance taken by technical problems, and so on. Two ethnically different negotiators sometimes may be closer in terms of styles than two nationals may be from different localities, employed in different professions, and so on. Many factors are involved in the interactive dimension of negotiations; hence it is often difficult to separate group traits from individual traits, apart from the fact that negotiating styles may not be independent of the type of issue, of the particular context and circumstances, and of the specific personality matching or mismatching of parties.

The Rhine negotiations do not permit a clear-cut position to be taken on this issue. In interviews many delegates expressed that the various delegations showed some definite characteristics and that negotiating styles differed. The French delegation often was described as showing a tendency to approach issues by concentrating on "principles," procedures, and legal aspects and to back positions by elaborate and obstinate argumentation. In contrast, the Dutch often were described as more direct, pragmatic, and results oriented. Yet these respondents also remarked that most individual negotiators were experienced and had developed a fair knowledge of the differing styles; hence they were able to decode the behavioral implications correctly and could make adjustments accordingly. This ability called for added caution and the need for formulating positions and for resorting to strategies and tactics in a more differentiated and subtle way.

An interesting point is to relate negotiating styles to national characteristics, values, and norms. Hofstede (1980) showed that one could point to cultural distances between the countries that we are surveying (his study, however, is based on a single broad corporate group). This distance can be reflected to some extent in negotiating styles. A more recent contribution, however, concludes that "despite a few divergences, the attitudes and the behaviors of the Europeans are close" (Mermet, 1991, p. 271). Stoetzel (1983) presents a more differentiated point of view, but he does not deny a certain homogeneity of the European culture as a whole despite its diversity on certain points. In addition, in such negotiation as those on the Rhine, there are many commonalities between high-level negotiators and experts; this commonality may tend to relativize, in this particular case, the usual cross-cultural differences that often are observed in international negotiations.

The role of language in negotiation has been an important theme of recent research. If language as a major vector of communication has a bearing on the process in a commonly shared language encounter, it is clear that the interference is categorically amplified when the parties—whatever the language used in the negotiations—do not share the same mother language. In the case of the Rhine, formal negotiations have been (and are) conducted in French or German or both. This usage does not seem to have constituted a major handicap for the other delegations, as their members generally speak several languages. However, the problem is not negligible; this can be inferred from the fact that as a trade-off for not using Dutch (the Netherlands being the most concerned state), the consensus was that the secretary-general of ICPR would be Dutch.

Other Factors

So far, the main factors that embody substantial cultural characteristics have been discussed. In this section other factors that do not show the same degree of cultural involvement are studied.

Among these other factors, interests are obviously prominent. *Interests* refer to bottom-line arguments derived from a comparison between benefits and costs defined in an extensive manner to include indirect impacts and externalities. The negotiators, whatever their cultural background, had to deal with hard issues couched in terms of expenses, revenues, financing, employment, turnover, growth, and the like. Their stakes and positions in the negotiations were based intrinsically on finding reasonable compromises, trade-offs, or other devices that were acceptable from a socioeconomic perspective.

Thus it is essential to view the Rhine negotiations not only as a matching or mismatching of cultures but also as parallel and fundamental confrontations of joint and diverging interests. Specific interests were presented and defended by all delegations to serve as a basis for unilateral justification of action and behavior in the negotiations. The main issues were project financing, distribution over time of cost-generating decisions, the valuations of direct and indirect damages (principally for the downstream state), and employment consequences (notably regarding the French potash mines, the main contributor of chloride pollution).

Another factor that can be identified as having had an impact on the negotiations is the distribution pattern of causes (contributions to) and consequences of damages. Gradually the negotiators took the view that the responsibility was global, as all countries shared in one way or another (though obviously not to the same extent) in the pollution (e.g., not only chlorides but also toxic substances, not only mines but also municipal waste, not only recurrent but also exceptional, accidental discharges) and the benefits of any plan or action would be not only for the downstream actors but also for all actors along the river. Compared to specific self-defense interests, this view introduced into the negotiations a value-creation component.

Technological dimensions and their complexity (e.g., damage measurement and definition of norms) should not be ignored. Such factors—apart from the fact that they involve engineers and experts as co-negotiators with their own standards and behavior—certainly have colored the negotiation in a substantive way—for example, issue formulation, search for and choice of options, and feasibility criteria. At one stage the Rhine negotiations focused on the technical content of proposals suggested by experts to find a temporary solution to the problem of how to stockpile salt residues at the site of the mines.

Contrasting with the institutional factors, which are characterized by their high degree of durability and their associated cultural base, one may consider the role played in an exogenous way by the political game, which is influenced by power shifts, adaptation to circumstances, and opportunistic orientations. The composition—and perhaps also the policy orientations of the various delegations—was certainly not immune from such influences. Interactions between negotiating teams were influenced to some

extent by the changing proximity or distance separating the political orientations of the member states.

Finally, the design of the negotiation structure (e.g., procedures, role of
the ICPR, frequency of encounters, and the mixture of bilateral versus
multilateral diplomacy) also may be analyzed in terms of a superstructure
corresponding to shared practices and values. The negotiating structure
can be considered as a specific factor that has had implications in the negotiating process.

Influences of Cultural Components: An Evaluation

Concentrating on the culture-based components of the negotiations, we
are now in a position to evaluate the impact of these factors on the negotiation
pattern. This evaluation studies culture's impact on actors, structure,
strategies, process, and outcomes. Two criteria are used:

1. Whether the influence is deemed to have facilitated a cooperative mode of
   interacting or a distributive/conflictual mode
2. Whether the influence may be considered as strong or weak

This analysis leads to an overall evaluation of the importance of culture
in the negotiations on the Rhine.

Cooperative Impact
Versus Distributive Impact

Homogeneity (H) may be viewed as a major cooperative factor. The
actors shared many commonalities in their cultural background, and this
feature was backed by political will to solve the problem. Thus this
background gradually generated a constructive climate. This climate was
somewhat mitigated, however, by the play of diverging interests (basically
not a cultural component) and, as regards other culture-linked factors, by
the varying degree of involvement of actors due to the differences in the
emotional (E) responses to the issues and in the acuteness of the sensitiveness to environment and ecology (EE). This factor lost its impetus, however,
as negotiations progressed. Negotiating styles and language (NSL) and
institutional factors (IDN) seem to have played a rather neutral influence,
though cross-cultural differences observed in this respect did produce
occasional difficulties and conflictual episodes. Altogether the strength of

the H factor seems to have been the main influence making the negotiations more cooperative than distributive.

Actors, Structure, Strategies, Process, and Outcomes

Actors in the Rhine negotiations are both the nations themselves (and the ICPR in a coordinating role) and the individual negotiators. This distinction is useful because the decision-making mechanism is influenced greatly by policy orientations (including such factors as historical background, perception of self-interest, and attitudes toward cooperation), but the actual negotiations are conducted by career diplomats, high-ranking civil servants, and experts. These individuals, although dependent on their mandates, bring to the negotiations their professionalism, their traditions, and their styles. Much of the climate of the negotiations depends on their interactions. Thus complex forces are simultaneously at work. Some of these factors are cooperative because of the individual links that traditionally develop between diplomats and because the experts have many common interests and approaches. At the same time, the need to present convincing positions and to defend state interests may lead to competitive episodes. In the Rhine negotiations, a balance seems to have been reached between these various elements. Individual profiles and state orientations produced a style of negotiation in which the classical dilemma between interest-based factors and interdependence-based factors was solved generally in a constructive manner.

Structure is also a combination of culture-linked and "other" influences. The choice and formulation of issues, the organizational pattern, and the impact of antecedents and context reflect both cultural practices and specific factors. A conference diplomacy type of culture certainly has emerged from the increase in intergovernmental and supranational bodies (especially in Europe with the EC, EFTA, Council of Europe, WEU, previously OECE, etc.) and meetings. Contextual factors also can be seen as influenced by culture, but at the same time structural elements of the negotiations have been instrumental, rather than cultural.

Strategies also exhibit a mixture of culture and other influences. The balance is once again between the defense of self-interests and the need for cooperation. Thus the basic strategy orientations and moves are different in each country and reveal cultural traits (e.g., negotiating styles), as well as specific features linked to the substance of the issues.

The *process* of the Rhine negotiations had a unique character. It was characterized by the complexity of the networks involved: expertise at the lower echelons, coordination by ICPR, and diplomacy at the upper level.

Estimated Impact on Outcomes

Origin of Factors		Cooperative/Integrative		Conflictual/Nonintegrative	
	Culture-Linked	Weak	Strong: H	Weak (**) E, EE, SP, NSL	Strong:
	Other (Autonomous) Specific Factors	Weak IDN	Strong: DP T(a) Po(c)	Weak (**) T(a)	Strong: (*) I

NOTE: (*) potentially strongly conflictual in this case
(**) potentially mildly conflictual in this case
(a) Factor T is estimated to have been either strongly integrative or mildly conflictual (e.g., measurement standards), depending on issues.
(c) Po has been classified as strongly cooperative due to the development of a political will to solve the problem.

Figure 8.2. Factors Accounting for Outcomes in the Rhine Negotiations

Network complexity also has led to specific modes and timing of negotiating episodes. In this process cooperation is facilitated both by culture-linked influences and by such "objective" factors as common goal, shared feeling of responsibility, and joint benefits, as well as the sheer weight of technical arguments. Competitive influences are also dual in nature: emotions and sensitiveness to ecology, for instance, on the one hand, and appraisal of the extent of damages, the distribution of costs, and timing, on the other.

The *outcomes* were the result of these various components. They took the form of conventions that governments agreed to implement. The result of the negotiations may be regarded as a combination of cultural and specific (autonomous) forces acting either cooperatively or competitively. This combination is shown in the simplified matrix in Figure 8.2, in which the degree of influence on process and outcomes is estimated and indicated by symbols: a strong influence or a weak or neutral impact.

The figure displays five factors—one cultural factor and four other factors. Most of the factors have helped create predominantly cooperative negotiations; however, one specific autonomous factor (the divergence of interests) has potential distributive capacity. This distributive element has been dealt with constructively—as should be the case in positive negotiations—thus permitting movement toward mutually acceptable, if not fully satisfactory, agreements. In this respect good negotiating behaviors and strategies by the actors (including the ICPR and the working groups) have contributed to this result. Finally it may be added that this essentially analytical approach leads to roughly the same conclusions as those derived from a more intuitive, qualitative, and traditional approach (see Ruchay, 1990).

Concluding Remarks

Cultural components have had an impact—although mixed with other specific, autonomous factors—on the Rhine negotiations. They have been intertwined in the situational factors, or they have operated autonomously, shaping and coloring the behaviors of negotiators. Their impact, either cooperative or competitive, seems to have been most pronounced on the formal aspects of the negotiations, the attitudes of the negotiators, or the climate under which the negotiations took place. On balance they may be assessed to have been more cooperative than conflictual, essentially due to the strength of past relationships, the quality of multinational expertise, the role of ICPR, the increasing feeling of shared concern and responsibilities that helped develop a spirit of cooperativeness, and the sense of political will to act jointly and responsibly.

, Have these conclusions a general validity? It should be noted that the context of these negotiations was specific. The problems at stake, although sometimes having far-fetched implications, were (and are) technically solvable in a reasonable time span. All countries are both contributors to and potential benefactors of a pollution-free Rhine. The countries concerned are part of a relatively homogeneous, economically developed, and democratic milieu. When negotiating an issue, they cannot ignore the multiple aspects of cooperation in other issues and fields; they are conscious of the increasing institutional interdependence.

These characteristics are not often present, but rather most often absent, in environmental regime, especially river negotiations. In these types of negotiations (such as the ones described in this book), developmental implications are important. Intracountry or ethnic (e.g., majority-minority) rivalries are a crucial factor; there may exist difficult relocation problems. Financing requirements are a constant constraint (though also an opportunity). Cultural differences may be deep rooted, reaching sensitive areas such as religion, societal contexts, and the basis of political life.

Some lessons from the Rhine negotiations, however, may be applied to all types of negotiations on river regimes: negotiations in highly industrialized countries, as well as negotiations in industrializing nations. The role of intergovernmental organizations (such as the ICPR) is to realize that there are common and conflictual interests, to include viewpoints of users in addressing issues and formulating their solutions, to give attention to the implementation of plans, and to contribute and develop skills to ensure a mutually satisfactory outcome (see Scudder, 1991).

Notes

1. Luxembourg's concern for the Rhine derives from fishing interests.

2. Recently the tendency has been for the ministerial conference to delegate authority for certain matters to the secretariat of the ICPR and to the working groups.

3. In Figure 8.2 these factors are indicated by a symbol; for example, the homogeneity factor will be referred to as factor H.

9

Turkey, Bulgaria, Romania, and the Soviet Union: The Black Sea

VLADIMIR PISAREV

The significance of the Black Sea is based on its geographic position at the crossroads of Europe and Asia and on the role it plays in the transportation system, connecting continental areas with the Atlantic Ocean, as well as on the economic, political, and military interests of coastal states and other countries that use it.

If the use of and the anthropogenic load on the marine environment is to continue to grow, then some restructuring in the priorities of coastal states must take place. The coastal countries' drive toward protecting the vulnerable marine environment of the Black Sea is becoming as important as their other top priority interests in the region.

Ecology of the Black Sea and the Interests of Coastal States

Natural and geographic features of the basin play an important role in the environmental situation in the Black Sea.[1] The shallow and most vulner-

Figure 9.1. The Black Sea

able parts of the sea stretch to the west of the Crimean Peninsula and farther along to the coasts of Romania and Bulgaria. It is in this area that the exploration and exploitation of the oil resources of the continental shelf are taking place. Major seaports, which are the centers of coastal navigation and international sea trade, are located here. Their operation requires ongoing dredging in harbors and sea channels. Industrial, agricultural, and domestic wastes are carried into the Black Sea by the Danube, the largest river in the region, which crosses eight European nations, three of which are Black Sea coastal states (see Figure 9.1).

The interests of the former Soviet republics (Russia, the Ukraine, Georgia), which are now independent coastal states of the basin, in relation to the protection of the Black Sea are determined by the need for stabilizing and subsequently reducing the marine environmental load under the conditions of the inevitable expansion of agricultural production, as well as foreign trade operations through seaports and the basin's growing role as a recreation zone.

Romanian concerns about the protection of the region are based on the need for improving the ecological situation in its area of marine jurisdiction. The urgency of the problem is caused by such sources of pollution as the Danube discharge—in particular, effluents from industrial enterprises on the Romanian bank of the river, oil development of the continental shelf, and the dumping of waste, which originates from Romania and sometimes Western Europe, into the coastal areas.

The ecological situation in the Bulgarian areas of marine jurisdiction, which as a rule are very shallow, is on the threshold of a crisis (Burgas Bay). In addition to the local sources of contamination, pollutant fluxes are brought into the sea by the western branch of the Black Sea current, which transports anthropogenic impurities from the Danube's estuarine waters, as well as other runoffs. The ecological interests of Bulgaria are oriented toward a rapid reduction of pollution entering the coastal waters and the coordination of international monitoring of and water protection measures for the Black Sea and Danube regions, as well as toward the implementation of the European environmental standards.

In Turkey's Black Sea areas, which are deep and have not been threatened by large amounts of pollution because of the small industrial concentration on the coastal zone, the environmental situation is not as acute as in the three other states. However, in Turkey the growing understanding of the transboundary nature of the ecological threat caused by the Black Sea water circulation, the reality of common regional problems (poisoning of the water by hydrogen sulfide), and the realization of the futility of any attempts at finding a unilateral solution to marine protection problems have predetermined the country's interests in reaching an effective regional agreement. Taking into consideration the intensive water exchange through the Bosporus Strait and the Dardanelles, Turkey hopes that an agreement would play an important role in protecting the Black Sea Straits.

Along with protecting the Black Sea against pollution, the coastal states also regard the development of ecological cooperation in the region as a means to reinforce their positions in bilateral and regional, as well as in pan-European and global, relations.

For the Soviet Union, the orientation toward quadrilateral negotiations meant the opening of a new channel of constructive regional interaction and, in particular, an improvement in relations with Turkey, the need for which was realized during the period of radical change in the political systems of the former socialist countries of Eastern Europe and the Soviet Union.[2] For Romania and Turkey, which for economic and political reasons have not signed most of the basic international agreements on the Black Sea protection,[3] the development of a convention to protect the Black Sea against pollution presented the opportunity for making up for nonparticipation and for adjusting the document to reflect their own interests on a more balanced—from their point of view—basis.[4]

In Turkey participation in the negotiations apparently was regarded as preserving and reinforcing its own sovereignty in the Black Sea Straits, regulated by the Montreux Convention. Among Turkey's interests, linked with the elaboration of the Black Sea protection agreement, use of the negotiating processes of the forthcoming convention plays an important role in strengthening good relations with the people of countries that in the past were under the Turkish yoke and still continue to distrust the intentions and initiatives of Turkey.

In Romania the decision to participate in the negotiations, which was taken during the Ceausescu rule, seemed to be regarded as a way of solving the environmental issues and also upholding the "special position" of Romania within the bloc of socialist countries. Bulgaria, which initiated the negotiations, regards them as a way of reinforcing its own position in the broader fabric of Black Sea cooperation between the Balkan States that have similar interests not only in ecology, but also in navigation, energy, fishing, recreation, and tourism.

Negotiations and Problems

In 1969 Bulgaria put forward the idea of convening a meeting of Black Sea countries to elaborate a convention on the protection of the environment in the region. At that time Turkey opposed the idea of such a conference and proposed instead to conduct such negotiations involving not only Black Sea states but also those countries not in the region that also pollute the seawater of the basin. It proposed the European Economic Commission (EEC) as a forum for such negotiations. In 1975 Bulgaria presented a draft convention on the protection of the Black Sea, which used ideas from the Helsinki Convention on the protection of the Baltic Sea. In 1978 Romania came up with the idea of regional cooperation within the framework of two agreements: one on the protection and development of the Black Sea's biological resources, and the other on marine scientific research. Later a joint draft treaty was developed by three socialist countries. However, it failed to serve as a basis for regional negotiations because Turkey's position remained unchanged.

The protracted process of Turkey's entry into the multilateral negotiations and the difficulty of starting the negotiating process itself at that time could be explained by four factors: (a) the negotiating countries belonged to different social systems and military-political blocs, (b) some bilateral issues were pending between the states of the region, (c) a lack of experience in constructive settlement of regional problems within the multilateral process involving the participation of all Black Sea states, and (d) prejudices and mistrust of a historical origin among the countries of the region.

In 1985 the USSR appealed to the Black Sea countries to start the elaboration of joint measures to protect the marine environment, having in mind the deteriorating environmental situation in the region. The Soviet draft convention, which was supported by Romania and Bulgaria, became the basis for trilateral negotiations that began in 1986. Irrespective of Turkey's nonparticipation, the draft that was developed did take into account its interests. It was hoped that the draft of such an approach would make it possible for Turkey to join the agreement later.[5]

In November 1988, diplomatic efforts to secure the participation in the negotiations of all countries in the region at last succeeded.[6] Starting in Bucharest, the meetings of experts designated by the ministries of foreign affairs of the Black Sea states took place, in turn, in each capital. Between 1988 and 1991, eight such meetings were held.

The final draft convention (1991) stipulates that contracting parties shall individually take all necessary measures to prevent, reduce, and control pollution in the Black Sea and to protect and preserve its marine environment in the area covered by the convention, including the territorial waters and exclusive economic zones of each party. The convention regulates all measures to combat pollution from land-based sources, from the atmosphere, and from vessels, as well as pollution from activities on the continental shelf. Also three protocols form an integral part of the convention: on pollution from land-based sources, on cooperation in combatting pollution from oil and other harmful substances in emergency situations, and on the dumping of waste.

Practically all of these problems were the subject of dispute, reconcilement, and compromise during the negotiations. Pollution from vessels is a good example of such problems. The essence of the dispute was whether universal international documents—the UN Law of the Sea Convention of 1982 and the MARPOL 73/78 Convention—should be taken as a basis for Black Sea negotiations, considering that their provisions deal effectively with that source of pollution,[7] or should some other solution be looked for. At the start of the Black Sea negotiations, only the USSR and Bulgaria were parties to the MARPOL Convention. The nonparticipation of Turkey and Romania was caused to a large extent by the fact that membership of the MARPOL 73/78 Convention places on the parties a heavy financial burden connected with improving the design of their tanker fleet and equipment at oil terminals and ports by employing devices for the treatment of ballast. For Turkey the question of joining the universal convention was linked to its unwillingness to include the Bosporus Strait in the area of application of the new convention on the protection of the Black Sea, which is referred to as a special area in the MARPOL Convention.[8] The USSR and Bulgaria could not but take into account these circumstances because the Black Sea Convention is a comprehensive document and reaching compromise on all aspects of the issue requires proper regard for the peculiarities of other participants' positions and approaches.

The compromise that was reached includes eliminating from the draft convention any reference to the MARPOL Convention and any mention of the Black Sea as a special area. However, the inclusion of Article VI on pollution from vessels must be regarded as a step toward securing a comprehensive, combined, regional approach to the protection of the Black Sea against pollution. It is important to note that this article provides that states shall take measures to prevent, reduce, and control pollution from vessels in accordance with the generally accepted international rules and standards.

During the summer of 1988, an incident in one of Turkey's Black Sea ports was given wide publicity. Germany's (as it was then West Germany) vessel *Petersberg* illegally attempted to unload toxic wastes on Turkish territory. The event, which evoked protests from environmental organizations and a negative public reaction, took place just before the opening of the first round of negotiations on the protection of the Black Sea, in which Turkey was a party.

The opportunity for taking into account and positively reacting to public opinion, which required the prevention of any such incidents in the future, became the basis of the Turkish initiative during the negotiations. The delegation from Turkey proposed to include in the draft convention a provision on the control of transboundary movement of hazardous wastes. Discussions focused, in particular, on provisions concerning the inspection by a coastal state of vessels navigating in its territorial waters or exclusive economic zone in such cases where there are grounds for believing that they represent a danger to the marine environment or territory of the coastal state. Soviet experts, while expressing their understanding of Turkish concerns, underlined that Turkey's proposal exceeded the scope of the convention under discussion, which regulated only the measures related to the protection of the marine environment. As for the transboundary movement of hazardous wastes, such an issue, according to the Soviet view, must be treated in a different context.[9]

The comment by Soviet experts, though legally quite justified, did nothing to promote the solution that was supported widely by public opinion in Turkey. Meeting Turkey halfway, the parties agreed to include in the draft of the convention an article on the transboundary movement of hazardous wastes. The parties reworded the basic principle of the article, which became a provision for cooperation in preventing, reducing, and controlling the pollution of the marine environment caused by such transboundary movement (Article XI).

This approach fully corresponds to the principles of the international Law of the Sea, in which the classification of measures to protect the marine environment is based, not on the types of pollutants, but rather on their sources (e.g., vessels, land-based sources, the atmosphere). Transboundary movement of hazardous wastes (in this case, as transported in international sea trade) is fully covered by such a classification and is regulated by Article VI on the pollution of the sea from vessels. Identification of this source in a separate article reflected the readiness of all sides to come to a settlement in the dispute. It is assumed, however, that the implementation of the article would take into account the relevant provisions of other international instruments, such as the Montreux Convention and the Law of the Sea Convention of 1982.

The establishment of the commission for the protection and preservation of the marine environment of the Black Sea was the subject of serious discussions. The USSR, Bulgaria, and Turkey suggested that the commission should have the status of an intergovernmental organization and should be empowered with the authority that would guarantee effective implementation of the convention's provisions. The question of the permanent secretariat and its headquarters was presented from the same standpoint. In contrast to these three states, Romania insisted on maximum restrictions for the commission's authority and agreed only to empower it with consultative functions. Its position was against the establishment of the secretariat as a permanent body of the commission. Agreeing later with its opponents' proposals on this point, Romania insisted that the commission's headquarters should be established in Romania. Turkey and Bulgaria also proposed their capitals as the headquarters for the commission's secretariat. Soviet experts, acting constructively, brought forward a number of criteria that opened the possibility of resolving the dispute objectively and on an unbiased basis. Having in mind the urgent need to set up an effective system of communications between all parties to the convention, they proposed, as a basis for such criteria, that the host country should be capable of supplying the headquarters—at a minimum cost—with all of the necessary technical means and communication equipment. Comparison of the data received from the three applicants showed that the proposal from Turkey agreed best with the criteria.

Structure of the Negotiations

The basic structural element of the negotiations was the meetings of experts from the four participating countries. This element, as well as the scope of interstate issues discussed and the elaboration of agreed solutions aimed at drafting the convention to be adopted by a diplomatic conference of the coastal states, predetermined the high status and significance of the negotiations. At the same time, the unofficial status of consultations facilitated the process by removing or mitigating some structural constraints, such as rigid instructions to the delegations from their capitals. The unofficial status of the negotiations and a ban on mass media involvement also promoted more freedom for participants in the negotiations. However, it did not dismiss the role of such constraints as precedents, which were referred to by all participants with regard to the elaboration of similar conventions on the Baltic and Mediterranean seas.

The dimensions of the negotiating process were determined to a large extent by the nature of the issue itself and by the special role of professional ecologists in their search for scientific and technical solutions. Meetings of experts during the negotiations and the intercessional periods provided broad opportunities for clarifying interests and approaches of all parties and for understanding and taking into consideration the real problems confronting the opponents. The joint efforts of the delegates in reconciling their positions thus were promoted efficiently. It was not by chance that compromises often were reached even before some of the issues were discussed at an official level.

At the same time, the unofficial status of consultations complicated the course of negotiations at times when some participants did not manifest a sufficiently constructive approach. The approach taken by the Romanian delegation on the Black Sea issue can be cited as an example. Romania regarded its participation in the negotiation process not so much as finding a joint solution to the environmental issue by the Black Sea states, but as preserving its possibilities of influencing the system of regional control mechanisms that were to be created. The delegates noted Romanian attempts to slow the negotiating process, to involve the participants in futile discussions, and to impose revisions of already agreed provisions. This was a policy of Ceausescu's government, and until his overthrow it was implemented persistently during negotiations. A gradual shift of Romania toward a more constructive approach became apparent after the crash of the totalitarian regime.

Substantial changes in the structure took place at the conclusion of the negotiations. In 1991 the process of so-called sovereignization of the constituent republics began in the USSR, and the question of representation in the convention arose because Russia, the Ukraine, and Georgia border the Black Sea. The urgent need to settle this problem before convening the diplomatic conference was the reason for the Soviet request presented to the participants of the negotiations in the spring of 1991 to postpone the final meeting scheduled for next summer. After the abortive coup in the

USSR in August 1991, the official declarations of independence by former Soviet republics, and the disintegration of the Union, the prospects of solving the representation issue turned out to be fully dependent on a comprehensive political settlement of relations between the former constituent republics and the former Soviet Union.

The negotiating process provided for plenary meetings and meetings of ad hoc working groups. Personal contacts and unofficial meetings became common in the relations between the Black Sea negotiators. Under these conditions personnel changes and replacements in the delegations of other parties to the negotiations were regarded by Soviet participants as a negative phenomenon adversely affecting the negotiating process. English was the official language of the negotiations, and all delegates who were fluent in English were equal from this point of view. Soviet participants emphasized that, notwithstanding the difficult nature of the negotiations, the meetings were characterized by a spirit of openness, trust, and constructive cooperation.

Cultural Factors and the Negotiations

A review of the prerequisites for the negotiations, the key issues to be settled, and the experts' meetings themselves presents an opportunity for estimating the role of culture at various stages of the negotiations and in relation to the major disputes in question.[10]

Three groups of cultural factors that influence the actors' perceptions of the issue, as well as their expectations of and approaches to the settlement of disputes, have been identified. The first group—historic-cultural and ethno-cultural factors—is based on a confrontation between Islamic and Christian cultures in the region. The confrontation is rooted deeply in the past epoch of Christianization of the Bulgarian Kingdom and Kiev Russia during the 9th to 10th centuries and in the conquest of Byzantium by the Ottoman Empire in the 15th century. The Ottoman yoke and the struggle against it were "the first clash on the European continent between Christianity . . . and Islam . . . two different philosophies and perceptions about values and beliefs in life" (Bokova, 1991, p. 89). The defeat of Bulgaria, the dominance of Ottoman rulers over Danube principalities and laying them under tribute, the Turkish policy of assimilation of the local population, and the centuries-old struggle of the Balkan peoples (supported by Russia) against the Turkish yoke contributed to the formation of cultural stereotypes, which even now influence the entire spectrum of interstate relations in the region.

The second group of cultural factors defines the emotional perception of the Black Sea issue by the actors. In this perception the traditional view of the region predominates; it is based on historically shaped notions of the value of the Black Sea for a given state. For Russia the key element in such a perception, which was shaped over the centuries, is the role of the Black Sea as a defensive bastion at its southern border, as well as its trade and transportation waterway securing access to the Mediterranean Sea and the Atlantic Ocean.

The starting point in the Turkish perception of any regional negotiation is the issue of the Black Sea Straits. Historically such a perception is influenced by cultural stereotypes, formed in the process of confrontation and cooperation with Russia in the area of military and commercial navigation through that strategic waterway.[11]

Romania, which formed a unified state by amalgamation of the Danube principalities[12] and acquired an outlet to the Black Sea (through the port of Constantsa) only in 1878, perceives the regional issues, to a large extent, in the traditional context of interactions among the states of the Danube basin. In Bulgaria the Black Sea protection, as any other regional issue, is regarded in the context of its relations with Turkey and against the background of tensions and mistrust generated by the ethno-cultural conflicts of the past.

The third group of cultural factors can be explained in terms of the nature of political systems of Black Sea states. These systems, which to a certain degree are derivatives of the basic components of culture, are important instruments of adaptation, create their own stereotypes, and can themselves be regarded as the constituent elements of culture. They are less stable and more dynamic and susceptible to changes in situations; at the same time, they affect more directly and tangibly the relations in the region, the formulation of ecological policies of governments, and the behavior of actors in the negotiations. Within the scope of interstate relations, it is the radical changes of political systems in the USSR and the former socialist countries of Eastern Europe, as well as the abandonment of the ideology of interbloc confrontation, that have played a major role in the transition from protracted preparatory consultations on the protection of the Black Sea to the stage of direct negotiations.

At the state level, it was the features of the political systems that have predetermined a modest place of environmental protection issues within the system of national priorities and a low level of ecological culture in some Black Sea states; this feature is characteristic not only of large groups of the population but also of the decisionmakers of those states.

By the late 1980s, both the perception of environmental issues and the approach to their solution began to change in a constructive way. This change was caused by a parallel development of two processes that positively affected the interaction of cultures of the Black Sea states. The first was the consolidation of the global ecological movement, based on the concepts of interdependence, sustainable development, and cooperation. Like the world's seafloor, which has been declared by the UN General Assembly as the Common Heritage of Mankind, the Black Sea has been perceived as some kind of a "regional commons" or "regional heritage," which has in itself a unique value that combines the roles of the region as an economic and ecological resource, a natural preserve, a center of centuries-old culture of humankind, and a common vital space of good relations and cooperation.

The core of the second process that positively affected the perception of the Black Sea protection issue is a growing impact of the inertial forces of regional cooperation, which is gaining momentum in many political, economic, and ecological areas. New bilateral treaties on friendship and cooperation have been signed (Turkey-USSR; Romania-Turkey); negotiations on air and sea boundaries between the countries of the region already have resulted in the resolution of some of the long-standing disputes; the initiative of Turkey on the Black Sea zone of economic cooperation has received support from the USSR and Romania; the green movement, which is unprecedented in its scale, continues to affect positively the ecological cooperation in the region.[13]

Negotiation Process:
Strategies and Culture

Three stages are conspicuous in the negotiation process: (a) the preparatory stage (1969-1988), (b) the stage of direct negotiations (1988-1990), and (c) the conclusive stage (began in 1991). Each is characterized by a line of interaction between the parties and by key factors, strategies, and specific measures directed at the development of agreed solutions.

The history of the formation of the negotiating process and the set of negotiation problems dealing with the involvement of all of the Black Sea states give the reason for claiming that it was during the preparatory stage, the most protracted and difficult stage of the negotiations, that the cultural factor played the most important role; at this stage the interactions between the states involved were developing in two parallel ways.

The interaction between Turkey and the three socialist states was affected by interbloc confrontation and was highly politicized. If political systems are considered to be components of culture, we can study the destructive influence of the cultural factor, which did not make for multi-lateral environmental cooperation in the region. In the mid-1980s the influence of this factor declined because of the warming of the political climate of international relations. However, stable behavioral stereotypes that were formed under the influence of deep-rooted historical perceptions and distorted assessments of other parties' intentions continued to affect the course of preparations of the negotiations in a negative way.

Based on such stereotypes, these traditions, which in the past helped reduce the uncertainty in relations between the states of the region, now have exhausted their stabilizing potential and have become an obstacle in the positive interaction of national cultures in the Black Sea region.

Inside the "socialist concord" of the Black Sea states, the interaction of the members was also extremely politicized. Unified culture, "socialist in content and national in form," did not reflect the peculiarities of issues' perceptions in the USSR, Bulgaria, and Romania, but rather served as a screen to mask deep differences in priorities of the Black Sea protection problem in those countries, in their approaches to its solution, and in the forms of its interconnection with other economic, political, and social problems of the three states.

The second area of the Black Sea states' interaction is evident in three types of forums: (a) their joint participation in the third UN Law of the Sea Conference (1973-1982); (b) the work of specialized international maritime organizations developing universal agreements on the protection of the marine environment, such as International Maritime Organization; and (c) the regional conferences, which resulted in signing the Baltic and Mediterranean seas conventions.[14] In these precedent-setting documents, the concept of *ecological interdependence* in its global and regional dimensions has been developed. Within the interacting cultures, as it were, emerged an understanding of the need for joint and coordinated steps to put an end to the ecological crisis in the Black Sea region. Such understanding has increased the possibilities of different national cultures inter-actively coping with the ecological crisis in the region, which is a threat to the traditional use of the marine environment and its resources in the interests of economic and social development and a threat to the quality of life of all people living in these countries.

From the standpoint of preserving cultural traditions, which are vital for the survival of the environment and which are oriented toward stable and sustainable qualities of the environment, the ecological crisis has complicated the functioning of these traditions as generalized models for forecasting appropriate processes. Thus within the framework of national cultural value systems, the ecological crisis in the region has provoked a drive to uncertainty avoidance, which is a fundamental incentive for changing the situation. This desire has become a hallmark of the strategies of all potential participants of the negotiations.

The place of pride in the Soviet strategy was taken by a policy aimed at identifying and settling regional disputes that blocked the start of direct negotiations. A repudiation of the confrontation policy and due account of the interests of opponents have been taken as a basis for compromises.

The strategy of Bulgaria, which initiated the negotiations, also was based on a similar constructive approach; however, some elements of wariness, caused by Bulgaria's ethnic conflicts with Turkey, were evident.

Romania's strategy at the preparatory stage was characterized by its policy of delaying the start of quadrilateral negotiations and of reducing the range of topics for the Black Sea states' cooperation on the protection of the basin from pollution.

Turkey's policy at this stage was affected by domestic pressures from environmentalists and by its realization that it was in Soviet and Bulgarian interests to have it as a party to multilateral negotiations. These considerations determined Turkey's strategy, in which a major element was its policy line on a settlement at the preparatory stage of certain concomitant problems of regional relations that, in Turkey's view, were urgent.

Against the background of such interactions of all of the actors, the common strategy of the preparatory stage emerged. It focused on the creation of conditions necessary for direct negotiations through the elimination of any obstacles.

The stage of direct negotiations began in the autumn of 1988. At that time some new dimensions of interaction had emerged between the parties because of active involvement of ecologists and lawyers in the negotiating process. Their professionalism, their emphasis on settlement of scientific, technical, and economic issues, and the establishment of legal foundations of a new regime played an important role in reducing the level of politicization of the negotiating process.

Positive changes in the international arena accompanying the disintegration of the socialist camp and the radical changes that occurred in the USSR and in East European states put an end to the era of domination of ideology-based values at negotiations in which representatives of the socialist camp participated. Those values are now being replaced by other values based on respect for statutory laws and the laws of nature. Concepts of ecological balance and interdependence and respect for internationally recognized principles, rules, and precedents are gaining higher priority in value orientation of participants from the former socialist states.

The transcultural character of those values, together with the multilateral nature of negotiations, has played an important part in "diluting the impact of national cultures" (Lang, Chap. 4) and in mitigating ethnically oriented controversies. The transition from confrontational thinking to cooperation and mutual understanding does not mean that parties to the negotiations have abandoned the basic goals they set for themselves. The strategies for achieving these goals have changed. This change is a result of the accelerated process of creating a common approach based on precedents and a more unified perception of the ecological problem. According to this perception, the marine environment is regarded as a common regional entity that requires coordinated efforts of all coastal states for its protection.

The strategy of Turkey, after its entry into multilateral negotiations, was invariably constructive, based on common human values and free of any attempts to resort to religious or ethnic arguments. The Turkish delegation was quite skillful in forming blocs with representatives from other states. It preferred to settle its disputes with Bulgarian delegates (e.g., the 1989 controversy over the venue of the next meeting) through third party meditation.

The strategy of Bulgaria was aimed at creating efficient instruments for regulating protective measures in the basin, including such elements as allowing for concessions, compromises, and temporary coalitions (not only with the Soviet side).

The Romanian strategy was oriented toward a maximum reduction of its international commitments within the framework of the convention and toward preserving its possibilities of influencing any future developments in that area. The Romanian delegation required the deletion from the regulation list of some sources of marine pollution (in particular, those related to the activities on the continental shelf) and the exclusion from any reference to such precedents as the UN Law of the Sea and MARPOL conventions.

The Soviet delegation, from the very start of the negotiations, used a strategy of cooperation and searching for compromises within the framework of universal international law. The best example of this approach was the solution to the problem of the transboundary movement of hazardous wastes. The compromise that was reached secured a reconcilement of the rules set by the UN Law of the Sea, on the one hand, and of the interests and desires of Turkey, for whom the problem proved to be very painful, on the other hand.

A review of the different negotiation settlements reached by dealing with the elaboration of the Black Sea Convention presents an opportunity for estimating the peculiarities of the cultural interactions that include norms, principles, and rules of customary and treaty law.

Two groups of states participated in the negotiations in the Black Sea Convention. On one side were the USSR and Bulgaria, which are members of all major international agreements dealing with the ecological protection of the region.[15] Romania and Turkey, which did not join most of these agreements, were on the other side.

The position of the first two states in the negotiations on the Black Sea was based on the desire to minimize the level of political and legal uncertainties through reliance on thoroughly elaborated, universal, and relatively rigid international rules relating to the protection of the marine environment. The second group emphasized the elaboration of protection measures to specific circumstances; these measures did not necessarily correspond to existing international agreements. Special attention was paid to the practical possibilities of the Black Sea states to comply with the measures. During the negotiations these two approaches were brought together as closely as possible and reconciled; this is the essence of the compromise.

The key factor at the conclusive stage of the negotiation was the emergence of the sovereign and independent former Soviet republics as new actors in the process in 1991. The countrywide Soviet system of decision making began to collapse; a similar situation was developing in the area of a single diplomatic representation, which at the previous stages of the negotiations was a guarantee that no separate national culture would become dominant in the formulation or realization of state policy. Previously, complete rejection of any emphasis on national peculiarities and traditions and deliberate neglect of differences in approaches or assessments, which could be caused by ethnic prejudices, were in this instance the highest manifestation of the diplomatic culture of the Soviet side and substantially contributed to the efficiency of negotiations.

Under the new conditions, contradictions between the parties that were formerly members of a single union were aggravated by the disintegration of the structural framework of a homogenized Soviet culture, which was actually a stiff conglomerate of cultures of different constituent republics. Political disintegration provoked an erosion of three fundamental elements: (a) the states' perception of the Black Sea issue itself, (b) the realization of the urgent need to resolve the issue, which was a high priority not only for the USSR but also for individual republics, and (c) the perception of the ecological challenge as one of consolidating bases on which former republics could develop an integrated approach.

Thus, at the conclusive stage of negotiations, the political factor again has become dominant in the complex process of interaction of national cultures. In 1991 the negotiating process was practically stalled because one of the four parties—the USSR—ceased to exist. It is now reasonable to expect that it will be replaced by the former Soviet republics that have borders along the Black Sea coast. A decision on this issue has not yet been taken, although the newly created states understand quite well both the urgency of the Black Sea protection problem and the need for working out an appropriate regional agreement. By the spring of 1992, these states had reached an agreement on the draft convention on the protection of the Black Sea, which is now ready for presentation to a regional diplomatic conference. Although such a conference has not yet been planned, in the course of the negotiations a positive precedent of resolving a regional issue with the participation of all interested parties has been established; this fact in itself is already a contribution to their successful completion.

Conclusion

Assessing the results of the negotiations on the protection of the Black Sea and the role of culture in that process requires that the time factor and the special features of the subject of the negotiations be taken into account. The beginning of direct negotiations was preceded by an almost 20-year preparatory stage. At this stage environmental problems were not at the top of the basin states' national priorities, meetings of the negotiators were sporadic, and the peculiarities of political systems with deeply rooted historic and ethnocultural perceptions and the resulting assessments of the other parties' intentions (which often were distorted) played a key role in the negotiations.

During these years the environmental protection movement entered the international arena; it was based on the concepts of interdependence, sustainable development, and cooperation. The formation of a global ecological culture has been gaining momentum and has resulted in a growing role of environmental protection issues in national priorities. Ever more ecologically oriented interaction of basin states promoted the perception of the Black Sea as an indivisible regional value. A "tragedy of the commons," caused by pollution of the common sea, began to be perceived as a common problem requiring a concerted approach to find a solution in the interests of all states in the region.

The draft convention is the result of a compromise, and it provides an opportunity for all negotiating parties, which are ready to share the burden of its implementation, to benefit from it.

Theoretically the analysis of joint efforts of the Black Sea states indicates that regional negotiations on environmental protection are progressing under a growing influence of the global ecological culture. This influence can be seen in a relative reduction in unfavorable aspects of the interaction between traditional cultures (which is most tangible at the stage of taking a political decision concerning the participation in the negotiations).

I must note the increasing role of the professional culture of delegates, which during direct negotiations facilitates overcoming barriers related to the peculiarities of national cultures and helps in promoting the effective development of the negotiating process. From the point of view of applications, the latter trend can be activated by consistently including professional ecologists in the delegations at the earliest possible stages, in addition to the full-scale participation of international environmental law specialists.

Notes

1. The northwestern part of the Black Sea, in places reaching 200 km in width, is shallow (30-60 m in depth). To the southeast, at capes Kaliakra and Tarhankut, the sea is deep. The water masses of the Black Sea consist of incoming salty Mediterranean water, brought in by a bottom current through the Bosporus Strait, and fresh water from continental runoff and precipitation. The counterclockwise flow of water, about 60 km wide, dominates the current system of the basin.

2. As the preparation of the draft convention was completed by 1991, before the emergence of independent states in the territory of the former USSR, in this analysis I refer to the Soviet Union as a de facto of the negotiations.

3. International conventions regulating various aspects of protection of the marine environment from pollution are as follows (Black Sea states that have signed these conventions are indicated in parentheses): UN Law of the Sea Convention, 1982 (USSR, Bulgaria, Romania); the International Convention for the Prevention of Marine Pollution from Ships, 1973, as modified by its Protocol of 1978 (MARPOL 73/78) (USSR, Bulgaria, Turkey); Convention on the Prevention of Marine Pollution by Dumping of Wastes and Other Matters, 1972 (USSR); International Convention on Civil Liability for Oil Pollution Damage, 1969 (USSR); International Convention Relating to Intervention on the High Seas in Cases of Oil Pollution Casualties, 1969 (USSR, Bulgaria).

4. Romanian nonparticipation in most of the international agreements dealing with the issue of marine environment protection and imposing some obligations, compliance with which requires major capital investments, is explained largely by its policy of relying on its own efforts to solve the problem. The Turkish refusal to sign the UN Law of the Sea Convention of 1982 is not related to marine environment issues, but is based rather on its disagreement with some of the articles defining the regime of the territorial sea and straits used for international navigation, as well as with the provisions regulating the delimitation of the continental shelf between neighboring states.

5. Participants of trilateral meetings regularly invited Turkey to take part in such consultations and sent drafts of the documents they had elaborated.

6. The main obstacle—Turkey's apprehension concerning negotiations with the bloc of socialist states—was removed by advance notification from the three states to Turkey's foreign office and by the circulation of all draft documents prepared by them. An important role in the process was played by the diplomatic consultations of Turkey with the USSR and Bulgaria, which took place several months before the opening of the negotiations. During the consultations, the states revealed their readiness to take into account both the interests and principal approaches of Turkey.

7. Among members of these international agreements are more than 50 states, including those whose vessels call at the Black Sea ports.

8. Turkey joined MARPOL 73/78 only in 1991.

9. Discussion of this issue had been initiated by the USSR in UNEP and resulted in the signing of the Basel Convention (1989) on the transboundary movement of hazardous wastes and their disposal.

10. In my evaluation of the role of cultural factors in the negotiations, I share the view of those authors who view the role of culture as an adaptive mechanism functioning under the conditions of changes in nature and society and as consisting of "shared and enduring meanings, values, and beliefs." I also include political systems, customs, and treaty law among the components of culture, which play an important role in the process of adaptation (Faure & Sjöstedt, Chap. 1; Markarian, 1983).

11. With the seizure of Constantinople by the Turks in 1453, a period of absolute domination of the Ottoman Empire began. The empire converted the Black Sea into its internal sea. After its consolidation on the Black Sea coast in the late 17th century, Russia spent about seven decades in wars and diplomatic struggles before it achieved international recognition as a Black Sea power and before it obtained the right for its ships to navigate through the straits. According to the Kuchuk-Kainardgy Peace Treaty of 1774, the straits were declared open to the Russian merchant ships. Until 1833 the regime of the Black Sea Straits was regulated by bilateral agreements between Turkey and Russia. From 1840 to 1941, the multilateral London Conventions established a new regime of navigation through the Black Sea Straits. The regimes, which were unfavorable for Russia, remained practically unchanged until 1923, when the Lausanne Convention was signed. The convention, however, fell far short of taking into full account the security interests of the Black Sea states. In fact, it deprived Turkey of its sovereign rights over the straits and opened them to warships of noncoastal states. The present regime of Black Sea Straits is regulated by the Montreux Convention (1936). A key element of the document is a combination of complete freedom of international merchant shipping with the preferential rights of Black Sea coastal states in military navigation through the straits within the framework of the security of Turkey and the security of coastal states in the Black Sea. Turkey plays a special role in protecting the viability of the convention and in ensuring strict compliance with its provisions.

12. In the mid-16th century, the Ottoman Empire seized Transylvania, Moldova, and Valahia. Unification of the last two principalities within the framework of a single state—Romania—took place in 1862. The Romanian constitution of 1866 deprived the ethnic Turkish population of civil rights. Romania's proclamation of its independence from Turkey put an end to the Turkish suzerainty in 1878.

13. In October 1990 the world green movement "Ecoforum for Peace" organized the international conference EcoBlack Sea-90 in which delegates from 15 countries, including the USSR, Bulgaria, and Germany, took part. The concept of preventing an ecological disaster in the Black Sea was discussed by the participants.

In July 1991, Georgia greens initiated an international conference that declared the Black Sea "a zone of environmental disaster" and adopted the program of scientific cooperation to preserve the Black Sea, in which all countries whose waters flow into the Danube and the Black Sea were to participate. The delegates formed a working group to plan "SOS Black Sea," an international campaign to protect the sea. Among the participants of the conference were delegates from Georgia, Turkey, the Ukraine, and Bulgaria.

In September 1991 an international seminar on cooperation between countries of the Black Sea basin and nearby regions, in the interests of peace and good relations, took place in Pitsunda. Delegates from Russia, Bulgaria, the Ukraine, Georgia, Yugoslavia, and Germany adopted a final document in which the Black Sea is proclaimed Common Heritage of Mankind and, on the basis of rich cultural traditions of ancient civilization of the region, expressed their deep concern about the grave ecological situation, ethnic conflicts, and the need for cultural ties within the region. Calling for consolidation of political and economic stability in the region, they urged to expedite the course of negotiations, to sign a convention on the protection of the Black Sea from pollution, and to create ecological centers for monitoring the situation in the basin.

14. It is significant to note that, in general, at all of these forums the Black Sea states were represented by the same career diplomats and ecological experts who are now involved in the development of a regional convention to protect the sea against pollution.

15. Bulgaria did not join the Convention on the Prevention of Marine Pollution by Dumping of Wastes and Other Matters (1972).

10

Turkey, Syria, Iraq:
The Euphrates

RANDA M. SLIM

In the Middle East, water as a resource is valued more than oil. In one scene from *Lawrence of Arabia,* Ali kills the intruder who was drinking water from his well without his authorization. Arabic poetry and prose are replete with references to water. Romances used to flourish around wells and village fountains. Water is equated with life and honor; having access to it has always been equated with power. Hence people and countries in this region have always struggled for access to water. Population growth, high rates of industrialization, and rapidly depleting sources of groundwater make that struggle more acute today. In the Middle East, rivers have always been considered as a more reliable source of water than underground aquifers, which are subject to depletion and high rates of salinization. Civilization is reputed to have begun around two of the rivers in the region: the Euphrates and the Tigris. I focus in this chapter on the dispute involving Turkey, Syria, and Iraq over the distribution of Euphrates water.

Figure 10.1. The Euphrates-Tigris Basin

The River Dispute

The Euphrates River rises in Turkey (see Figure 10.1). Approximately 88% of the mean annual flow of the Euphrates is generated within Turkish territory. After flowing through Turkey, the river enters Syria at Jarablus, continues for a length of 680 km, and enters Iraq at Abu Kamal. Almost all of the remaining 12% of the mean annual flow is generated inside Syria. In Iraq the Euphrates combines with the Tigris, which also rises in Turkey, at the spot reputed to be the original Garden of Eden. Here it forms the Shatt al-Arab, which flows into the Persian Gulf. Except in times of unusual rainfall, Iraq's contribution to the Euphrates water is almost nil.

In the past the Euphrates, with its abundant volume of 32 billion m^3 per year, seemed capable of sustaining life along its banks indefinitely. However, the powers of the river are beginning to look finite in the light of the rapidly growing populations of the three states through which it runs and their ambitious new development plans.

Iraq's use of Euphrates water for irrigation dates back 6,000 years and reached a peak under the Abbasids. It was the first of the three riparian states to build a dam on the river. Built in 1913, the Hindiya Dam made possible the diversion of the water into reconstructed medieval irrigation canals. Syria was next to try to control the flow of the river. Because the Euphrates is Syria's largest river, Syria is the most dependent of the three on its water to generate electricity and to meet irrigation needs. With a great deal of help from the former Soviet Union, the Syrians built the al-Thawra Dam on the Euphrates, 40 miles south of the Turkish border. Syria also began, in late 1976, to fill Lake Assad, whose total storage capacity reaches 14.2 billion m^3. This dam, too, was built to exploit Euphrates water for irrigation and hydroelectricity.

In the late 1970s, Turkey followed Syria's lead, and a master plan was produced for the Southeast Anatolian Project (known by its Turkish acronym, GAP), the primary cause of the dispute between Turkey, Syria, and Iraq. GAP is a $20 billion program for building irrigation and hydro-electric projects along the Euphrates and Tigris rivers. It will provide for the construction of 21 dams and 17 hydroelectric plants. The centerpiece of this plan is the Ataturk Dam, which will be the fifth largest rock-filled dam in the world and the largest dam in Turkey, and which will irrigate an area of 875,000 hectares. Its construction began in 1983 and was scheduled for completion in 1992. Other Turkish dams on the Euphrates include the Karabaya Dam, built upstream of the Ataturk Dam to regulate the river and produce power; and farther north, the Keban Dam, which serves the same purposes and was completed in 1974. Once complete, GAP will more than double the amount of irrigated land in the country, increase agricultural production in the southeast twentyfold, and generate four times the amount of hydropower now produced in Turkey. One senior Turkish government official remarked, "The whole look of the region will change from the Middle Ages to the modern era in one bound" (Reed, 1987, p. 28). It is important to note that the rural southeast region of Turkey is populated mostly by Kurds, who have always harbored separatist dreams. A central political premise on which the GAP initiative is predicated is that as long as the rural Kurdish areas remain poor, the locals will be susceptible to Marxist and nationalistic ideas. Conversely, a thriving economy with many job opportunities would strongly inhibit the inhabitants from toying with such destabilizing ideas.

While having a stabilizing effect on Turkey's domestic problems with its Kurdish population, GAP would likely have destabilizing effects on the domestic insurgencies in Iraq and Syria. Syria and Iraq are concerned that Turkey will restrict the flow of water from the Euphrates River, a vital resource for both of them. It is estimated that if the three nations fail to negotiate a water-sharing agreement by the time the GAP project is fully developed, Syria could lose 40% of its Euphrates water and Iraq up to 90%. Syria relies almost entirely on Euphrates water for drinking, irrigation, and industry and partly for electricity. It is estimated currently that to meet the needs of its population, Syria must expand its irrigated areas to three or four times their present size. An erratic flow of the Euphrates River over the next decade, caused by the GAP project, would jeopardize Syria's much-needed agricultural development plans. Syrian towns already suffer water and power cuts. With its population increase at 3.7% per year, Syria would run short of water by the end of the century even without GAP. With it, Syria faces a water catastrophe. So Syria stands to lose the most if GAP is completed without having reached a water-sharing agreement. In addition, a water shortage might spur Syria's urgent quest for additional sources of water, thus leading it into potential conflict with Israel over the Yarmouk River, a tributary of the Jordan River.

Iraq has less to worry about. Its big advantage over Syria is that it can make up for the depleted Euphrates with Tigris water. Most of Iraq's newest dams, including the Saddam and the Bakman, are on the Tigris or its tributaries. Iraq's problem lies in the fact that intensive water use by Syria and Turkey would affect the quality of Euphrates water, notably its salinity and pollution levels. Higher salinity would seriously affect 40% of the agricultural land in the Euphrates basin and gravely damage Iraqi industrial and water-treatment plans. Another problem for Iraq lies in the fact that the majority of Iraqis who are involved in agriculture in the Euphrates basin are Shi'a from the central and southern provinces of the country. The regime has worked very hard to improve their economic lot and to promote their loyalty and political quiescence. A reduction in the region's agricultural output and, consequently, its standard of living would have grave political repercussions. Yet it is with Iraq that Turkey has the best potential for balanced relations. In part, this potential exists for geographical reasons. Iraq is virtually landlocked, and Turkey provides it with a much-needed outlet to the sea. Turkey is also Iraq's most direct land bridge to Europe.

Twice—in 1974-1975 and in 1984—Syria and Iraq almost came to blows, in part over a temporary dearth of Euphrates water. In 1986 the Turks uncovered an alleged Syrian plot to blow up the Ataturk Dam. Tensions over the Euphrates River came to the fore in mid-January 1990 when, for

1 month, Turkey virtually halted the flow of the river to begin filling the Ataturk Dam reservoir. Despite vigorous protests from Damascus and Baghdad and Iraq's attempt to convince Turkey to limit the halt in river flow to 2 weeks, the river remained "closed" for an entire month. Then, on March 8, 1991, Turkey reduced the flow of water from the Euphrates River. According to the Turkish foreign ministry, the reduction was "for technical reasons." During the Gulf War, Turkey and Syria considered using water as a weapon against Iraq but later decided against it. This decision was based on the fact that Syria would suffer as much as Iraq if Turkey cut the flow of Euphrates water. Such public deliberation over the use of river water as a weapon has set a precedent in the region that could be followed in the future by any other riparian state that decides to go to war against its neighbors.

Each of the three riparian governments in this dispute perceives no less than the very existence and survival of its people and nation to be at stake. Talking of the heavy demand on the Euphrates, one Syrian official said, "It is a problem of 'to be or not to be' for Syria." The confluence of the Euphrates and Tigris in the Shatt al-Arab is referred to by Saddam Hussein as "the vital vein of Iraq's economy." For Turkey this dispute involves threats to its sovereignty and to its right to control the natural resources in its territory. In July 1990 the Turkish minister of public works said: "We oppose the concept of sharing the Euphrates and Tigris rivers, which are the Turkish people's resources. We said that this is like Turkey asking the Arab countries for the right to share their oil." Over time, the dispute has come to assume a zero-sum character—if one wins, the other loses. Part of the problem is that each of the three countries' other domestic problems is entangled with the river dispute, thus rendering the latter more difficult to solve. The ideological conflict pitting Syria against Iraq has made negotiations between the two countries over the Euphrates River almost impossible. And Syria's support of Kurdish and Armenian insurgents in southern Turkey has made a negotiated agreement over the Euphrates River unpalatable to Turkish decisionmakers.

Tripartite talks involving the three riparian states have been held intermittently since the 1960s. But little is known of the discussions among the three states because all three countries have taken great pains to keep the records of the talks hidden from public scrutiny. In 1982 a joint Turkish-Syrian-Iraqi committee was formed to establish precise flow levels. But this committee has so far met rarely, and its talks have been limited mainly to technicalities. In July 1987 Turkey entered into a gentlemen's agreement with Syria to prevent any terrorist activities against the other originating in their territories. In return Turkey promised to try to guarantee Syria a minimum average annual flow of 500 m^3/sec of Euphrates water. But the

Turkish authorities insist they have no obligations toward Syria and Iraq by emphasizing that international law acknowledges the absolute sovereignty of nations over the resources they control. In March 1990, talks were held in Ankara between Syria, Iraq, and Turkey to discuss a Turkish plan for sharing water from the Euphrates and the Tigris. Three days later, the talks broke down. Turkish government sources claimed that Syrian and Iraqi representatives insisted on a system under which the supplies would be shared on the basis of each country stating its water needs. "But the added figures exceeded the total potential of the basin," one official said. On April 17, 1990, Syria and Iraq signed an agreement in Tunisia allocating 50% of the Euphrates water to Iraq. On June 16, 1990, Syrian and Turkish representatives concluded an unsuccessful 3-day effort to divide the Euphrates water between the two countries. On June 28, 1990, another tripartite ministerial meeting over the sharing of Euphrates water ended in failure after 2 days of talks. In mid-July 1990, Turkey refused Syrian and Iraqi demands for a guaranteed water flow rate of 700 m^3/sec. Turkey made a counteroffer, which Syria and Iraq rejected, to supply this flow rate in the summer (though maintaining a much lower rate in the winter), in order to maintain the current 500 m^3/sec annual rate. Despite persistent pressure from Syria and Iraq, Turkey has so far been unwilling to commit itself to a basinwide water-sharing agreement. To date, the only formal agreement relevant to the Euphrates water is the Turkey-Iraq friendship treaty, concluded on March 29, 1946. This treaty stipulates that Turkey should inform Iraq of any conservation works on the Euphrates and Tigris rivers and would try to adapt these projects, to the extent possible, to meet the interests of both states.

All three parties to the dispute belong to the same region, share many similarities, and yet are separated by many differences. Two of the parties —Syria and Iraq—are Arab and share a similar cultural heritage, as well as similar political ideologies, although the latter has so far been more of a source of conflict than of harmony and rapprochement between the two countries. Turkey straddles two continents—Europe and Asia—with the majority of its inhabitants subscribing to the Muslim faith. Most Syrian and Iraqi citizens are Muslims as well. All three countries share population problems such as that posed by the minority Kurds. All three countries value water as a symbol and attribute of power in the region. In this tripartite cultural system, cultural variables operate at two levels: the Arab-Turkish level and the Syrian-Iraqi level.

It has been hypothesized that the greater the heterogeneity of the societies of the disputing parties, the more important the role of culture in their interactions. Such heterogeneity is clearly a distinguishing characteristic of the three societies I focus on in this chapter. In each, different ethnic groups have lived side by side for generations. Despite their physical proximity, these groups have managed to remain exclusive, keeping their own language, religious institutions, and group identities. Hence the social pattern that is typical of most countries in the Middle East resembles that of a mosaic in the close yet formal relations that have so far existed among the different groups within societies. Assuming, then, that cultural factors have and will continue to play a role in the Euphrates River dispute, how do they affect the actors' behaviors? What are these cultural variables? And what is the historical context within which these variables operate?

Historical Context

In a study of Turkish values, Helling (1959) found that the majority of the Turks he sampled viewed the Arabs as very religious, backward, ignorant, lazy, dirty, indolent, slovenly, uncivilized, undependable, cheating, sly, and tradition loving. Many of these perceptions have not changed since 1959. If a similar study were conducted using a sample of Syrians and Iraqis, one likely would find them viewing the Turks as arrogant, untrustworthy, opportunistic, and aggressive. Despite overt expressions of friendliness between the Turks and the citizens of different Arab countries, this mutual antipathy, still latent in people's psyches and minds, is explicable from the history of the relationship between Turkey, on the one hand, and Syria and Iraq, on the other hand.

The Arabs, including Syrians and Iraqis, still smart from their lengthy domination by the Turkish Ottoman Empire. In March 1990, while commenting on the evolving Euphrates River dispute, the Turkish foreign minister spokesman, Murat Sungar, complained, "It is all of a sudden an issue of the Arabs against the Turks" (Franklin, 1990, p. 28). There is still a tendency among Arab policymakers to blame the underdevelopment of the new Arab states on Ottoman policies that deprived Arab provinces of funds that were diverted instead to other parts of the empire. In fact, recent writings by Turkish scholars tend to confirm these Arab perceptions.

Another indirect consequence of the Ottoman Empire's control over Syria and Iraq is the lack of a cohesive national identity in these two societies. To maintain its grip on its faraway provinces, the Ottoman authorities ascribed to the old dictum of "divide and conquer." Hence the Turks deliberately fomented hatred between the ethnic groups that coexisted in the provinces they ruled. Ironically, at the end of World War I, the new republic of Turkey found itself suffering from a similar plight. The Ottoman authorities worked so hard on promoting loyalty to the empire and to the dynasty (an ideology known as *Ottomanism*) that when the empire died and the dynasty went into exile, the Turkish people were left without an overpowering national structure to claim their allegiance. With the rise to power of Mustafa Kemal, the Turkish nationalist leader better known as Ataturk, the idea of a territorial state based on the Turkish nation in Turkey began to emerge. However, all three countries are still in search of their national identities. Every now and then, they try a new brand, from pan-Arabism and Islamism in Iraq and Syria to Turkism and Westernization in Turkey. The lack of a cohesive national identity inevitably affects each of the three countries' foreign policy, which, of course, includes their positions and negotiation behavior with regard to the Euphrates River water dispute.

The history of the relationships between Turkey, Syria, and Iraq is marred further by two still controversial territorial disputes. The first surrounds the frontier between Iraq and Turkey over the status of Mosul. The second and later dispute surrounds the frontier between Turkey and Syria and focuses on the Sanjak of Alexandretta, or Hatay as it is known in Turkey. The Treaty of Lausanne, which established the international borders of Turkey in July 1923, failed to address the future of Mosul. Turkey claimed that the area, heavily populated with Turks, belonged to the defunct Ottoman Empire. Great Britain, which at the time held the League of Nations mandate for Iraq, claimed Mosul for that country. When the dispute was taken up by the Council of the League of Nations, it found in Britain's favor. The Turks eventually recognized the status of Mosul as part of Iraq and signed a treaty to that effect with Britain and Iraq in 1926. Although Turkey claims that it does not harbor any designs on Mosul, the economic, demographic, and security implications of the loss of Mosul for Turkey continue to excite Iraqi suspicions about Turkey's intentions in the area.

The Sanjak of Alexandretta originally was attached to Syria. In 1921 Ankara agreed to compromise with the French, who at the time had the League of Nations mandate for Syria. Turkey agreed that the Sanjak would be administered under the terms of the mandate in return for cultural concessions to the Turkish population in the Sanjak. In 1936, when the French proposed to grant independence to Syria, Turkey became concerned about the future of the Sanjak. With the implicit help of the French, the Turkish army marched on the Sanjak and in 1939 formally incorporated it as Hatay into the new republic of Turkey. The Syrians still refuse to accept the loss of the Sanjak. The area of Hatay is still shown on Syrian stamps and maps as part of Syria.

Recently the Turkish foreign minister visited Syria to discuss the Euphrates River dispute with his counterpart. He abruptly interrupted the talks and left the Syrian minister's office, denouncing claims made by his Syrian interlocutor over Hatay. For Arab nationalists in general, and for Syrian ideologues and territorial nationalists in particular, Turkey's control of the Sanjak is a grave injustice that must be redressed. Interestingly, it appears that Turkey tried to link an agreement with Syria over Euphrates water with a Turkish-Syrian accord on the Orontes River. The Orontes River rises in Lebanon, flows into Homs Lake in Syria, through the Syrian cities of Homs and Hama, and then enters Turkey. Syria rejected this linkage because the Orontes flows through Turkey in Alexandretta, the province that the Syrians still claim as their own. A large part of Syria's problem in the Euphrates River dispute lies in the fact that no matter what guarantees Syria would be given about the waters, they would result from decisions taken solely by the Turks, whose intentions can never be fully trusted.

Turkey still regards the Arab uprising led by the Sherif of Mecca in 1916, in collaboration with Britain and in opposition to the Ottoman Empire, as a monumental act of betrayal. Despite the collapse of the Ottoman Empire and the establishment of the Turkish republic with its different political ideologies, its leaders were reluctant to establish friendly relations with Arab countries. A former president of Turkey, Celal Bayar, remarked in a personal interview that the Turkish leaders "were not disposed to re-establish a close relationship with a nation [the Arab] which had 'stabbed the Turkish nation in the back' " (Robbins, 1991, p. 190). Even today, it is normal for educated Turks to refer to the experiences of World War I as proof of the untrustworthiness of the Arabs.

The lack of a cohesive national identity in each of the three societies, the vulnerability of each to ethnic strife, and the history of the relationships between them provide an important context within which cultural variables operate. As noted, these variables operate at two levels: the system level, meaning the interaction between the Turkish and Arab cultures, and the subsystem level, meaning the interaction between the Syrian and Iraqi cultures. That the latter level is an encounter between two Arab countries vying for the same finite and scarce resource makes the conflict all the more vicious and intractable. The focus here is on the political culture prevalent in each of the societies and how it has shaped their decision-makers' behavior in the dispute.

Political Culture:
The Turkish-Arab Dimension

To understand the Turkish political culture, one needs to go back to the Turkish revolution in 1908, which overthrew the old political order, and to the Kemalist republic, which took its place. Kemal's Turkism in the early 1920s revolved around the idea of a territorial nation-state based on

the Turkish nation in Anatolia—present-day Turkey. Kemal also introduced the movement toward secularization and the accompanying attempts to Westernize his people. According to Lewis (1968, p. 485), "The
two terms most frequently used [among the Turks] to denote their revolution are nationalism and Westernization." Kemal abolished all kinds of
Muslim clothing, closed the religious schools, and made religious authorities
subject to government control. Old Islamic concepts of loyalty, authority,
and identity were replaced by new concepts of European origin. The
people, not God, became the source of sovereignty. The nation replaced
God as the object of worship. Although Turkey has renounced formally
much of the Kemalist doctrine, notably its secularism, the Kemalist concepts of authority and loyalty to the nation are still strong among the
decision-making elite and are likely to affect their behavior in the negotiations over a dispute that touches the Turkish sense of sovereignty.

Unlike their neighbors, the Turks began immediately to rid themselves
of the Ottoman influence, making the new political culture more democratic and free of the ghosts of the past. Today's Turkish decisionmakers
are not obsessed with the problem of foreign rule. In fact, modern Turkish
leaders have accepted responsibility for the affairs of their country and
have shown a sense of realism and pragmatism that is derived partly from
their long experience in government. According to Lewis (1968, p. 484),
the Turkish elite "have been able to assess situations and define objectives,
to make decisions related to facts and to abide by them." This ability runs
counter to a tendency among the Syrians and Iraqis to focus more on
ideology and, sometimes, less on facts.

Another aspect of the Turkish political culture revolves around the
Turkish national identity. Like its neighbors, the Turkish population is an
ethnic mix consisting of Turks, a large population of Kurds, a Jewish
minority, a small but important Arab minority, 40% of whom are located
in Hatay near the Syrian border, and a group of Alawis, a Muslim religious
sect that also is based in Syria and to which the president and most of the
current Syrian decision-making elite belong. The Turks also are divided
into a secular, educated elite including army and civil employees, and a
very religious rural peasantry. The Turkish decision-making elite rolled
back most of Kemal's secular reforms to accommodate the Islamic tide
that was unleashed in the region by the Khomeini revolution in Iran and
in response to pressure from vocal and well-organized Turkish Islamists.
Yet these elite remain strongly secular in their orientation, a reality that
tends to arouse suspicions about the Turks in citizens of Arab countries.

All of these factors have been partly responsible for an uncertain
Turkish national identity—caught up between Islam and secularism, between loyalty to the nation and loyalty to the ethnic group, and between

the rest of the Middle East and Europe. Veiled rejection of Turkey's 1987 application to the European Community prompted Turkey to reorient itself toward the Middle East and to start carving a role for itself in that region. One such role could be that of the provider, or breadbasket, of the Middle East. GAP would considerably strengthen Turkey's aspirations in this direction, although in the light of the history between Turkey and the neighboring states, any such attempts are likely to be viewed with suspicion as another means for Turkey to reassume its dominant role in the region. The Gulf War also has endowed Turkey's role in the region with more prominence as one of the political centers of power. The fall of communism in the former Soviet Union and the increasing decentralization of the former empire is leading the former "Soviet" Muslim republics to look for patrons and allies in the Middle East. Because of ethnic and communal ties, many of these republics, such as Azerbaijan, consider Turkey to be their ally. This association will lead to a reconfiguration of the political map of the Middle East, in which three regional blocs—the Turkish, Persian, and Arab blocs—will compete for political power.

Most modern Arab chief executives, including the Syrian and Iraqi leaders, grew up in the days of anti-imperialism and the struggle for independence. Hence, unlike their Turkish counterparts, they are obsessed with the region's historical experiences. For example, it is well known that in any talks with Hafiz al-Assad, the Syrian president, one should expect to be treated to at least a 2-hour exposition on the history of the region. The tendency of Arab leaders to view any dispute in a much larger historical context involving a host of issues other than the one at stake makes conflict resolution a difficult task. Another indirect implication of Arab political experiences is their obsession with achieving self-sufficiency as a means to avoid repetition of past experiences. Agricultural self-sufficiency is viewed by both the Syrian and Iraqi decisionmakers as one means toward economic independence. Hence the GAP threat lies in its thwarting of such aims, especially for Syria.

An important characteristic of Arab political culture is the personality cult. Political power continues to reside with the chief executive. Thus most international decisions have to pass over the chief executive's desk. Technical commissions are formed to postpone decisions, rather than to make them. One implication is that even technical issues, such as the exact amount of Euphrates water to be distributed at different times during the year, assume a political character that renders them less liable to trade-offs. The personalization of power in Arab political culture is due partly to other cultural variables that have always characterized these societies. The core societal units in the Arab societies have always been the tribe, the village, and the extended family. The sheikh, the rais, or the father is always perceived as the provider of goods, the arbiter of intragroup disputes, and the ultimate dispenser of justice. Transposed onto the national scene, the nation's leader is expected to assume the same role. In the case of the Syrian and Iraqi leaders, their legitimacy rests very much on their responsiveness to the values and ideas of their populations and on their ability to deliver the goods, including food, electricity, and potable water. Once complete, it is clear that GAP would thwart agricultural development plans and ultimately would damage the leaders' image as a provider of goods in both Syria and Iraq. This cultural dimension lies at the heart of some of the Syrian and Iraqi leaders' concerns, and any negotiated agreement would have to assuage these concerns.

Another result of the tribal, familial pattern that forms the foundation of many Arab regimes is the tendency of Arab leaders, including the Syrians and Iraqis, to view the secular and democratic Turkish regime with suspicion. There is always the fear that the Turkish regime would export an alternative form of governance that is capable of subverting the power of the traditional regimes in the region. Such fears and suspicions inflame the malignant attribution of motives between parties in a dispute, a practice that Fisher (1980, p. 15) calls "one form of unconscious projection that wreaks havoc on negotiations." In 1990, prior to suspension of the Euphrates water flow, Turkey made an honest and serious attempt to release additional amounts of water to help Syria and Iraq store enough water to make up for their losses while the Ataturk Dam reservoir was being filled. According to the Syrian press, the Turkish motives were far from benign. They were interpreted as a kind of ruse employed by the Turkish government to divert the anger of the Syrian people.

Syrian and Iraqi societies are also a mix of different ethnic and religious groups, which makes the search for a cohesive national identity all the more necessary for these societies. One major value that has so far dominated the political consciousness of the people in the region is Arabism. The term refers to a sense "of belonging to a vast group supposed to share a common origin, characterized by a name and by common cultural features, and above all by all the bounds of the linguistic community" (Rodinson, 1981, p. 25). As such, Arabism is a powerful cultural symbol that sets normative standards with which people in Arab countries can identify. In 1980 a group of Arab social scientists studied the extent and potency of Arabism among the people in several Arab countries. They found that 8 out of 10 respondents believed that the Arabs belonged to a single nation and that they were culturally distinctive (Ibrahim, 1980). The Gulf War, and the intra-Arab division it has revealed, might have affected these beliefs, but, of all the citizens of Arab countries, the Iraqis and the Syrians have always been known to be among the strongest advocates of

Arabism—more so, for example, than the Egyptians, who have always been self-assured about their Egypt and their distinctive historical identity.

Arabism has affected leaders' conceptions of national interest. Both Syrian and Iraqi decisionmakers equate the respective national interests of Syria and Iraq with those of the Arab nation as a whole. So the dispute between Syria and Turkey over Euphrates water involves all other Arab countries as well and thus encompasses many issues. By opposing GAP, Assad is defending not only Syria's interests but also those of the whole Arab nation, thus escalating the conflict from one between two nations over a limited number of issues to one that involves all countries in the region and encompasses all of the contentious issues that have plagued the relationship with Turkey.

Another factor contributing to cultural misunderstanding between the Turks and the Arabs is each party's ignorance of the other's language and script. Turkish is not a popular language in Syrian and Iraqi schools and universities. Similarly most Turks neither speak nor understand Arabic. The Euphrates River dispute evokes many national symbols of independence and self-sufficiency and concepts of national sovereignty and national interest. Meanings ascribed to these symbols and concepts are very much language-specific, and, by ignoring each other's language, negotiators are likely to miss the subtleties that are at stake.

Thus the process and outcome of the negotiations between Turkey, Syria, and Iraq over Euphrates water would be affected by the different political ideologies to which each party ascribes, the different languages they speak, the different historical interpretations they hold, and their different conceptualizations of national interest.

Political Culture:
The Syrian-Iraqi Dimension

Both Syria and Iraq are Arab countries: Their citizens speak Arabic, the majority of their populations are Muslims, and their decision-making elites ascribe to the same political ideology, the Ba'ath, which espouses the ultimate goal of Arab unity. Both Syrian and Iraqi leaders are vying for regional leadership, and the Euphrates River dispute has become entangled with this competition. Each leader perceives that any compromise in his position in one conflict—the river dispute—would translate into a gain for the other side's position in the other conflict—the competition for regional leadership. In this dimension, then, cultural similarity obstructs, rather than expedites, international interactions. This obstruction is caused partly by the scarcity of resource(s) they are vying for: access to water, in the case of the Euphrates River dispute, and regional leadership. It is also due partly to personal animosities and jealousies between the Syrian and Iraqi leaders. The tradition of personalized leadership in the Arab countries sometimes makes a country's foreign policy hostage to its chief executive's personal feelings and agenda.

Another cultural similarity between the Syrian and Iraqi regimes concerns the basis of their political power. Assad is Alawi, a Shi'a religious sect that represents almost 12.5% of the Syrian population, whose majority is Sunni. Hussein is a Sunni in a country where most of the population (almost 50%) is Shi'a. Each leader has created pillars of support for his regime that competes with the country's traditional political institutions. Assad's top political advisers are Alawi, and he has staffed most critical positions in the army, security, and intelligence services with his relatives. The same phenomenon holds true in Iraq. Very few Shi'a occupy critical political posts in Iraq. Hussein has drawn heavily on fellow Sunnis, members of the Iraqi Ba'ath Party, and relatives. Hence national agendas easily can become identified with the protection of the interests of the group in power. In the case of Syria, some of those interests include the protection of the Alawi's rights in Hatay, a thorny issue that has affected the negotiations with Turkey over the Euphrates water dispute. They also include supporting Shi'a political power inside Iraq, a source of constant friction between Syria and Iraq, which indirectly has affected negotiations between the two countries over the river dispute. The Iraqi political elite also have supported Sunni Muslim groups inside Syria, such as the Muslim Brotherhood, and have used religious symbols in isolating the Syrian regime in a region that is dominated heavily by Sunni political regimes. Interestingly, any kind of rapprochement between Turkey and Iraq regarding the Euphrates is interpreted immediately by the Syrian political elite as a coalition of the Sunni, meaning the Turks and the Iraqis, against the Alawi.

Because both Iraqi and Syrian leadership draws heavily on the support of minority groups, the legitimacy of their regimes is limited. Hence the leaders' latitude in maneuvering on sensitive issues also is restricted. As noted, access to water is a very sensitive issue in the arid Middle Eastern countries. Thus the range of possible trade-offs on the different issues involved in this dispute would be quite narrow.

The Effects of Culture on Negotiations in the Euphrates Water Dispute

Having examined some of the cultural variables that so far have marred the relations among the three riparian states, I suggest it would be interesting to think of an analytical framework for investigating the nature of their role in the negotiations over Euphrates water. As noted, none of these negotiations have so far led to any successful basin-sharing agreement. In fact, one of the few things that is known about these negotiations is that the different parties frequently have limited themselves to advancing rigid positions during the negotiations and to constantly attributing the failure to reach an agreement to the other parties' rigidity and stubbornness.

One such framework that has been applied to water issues is the cognitive mapping approach developed by Axelrod (1976) and others. This approach helps clarify the players' interests and misperceptions of the different issues at stake, which, in the case of the Euphrates dispute, have been affected by the historical context of the parties, their political cultures, and the symbolism that water carries in an arid or semiarid developing region. According to Naff and Matson (1984), water issues in the Middle East are complex for two reasons. The first reason is that water in the Middle East is perceived as both an end and a means. It is linked directly to national survival in countries that do not have many renewable sources of water and where agriculture and animal husbandry have been the main sources of economic productivity. It is also a means to other ends and often is used as a bargaining chip. In the case of the Euphrates, an agreement over water sharing is likely to be traded for cessation of Syrian support of the Kurdish insurgency in Turkey.

The second reason is that water issues in the Middle East are intertwined with other issues, such as nationalism, economic development, foreign policy, ideology, and internal politics. Hence solving water conflicts might be a precursor or a means to establishing confidence-building measures that would help in paving the way for settling other seemingly unmanageable conflicts in the area.

For these two reasons, the Euphrates water dispute so far has proven intractable. Too much is at stake, and the parties still are mulling over how the different trade-offs could be worked out in a final settlement. A cognitive map of the general Turkish perspective of the Euphrates water issue shows that water is connected with agriculture. And agriculture is connected with the country's national interest, which is itself a function of internal politics and foreign policy. Development of major agricultural projects in southeastern Turkey, irrigated by water from the Ataturk Dam, would help quell Kurdish unrest in that region. It also would make Turkey the breadbasket of the Middle East and, consequently, an important broker in regional politics. More important, GAP is a means of bringing together what so far have been the two conflicting aspects of an emerging Turkish national identity: the Western element and the Muslim element. GAP is a technological achievement that would satisfy Turkey's need to be part of the industrial and developed Western world. At the same time, by becoming the breadbasket of the Middle East, Turkey would be reorienting itself toward the Muslim world and, in a way, acknowledging its membership in the club of so-called Muslim countries—a membership that, until recently, Turkey has been reluctant to accept.

The cognitive maps of the Syrian and Iraqi perspectives of the Euphrates dispute would include the same elements as those on the Turkish map. But unlike the configuration on the Turkish map, national interests on the Syrian and Iraqi maps coincide with the interest of the Arab nation as a whole. The problem is that the perceptions of the Arab national interest held by Syria and Iraq are mutually exclusive—hence the zero-sum character of the conflict over the Euphrates water. Ideology is also an important element on the Syrian and Iraqi cognitive maps. The fact that they share the same political ideology would, in other cases, provide the basis for cooperation. But set against a cultural context imbued with a strong personality cult and the close linkage between the leader's personal agenda and the national political agenda, grounds for cooperation turn into factors that intensify conflict. Naff and Matson (1984, p. 181) argue that "water has been the primary strategic factor behind the political and military maneuvering in the Middle East." It is now doubtful that the 1974-1975 Syrian-Iraqi "water crisis" was over water at all. That crisis was prompted by the long-standing feud between rival Ba'athist wings in Syria and Iraq and Syria's fear of Iraqi subversion with the Muslim Brotherhood. It could be argued that the water crisis was created chiefly to promote anti-Iraqi feelings inside Syria and to gain some regional advantage in their competition with Iraq for regional superpower status.

The symbolic nature of the water issue in the region also links this dispute with the notion of legitimacy. Leaders in Syria and Iraq have been reluctant to compromise their positions in this dispute because it lies at the core of the internal legitimacy of their regimes. Much of the rigid positioning around the negotiation table is meant to convey to domestic audiences the image of the leader as a protector of the nation's rights to a highly valued resource. For Turkey the Euphrates dispute is linked partially with Syria's refusal to recognize Turkey's territorial rights in Hatay. In such a context, it becomes easy to see one's interests as "rights" and to feel outraged when one's rights are denied. Because of its near total dependence on the Euphrates for domestic consumption, Syria sees its water needs as more legitimate than those of Turkey and Iraq. Syrian officials often point to the fact that Turkey has many other rivers in its territory and that Iraq could always tap the waters of the Tigris. Thus, according to some Turkish officials, even technical talks over Euphrates water often turn into a haggling over who has the most rights to the water and the legitimacy of the grounds on which each bases its entitlement rights.

Perception of Outcomes

Decisionmakers in the three countries hold different conceptions of what would be a fair outcome, partly determined by what each party perceives to be at stake in the dispute. Turkey perceives its control over its natural resources and, ultimately, its national sovereignty to be at stake. Syria and, to a lesser degree, Iraq believe that the very survival of their people and nations are at stake in the dispute. Thus the parties tend to make their claims by appealing to different standards of fairness. Because the Euphrates starts in Turkey, Turkey insists that it has absolute sovereignty over the river. Turkey would consider fair any outcome that recognizes its rights of ownership. Turkish decisionmakers base most of their argument on international law that acknowledges the absolute sovereignty of nations over the resources they control. Hence their refusal, on many occasions, to acknowledge responsibility for any damage incurred by Syria and Iraq because of GAP.

In 1990, though Turkey had endeavored to alleviate the difficulties imposed on Syria and Iraq by the diversion of the river, some side effects, such as pollution and environmental damage to the cultivated land, were inevitable. Despite evidence of the facts, the Turkish government refused to acknowledge them. Turkey regarded any acknowledgment of the Syrian injuries as a gesture toward compromise over certain rights that Turkey considered to be inviolable. This was a missed opportunity for eliminating some of the existing tension because, by giving rhetorical ground, the Syrian feelings of injustice could have been assuaged. Another opportunity was missed in January 1990 when Turkey announced its cut of the river flow. Turkey made the decision unilaterally, without any prior consultation with Iraq and Syria. The Turkish minister for public works announced: "We have to cut the water for a month. There can be no debate about this" (Williams, 1990, p. 8). A Syrian official source said Ankara's decision was "a unilateral one" and set "an unhealthy precedent" (Zaman, 1990, p. 9). Turkey could have involved Syria and Iraq in the decision-making process, providing a structure within which they could voice their grievances while still maintaining control over the final decision. In protesting against the cut in water flow, Syrian and Iraqi political elites really were voicing their anger at being left out of the decision making and at being faced with a fait accompli.

Syria and Iraq base their claims on the principle of need and of entitlement, rooted in the historical allocation of Euphrates water. Hence the Syrian and Iraqi decisionmakers frequently appeal to the terms of two international conventions—the Helsinki Rules of 1966 and the United Nations Convention of 1972, both of which state that water rights are to be shared according to population and need, with historical allocation and prior usage taken into account. Thus both Syrian and Iraqi decisionmakers would regard as fair any outcome that satisfies their populations' needs for water and electricity.

Because each of the disputing parties' claims is based on legitimate international legal standards, it would be hard to resolve this dispute without the establishment of an overarching convention or a universal standard of fairness that could satisfy the minimum rights of owner and user.

A Scenario for Settlement

Because it involves the vital interests of the three riparian nations in an interdependent manner, the Euphrates River dispute contains the seeds for peace. Naff argues: "Water can unite or divide the region. It can be a catalyst for cooperation and peace or for conflict" (Moffett, 1990, p. 4). Among the obstacles to any settlement so far have been the domestic problems facing each country. Turkey holds Syria responsible for the Kurdish insurgencies and links any potential settlement of the river dispute with the cessation of Syrian support of the Kurdish military factions. Syria considers such support to be its trump card in a high-stakes poker game and would be unwilling to part with it without prior agreement on the river dispute. A major agreement on water rights would assuage some of the mistrust Syria feels toward Turkey and would pave the way for cooperation on a whole range of regional problems. And although Turkish officials have insisted repeatedly that Turkey would never exploit its control of the Euphrates for political purposes, President Turget Ozal, in October 1990, remarked that Syria should cooperate with Turkey in ending Turkish insurgency in order to maintain its flow from the Euphrates. Such mixed signals from Turkish officials are likely to increase Syrian fears of sudden water cuts and distrust of Turkish assurances of their good intentions. Furthermore, because of its dependence on Euphrates water for most of its consumption and the lack of any alternative sources of water, Syria perceives its bargaining position to be very weak compared with the Turkish position. Hence its reluctance to be the party to make the first move in a process of "graduated and reciprocated initiatives in tension reduction" (Osgood, 1962).

For ideological and personal reasons, the Syrian and Iraqi leaders are bent on undermining each other's credibility as "the Arab leader," and the Euphrates River dispute gets embroiled in this conflict. But history has shown that such conflict did not prevent them from entering into agreements over the Euphrates River when they perceived their political survival to be at stake. With a change in the regional political situation, incentives could be found for both regimes to reach such an agreement.

It is clear that because of the particular nature of the dispute and the history of mistrust among the three parties, third party mediation is needed for settling the dispute. Twice in the past, third parties have intervened in this conflict. In 1974-1975, when Syria and Iraq were on the verge of war over Euphrates water, Saudi mediators successfully defused the conflict. In January 1990 the Kuwaiti government, ironically at the request of the Iraqi leadership, tried to mediate between the two Arab countries and Turkey when Turkey instituted its month-long cutoff.

Given the cultural misunderstandings that have marred the course of the conflict so far, the mediator also would have to perform the role of a cultural interpreter, to explain to each party the other's positions, to diffuse the historical mistrust that has set in between Turkey and the two other Arab countries, and to recognize the historical basis of Syria's and Iraq's rights to the water. Such a mediator also would have to play the role of a guarantor of agreement to assuage Syrian and Iraqi fears of future Turkish unilateral decisions to halt the flow of the river.

The negotiation process over the past 30 years attests to the fact that the tripartite structure often gave way to a series of bilateral agreements between two of the three riparian states. At different times, agreements were reached between Turkey and Syria, Turkey and Iraq, and Syria and Iraq over the sharing of the water. Three two-way coalitions were formed at different times, depending on the direction of the political winds. Such coalitions could give rise to an interesting package of solutions. A settlement package could include a final settlement of the two territorial disputes, termination of Syrian support of Kurdish and Armenian insurgents, a Turkish acceptance of Syrian and Iraqi historical rights to the Euphrates River, a cessation of Turkish and Iraqi support of the Muslim Brotherhood in Syria, and a cessation of Syrian support of the Shi'a and Kurdish groups inside Iraq. These moves could be undertaken simultaneously by the parties involved, with the mediator continuously monitoring their implementation. Currently the three parties disagree over the overall capacity of the river basin. The mediator would serve as an objective source of factual information, correcting some of the perceptions that have impeded the negotiation process. Initially a mediation process would involve a series of contingent bilateral agreements that would, in a sense, provide a set of confidence-building measures and pave the way for a tripartite negotiation process. The latter could be held under the auspices of an international organization such as the UN, which eventually would be the guarantor of the final settlement.

Conclusion

Steps have been undertaken to address the problem of water scarcity in the Middle East. One such step is the Multi-year Global Water Summit Initiative, which brings together national decisionmakers in the international development community to promote greater cooperation among riparian nations. The first summit was hosted by President Hosni Mubarak of Egypt in June 1990 in Cairo. It included representatives of 43 African states, development experts from international organizations, and observers from Turkey, Jordan, and Iraq. The second summit was to have been hosted by the Turkish president in October 1991 in Istanbul, but the beginning of the Arab-Israeli peace process pushed the second summit to the back burner. A third step of the peace process involves holding multilateral talks among the countries in the region to discuss such issues as water and arms control. This third round of talks was held January 29, 1992, and was boycotted by Syria and other Arab countries. Syria has conditioned its participation in the multilateral talks on achieving some agreement with Israel over the issue of territory in their bilateral talks.

President Ozal of Turkey has suggested building "a peace pipeline" to transport water from two of Turkey's rivers in central eastern Anatolia, the Ceyhan and the Seyhan, to potential recipient countries in the Gulf and the Levant. The plan involves building two pipelines: The largest one, known as the "western pipeline," would run through Syria and Jordan and would terminate in Mecca, in Saudi Arabia. This pipeline would feed the main population centers between Aleppo in Syria and the Hijaz in Saudi Arabia. The two largest recipients would be Damascus and Amman, the capital cities of Syria and Jordan, respectively. The smaller pipeline, known as the "Gulf pipeline," would run across to Kuwait and go as far as Muscat in Oman, feeding five Gulf states in the process. Estimates of the cost of this project have differed markedly. One feasibility study put the total at approximately $21 billion. The Gulf states so far have opposed this plan because of their refusal to be dependent on the Turks for their water resources, thus giving the Turkish government a more powerful position in regional politics.

Instead of focusing on such a grandiose scheme, partial solutions could be attempted in the short term. Kolars (1990, p. 68) argues for a more modest first link: a peace pipeline that would link Turkey, Syria, and Jordan and deliver water along the way to Aleppo, Homos, Damascus, and Amman. This link would provide Jordan with a much-needed water supply, thus diminishing the problem of the East Ghor Canal, a major component of the conflict over the Jordan River that involves Jordan, Syria, and Israel. A small feeder line from that pipeline also could feed the West Bank communities, thus eliminating some of the obstacles to a potential Israeli-Palestinian settlement. Such a pipeline also could allay the suspicions of the parties involved. Kolars suggests that "any unfriendly move by Syria toward Jordan's or the West Bank's trans-Syrian supply lines could be matched on the part of Turkey by the possibility of water shortages in the major urban areas of Syria." The interdependent nature of the effort would enhance perceptions of interdependence among regional parties, one prerequisite for a lasting regional peace settlement. What also is needed in the short term is an education campaign that aims at changing centuries-old traditions of water-wasteful farming and consumption.

Culture could be a facilitator, as well as an obstacle, in resolving international water disputes. A determining factor in the role of culture in water disputes is the regional context and, more specifically, the history of the relationship among the parties, the political culture of each society, its level of development, and the presence or absence of alternative sources of water.

11

Arabs and Israelis:
The Jordan River

MIRIAM LOWI
JAY ROTHMAN

In this chapter we outline the history and current status of the conflict over the water of the Jordan River basin and include an abbreviated discussion of efforts to resolve it. We then describe how cultural factors have played a part in the origins and persistence of the conflict and have hindered attempts to manage water disputes between Arabs and Israelis. Finally, we illustrate how culture may be employed as a constructive force in managing creatively this and other "protracted social conflicts" (Azar, 1990), which revolve primarily around issues of national identity and legitimacy.

We make the assumption that by virtue of the increased activity in promoting a Middle East peace process, political conditions have ripened such that the potential for progress in functional issues, such as sharing water resources, is enhanced. Although this enhancement may or may not be the case at the, our thesis regarding conditions necessary for cooperative water policy between Arabs and Israelis remains the same. For progress to be made on such issues as resource use and development, some degree of progress first must be achieved on the larger political questions dividing the parties.

We argue that by dealing with functional issues within the cultural context in which they are embedded, negotiations may gain momentum and be consolidated in creative and mutually satisfactory ways. In other words, by setting the stage whereby the larger political issues such as identity, recognition, and security are being discussed seriously, their ultimate resolution may be promoted by shifting focus periodically onto matters over which cooperation and agreement may be somewhat less intransigent ideologically. The disputants may begin to learn to work together on functional issues of clearly overlapping concern and thus build both the will and the momentum for tackling more complex political issues where self-interest does not overlap as clearly. Moreover, progress in resolving functional issues may provide parties with the confidence and concrete evidence that "making a deal" with their adversaries can result in real gains, and thus the perception of self-interest in cooperation may be enhanced.

The Jordan River Basin

The Jordan River basin is an elongated valley in the central Middle East. Draining an area of some 18,300 km², it extends from Mount Hermon in the north to the Dead Sea in the south and lies within the pre-June 1967 boundaries of Israel, Jordan, Lebanon, and Syria. Its water, which originates in rainfall and in rivers and streams in the riparian states, drains land east and west of the Jordan valley. Precipitation in the basin ranges from over 1,000 mm/year in the north to less than 50 mm/year in the south but averages less than 200 mm/yr on both sides of the Jordan River (Inbar & Maos, 1984). Much of the basin, therefore, is arid or semiarid and requires irrigation for agricultural development (see Figure 11.1 and Table 11.1).

Although the basin covers parts of four states, about 80% of it is located in present-day Israel, Jordan, and the West Bank. These areas are most dependent on its water. Moreover, coterminous with the political conflict in the region has been a dispute over the water resources of the Jordan basin. Until 1967 the water dispute engaged the four basin states. Since June 1967, when the two upstream states—Syria and Lebanon—lost their superior riparian positions to Israeli forces, it has engaged Israel, Jordan, and the West Bank. Syria, however, has retained its upstream status on the Yarmouk River and so is party to discussions concerning the water of that tributary.

Figure 11.1. The Jordan Basin

It is important to bear in mind just how little water there is in the Jordan system. This factor, coupled with the rising demands of states in arid and semiarid regions with high population growth rates and considerable

TABLE 11.1 Principal Surface Waters of the Jordan Basin

River	Source	Direction	Political Control	Discharge
Hasbani	Lebanon	South to Upper Jordan River	Lebanon pre-1967 Israel post-1967	138 mcm[a]
Banias	Syria	South to Upper Jordan River	Syria pre-1967 Israel post-1967	121
Dan	Israel	South to Upper Jordan River	Israel	245
Upper Jordan		to L. Tiberias	Israel	650
Lower Jordan		to Dead Sea	Israel, Jordan	1,200[b]
Yarmouk	Syria	Southeast to Lower Jordan River	Syria, Jordan, Israel	450

NOTES: a. In this chapter, a million cubic meters (mcm) is used as the standard measure of water volume. One m^3 of water equals 1,000 kg in mass, or 1 metric ton. Note that discharge figures for the Upper and Lower Jordan rivers include the contributions of tributaries and other sources.
b. Despite their quantity, the water of the Jordan River below Lake Tiberias is of poor quality. It is highly saline and cannot be used for most agricultural purposes. Over the years, this portion of the river has become little more than a drainage ditch.

agricultural sectors, illuminates the extent to which margins are narrow in the development and use of water resources. The Jordan system's total discharge of about 1,200 mcm (million cubic meters) into the Dead Sea, under "normal" climatic conditions and prior to extractions upstream, is equivalent to about 2% of the annual flow of the Nile (84 bcm [billion cubic meters]), 6% of the Euphrates (31 bcm), less than 2% of the Indus (97 bcm), and less than 1% of the Congo (200 bcm). Despite its size and the relative meagerness of its flow, the river is crucial for Israel and Jordan in their efforts to meet their development needs.

The Conflict Over Jordan Water

The roots of conflict over the water of the Jordan River system lie in the convergence of two phenomena: the scarcity of land and water in historic Palestine, and the competition between two peoples—Arabs and Jews—for these resources. Because a viable economy is dependent on a minimum degree of land and food security, the fact of scarcity impinged on the contending national aspirations of Arabs and Jews.[1] Although land was the basic requirement of settlement, without water it could not be made productive. Thus land became a central issue in the struggle for Palestine, and water came to be viewed as an extension of the land. Indeed the dispute over water resources in the Jordan basin is bound intrinsically with the larger Arab-Jewish conflict over Palestine/Israel.

Not only were land and water limited, but also, since the 1930s, when the partition of Palestine into Jewish and Arab areas was first being considered as a possible solution to tensions in the region, neither community perceived that the resources could be divided in a way that would be mutually satisfactory. Indeed the only sources of water on a scale large enough to affect the capacities of two independent states were the Jordan and Yarmouk rivers. Both the Zionist organization and the Transjordanian government commissioned projects for the development of the river system to increase the agricultural and settlement potential of the immediate region.

On May 15, 1948, one day after Israel was declared a sovereign Jewish state, the Arabs and Israelis fought their first of many wars. By the time the fighting ended, Israel had gained political control over a significantly larger area than previously had been allotted to it by the United Nations, including several important bodies of water: much of the upper catchment of the Jordan system, one of the three headwater tributaries, Lake Huleh, Lake Tiberias, and part of the western shore of the Dead Sea. Moreover, in the aftermath of the fighting, the resource bases of Israel and the Kingdom of Jordan underwent tremendous strain. Both countries experienced massive influxes of population: immigrants, on the one hand, and refugees, on the other. The Jordan system figured significantly in the development plans of both newly founded states.

In the early 1950s, the United States government became interested in the development of the Jordan valley, in part, in an effort to settle the refugees in neighboring Arab states and thus to relieve tensions in the region.[2] Through the United Nations Relief and Works Agency (UNRWA), it commissioned a study for the unified development of the Jordan-Yarmouk river system, emphasizing first irrigation, and second hydroelectric power production and disregarding political boundaries.[3] In October 1953 President Eisenhower appointed Eric Johnston, Personal Representative of the President, to carry out a mission to the Middle East to secure agreement from Israel, Jordan, Lebanon, and Syria to the development of the Jordan water on a regional basis, in line with the Unified Plan.[4] The ultimately unsuccessful mediation effort was conducted in four rounds of negotiations over a 2-year period.

Throughout the negotiating process, there was constant disagreement among the parties over allocations of water and locations of storage facilities, as well as conflicting views of rights, needs, and international legal precedents. Eventually both the Arab states and Israel, despite deep-seated suspicions, admitted that the plan that emerged was acceptable on technical grounds (Lowi, 1993). Nonetheless the League of Arab States, representing the Arab riparians, would not take a definitive position on the plan, on political grounds. It could not agree to cooperate with and enhance the development potential of a state with which it was engaged in a protracted political conflict that hinged on issues of identity and recognition. In 1955 the mediation effort came to a halt.

The Arab states, especially Jordan, wanted access to water resources, but they did not want to cooperate with Israel in the absence of an overall political settlement. The Jordan water issue could not be considered outside the context of relations in the basin, and those relations were part and parcel of the larger interstate conflict. Moreover, the dispute over Jordan water was a manifestation of a conflict that persisted within a context of nonrecognition. Hence there was reluctance to collaborate, even in technical matters.

After the Johnston mission, both Israel and Jordan reverted to their earlier unilateral plans to tap the water resources of the Jordan River basin. Jordan embarked on a scheme to extend an irrigation canal from the Yarmouk River in the north, southward along the eastern Ghor of the Jordan valley. Israel proceeded with its plan to integrate all of the water resources of the country into a comprehensive countrywide network—the National Water Carrier.

The Arab states protested vehemently against the Israeli plan to pump water from Lake Tiberias and transport it southward, outside the basin. They perceived it as a violation of the rights of Arab riparians and those living within the basin, a violation of international law, and a profound threat to the security and survival of the Arab states. In response the Arabs drew up a plan to divert the headwaters of the Jordan River—the Banias and the Hasbani—into Lebanon, Syria, and Jordan to prevent their access to Israel.

Work on the diversion scheme began in 1964. The sites in Syria soon became the scenes of repeated clashes between Israeli and Syrian forces. During this period confrontations occurred along the Israel-Jordan frontier as well. More often than not, water installations were targets of attack. Between 1964 and June 1967, tensions escalated rapidly in the region, culminating in a war whose geopolitical outcome would prove to be a major turning point in the conflict over Jordan water.

After 6 days of fighting, Israel more than trebled the territory it controlled by occupying the Sinai Peninsula, the Gaza Strip, the West Bank, the Golan Heights, and East Jerusalem. Its gains were also impressive insofar as water resources were concerned. By wresting control of the Syrian Golan Heights, it controlled the headwaters of the Banias tributary and was free to use its water at its own discretion.[5] In terms of the Jordan River proper, it was now in the advantageous position of upstream riparian in the basin.

Israel achieved substantial gains on the West Bank as well. The rich groundwater reserves of that territory, amounting to approximately one-quarter of Israeli water consumption, were now within its jurisdiction. Although Israel did have access to these subterranean sources prior to 1967, by virtue of the fact that the waters flow naturally westward toward the sea, it could now monitor and control their development and use within the West Bank proper and thereby ensure that they remain available for Israeli consumption.

No doubt, Israel's gains were the Arabs' losses. Of the three Arab riparian states, the Kingdom of Jordan suffered the worst blow. It lost the West Bank and, hence, its richest agricultural land. It "gained" several hundred thousand refugees, which added tremendous strain to the country's development potential. Moreover, Israel now controlled about 20% of the northern bank of the Yarmouk River, the kingdom's only abundant source of fresh water, as opposed to 10% before the war. This proximity placed severe constraints on Jordan's ability to tap that resource as it had planned.

In 1976 Jordan and Syria revived a 1953 treaty to exploit the Yarmouk water jointly by impounding it behind a dam at the Maqarin site. Jordan would use the floodwater—which until then had been going to waste—for badly needed irrigation in the valley, and Syria would have access to hydroelectricity. The Carter administration in Washington immediately took an interest in this scheme. As with the Johnston mission in the 1950s, the United States perceived regional water development as a stepping stone to regional peace because projects would require multilateral cooperation in the use of water resources. The government undertook to help finance the Maqarin project on the condition that Jordan reach an understanding on allocations with Syria, the upstream riparian, and with Israel, the downstream riparian.

Over a 3-year period, Philip Habib, then U.S. Assistant Secretary of State, shuttled among the three capitals, trying to get a multilateral agreement. Again there was constant haggling over quantities of water and their destinations. Syria wanted to use Yarmouk water upstream before it flowed into the dam, and Israel wanted to be guaranteed a certain amount of water for the West Bank, in accordance with the Johnston plan stipulations.[6] In the meantime Jordan's need for access to Yarmouk water was increasing: The country was facing severe water shortages.

Again water development in the Jordan basin brought into focus the larger conflict and some of the basic issues that were at its core: (a) control over land and, as its extension, control over water resources and (b) recognition and legitimacy of control. By 1981 the talks broke down. Syria would not approve the project because it would entail cooperation with Israel. And Jordan was reluctant to provide Israel with water that could be used for Jewish settlements in occupied territory. As long as there is no dam on the Yarmouk for Jordanian use, Israel is able, climatic conditions permitting, to divert the floodwater to Lake Tiberias for storage and use within its own territory.

The project resurfaced in 1987, when Syria and Jordan signed another treaty—this time to build a smaller dam on the Yarmouk. Jordan approached the World Bank for funding of the Unity (al-Wahda) Dam. Funding, however, was conditional on Jordan reaching agreement with the two other riparians. Talks between Jordan and Israel, mediated by the United States Department of State, were revived, albeit with very little success.[7] Within one year, they broke down.

The final and perhaps most striking example of conflict over water resources in the Jordan basin and its relationship to the larger political rivalry in the region is the case of the water supply of the West Bank (Lowi, 1992). Approximately 40% of the groundwater on which the state of Israel is dependent and one-quarter of its sustainable annual yield originate in this territory and flow naturally in a westerly direction across the 1949 Armistice Demarcation Line—the "Green Line"—into Israel. Three principal aquiferous basins underlie the West Bank.[8] Of them, as much as 95% (approximately 330 mcm) of the water of the western basin and over 85% (or 130 mcm) of the water of the northeastern basins are tapped inside Israel.

In an effort to protect this vital water supply for use inside Israel proper, the state has adopted stringent measures to minimize local use of the aquifers. West Bank Palestinians are subject to severe constraints on the use of local resources. Moreover, the unequal distribution of West Bank water between Palestinians, on the one hand, and Jewish settlers on the West Bank and Israelis inside the Green Line, on the other, has increased considerably over the last decade.

Given that groundwater represents some 60% of the total water consumption of Israel and that about 40% of this source originates in the West Bank, the significance of the territory's water resources is indisputable. Furthermore this dependence, coupled with the growing resource constraints experienced by Israel, exposes one of the major reasons why Israel will not easily rescind control over this territory. Largely because of the links between the water resources of the West Bank and the development needs of Israel, accepting an independent Palestinian state in the West Bank and Gaza Strip and, hence, relinquishing control of the territories' resources, is considered to be unacceptable by a significant portion of the Israeli political establishment. Without access to the rich groundwater supplies of the West Bank, Israel would be denied some 500 mcm of water per annum. It is primarily for these reasons that, under the rubric of the multilateral track of the Middle East peace process (Lowi, 1992), a water resources working group has been established.

Culture and the Jordan Water Dispute: The Importance of Cultural Factors

The history of the Jordan water dispute, as described above, elucidates the fact that the "question of Palestine" is central to all interactions between Arabs and Israelis. Probably no issue expresses the zero-sum nature of the larger political conflict more vividly than the competing claims to the land. Nonetheless, parties can find common ground by looking beneath the land issue itself to the meanings each attaches to it (Rothman, 1992, chap. 1). For centuries both Arabs and Jews have expressed their love of the land of Palestine/Israel as an integral part of the lives, dreams, memories, and myths of their people.

In a pastoral picture composed by an Arab in the 10th century, Palestine (Filastin) is described as a treasure: "Filastin is watered by the rains and the dews. Its trees and its ploughed land do not need artificial irriga- tion. . . . Filastin is the most fertile of the Syrian provinces" (cited in Said, 1980, p. 11).

A more recent praise of the land, as discussed by a scholar interviewing a Palestinian refugee exiled from his home, begins thus:

"We lived in Paradise": this remark, so often heard from older Palestinians in the refugee camps, would be dismissed by many as mere sentimentality. It is true that the dispossessed peasants have recalled their homes in Palestine from a present so bleak that their poverty and class oppression there tend to be blurred. But there is truth in their view of peasant life as good, for, in spite of poverty, "our land provided us with our needs." Village and clan solidarity formed a warm, strong, stable environment for the individual, a sense of rootedness and belonging. The proof of the strength of peasant social relations is that they survived in dispersion and helped Palestinians themselves to survive. They formed, too, an unbreakable umbilical cord that ties newborn Palestinians to the country that formed their forebears. (Sayigh, 1979, p. 10)

In the immediate post-1948 period, the humiliated Arab states sought to oust the "Zionist entity" from Arab soil and to return Palestine to its indigenous Arab inhabitants. The state of Israel was perceived as a foreign intrusion and a Western imperialist construct. Dealings with the "illegiti- mate" state were viewed as treasonous.

For Jews the memory of ethnic and religious persecution in Europe was vivid; they were determined to preserve the territorial and ethnic integrity of the Jewish homeland within secure borders. The land of Israel has meant refuge and renewal: "Through cruel and bitter trials and tribulations, through blasted hopes and despairs of the soul, through innumerable humiliations, we have slowly arrived at the realization that without a tangible homeland . . . we can have no sort of a life, either material or spiritual."[9]

Such aspirations were articulated positively in "The Hope," the Israeli national anthem ("Ha-Tikva"): "As long as in the heart, the Jewish spirit yearns with eyes turned eastward looking towards Zion, then our hope, and the hope of two thousand years, is not lost: to be a free nation in our land, the land of Zion and Jerusalem."

Arab expressions of aggression were interpreted as attempts at the annihilation of the Jewish homeland. For the new state, the perception of threat from an exceedingly hostile environment heightened its security concerns.

In sum, the conflict engaged two nationalist movements, each struggling for its right to national identity and national existence, while denying the adversary these same rights. Moreover, the organizing ideologies of both were defined, in part, with reference to the other. Withholding recognition of Israel by the Arab states and of Palestinian nationhood by Israel because of a perception of questioned legitimacy, marked the conflict at a very basic level.

To the Zionist movement, dominated by socialist trends from its inception through the 1930s, water was important insofar as it was part of the "ideology of agriculture" in Zionist thought (Laqueur, 1972, pp. 285-286). Of primary concern to the Zionists in their endeavors at promoting the establishment of a sovereign Jewish state was to restore to Jews what they lacked in the diaspora—an attachment to and productive relationship with the land—and to create what they considered to be the "ideal man." To socialist Zionism the "ideal man" is he who tills the land. And in keeping with socialist doctrine, he who tills the land has rights to it. It followed logically that if Jews would work the land after having "acquired" it, the Land of Israel (*Eretz Yisrael*) would belong to them.[10] Hence, in this early period, the emphasis on agriculture had both social and ideological components.

In time, however, agriculture became related to defense and defense imperatives, insofar as it was viewed as the means by which the Jews could be settled and an uninterrupted physical presence could be established throughout the country. Water, because it is an essential ingredient of agriculture, was and continues to be considered important by Zionists and the state of Israel. Moreover, it has always been perceived as linked to their ideological, economic, political, or security-related concerns.[11] Water would help make possible the absorption of increasing numbers of immigrants in *Eretz Yisrael* and also make it possible for Jews to work the land.

Prior to 1948 the Arab population of Palestine constituted a largely agricultural society that worked and lived off the land (Sayigh, 1979). Because, traditionally, agriculture was the principal economic activity, water—whether in the form of rainfall or surface flow—was vital to the livelihood of Palestinian peasants. They were both tied to the land and dependent on its resources. Water was perceived as an extension of the land.[12] With the settlement of Jews in Palestine and the establishment of the state of Israel, Palestinians were "denied" the land that they worked and that was their homeland.[13] This they viewed as a threat to their national survival (Kimmerling, 1983).

To the East Bank Arabs, water had a different significance. Prior to the establishment of the Kingdom of Jordan in 1946, the population of what then was called Transjordan was primarily nomadic or seminomadic (Konikoff, 1946, p. 19). To the bedouin, land per se is of no intrinsic value because they view all land as theirs and accessible to them. However, water obviously is important to the nomadic way of life because movements are determined largely by the search for water and grazing land for animals.

After the establishment of the Kingdom of Jordan, water was essential for the tasks of state building and economic development in a predominantly desert environment. Moreover, following the first Arab-Israel War in 1948-1949, the population of Jordan trebled due to the influx of Palestinian refugees (Gubser, 1983). All resources of the country were strained, and the Jordan valley was earmarked to become the settling ground of the refugees and the breadbasket of the kingdom (Khoury, 1964). Water was essential for domestic consumption, as well as for agricultural development.

Hence the combination of resource scarcity, acute population pressure, and the demands of economic development has caused the Israelis, Jordanians, and West Bank Palestinians to view access to increasing supplies of water as essential to their continued survival.

How Culture May Be Employed
to Facilitate Solutions

As is evident from the history of the Jordan water dispute and its relationship to the Arab-Israeli conflict, cultural factors may stimulate conflict and/or impede its resolution. However, a "cultural" approach may be employed consciously to assist adversaries in resolving their disputes.

Culture, particularly as it relates to a specific conflict, is a highly "reflexive" phenomenon (De-Reuck, 1990; Rothman, 1992). In brief, *reflexivity* is a form of analysis derived from a complex interplay between experience and context, self and other, internal and external. A reflexive analysis of conflict begins with the assumption that where one stands and who one is—one's context, identity, cultural norms, values, and priorities—influences what one sees, how one perceives and interprets events and invests them with meaning. Moreover, a reflexive analysis suggests that one's interactions and interrelations with others influence and shape oneself. Thus reflexivity pays close attention to the forming and influencing processes of relations between self and other, particularly those engaged in "intense" interaction, such as protracted conflict.

By describing reflexively their deepest motivations, traumas, hopes, and fears in the context of past and potential interactions, parties may begin to forge common ground and move beyond blaming: "You have taken our resources" or "You have rejected our legitimacy." This latter, adversarial approach encourages a dynamic that makes the other side defensive, mistrustful, and disinterested in further discussion. Instead a reflexive approach would begin with an exposition of self: "Our experience at the hands of adversaries, including you, but surely not limited to you, has threatened our culture and our values, undermined our well-being, and led us to feel a profound sense of injury, insecurity, and mistrust." We suggest, and some of our experience confirms (Rothman, 1992), that when parties in protracted conflict describe reflexively their motivations and the assumptions on which they act in the conflict situation, and illuminate the "cultural" dimensions at play, constructive dialogue and intercultural encounter become possible.

Rather than initiate a "deaf dialogue" (Cohen, 1990) through the conventional articulation of opposing national interests and competition over resources, a reflexive approach may encourage a "hearing dialogue" over converging needs and values. Thus parties may overcome attributional and ethnocentric biases in which each views the other as inherently aggressive and culturally inferior. Hearing that the other side is motivated by what could be called "cultural" hopes and fears, which often resonate with those of one's own group, a newfound sense of converging self-interest (in promoting and protecting each side's separate and unique identity, gaining recognition, safety, etc.) may begin to emerge.

Culture and Conflict Resolution

In an effort to suggest concretely how culture may be used to promote cooperation over water issues, which may, in turn, encourage a consolidation of efforts for peace at the political level, in this section we briefly summarize conflict resolution methodology that has been employed and developed in the Israeli-Palestinian context. Operating within the problem-solving workshop tradition (Burton, 1986; Kelman & Cohen, 1976; Rothman,

1989, 1991, 1992) a three-phased intervention methodology for helping parties move from conflict to cooperation has been developed. In the *adversarial* phase, parties blame each other for the conflict. In the *reflexive* phase, they articulate their own values, needs, hopes, and fears in the conflict situation. In the *integrative* phase, parties work cooperatively to solve common problems.

What follows is an analytical application of this methodology to the water dispute between Arabs and Israelis to illustrate how culture, in the context of the reflexive approach, may be employed to move parties from the adversarial to the integrative phases.

How Culture Has Stimulated Conflict
and Hindered Solutions:
The Adversarial Approach

Initially parties in a dialogue setting are asked to frame the conflict in terms of how they define it and analyze its causes. In deeply rooted, culture-based conflicts, parties generally blame the other side and attribute aggressive disposition to their adversary. This judgment leads to distributive, or "us versus them" (zero-sum), approaches to the dispute.

The history of the Jordan water conflict is replete with examples of this tendency. When Syria complained to the United Nations in 1953 that Israel was digging a canal in a part of the Demilitarized Zone (that had been established following the war of 1948-1949), Israel referred to the complaint as the unjustified act of a hostile neighbor, "bent upon Israel's economic strangulation."[14] In January 1954 the Arab League criticized the stipulation of the Unified Plan that Lake Tiberias, wholly within Israeli territory, be used as a storage reservoir for water that would go to Arab states. It maintained that it could not accept a scheme in which "Israel would have complete control of the waters on which Jordan would be dependent."[15] Israel, on the other hand, did not want a reservoir within its territory to be outside its sovereign control; otherwise "it is inevitable that in due course . . . it should lead to the creation of territorial claims, claims to the change of boundaries."[16] Furthermore, during the initial stages of the Johnston negotiations, the Arabs rejected the Israeli plan to transport a portion of Jordan water outside the basin, because of their reluctance to lend assistance to the economic development—that is, the strengthening—of the enemy state (Lowi, 1990, pp. 367-370). In fact, Israel's work on its national water system of pipelines was referred to by the Arabs as the enemy's "aggressive expansionist ambitions threatening all Arabs alike" (British Broadcasting Corporation [BBC], 1964a, 1964b). It prompted the Arab states to formulate a plan to divert the headwaters of the Jordan system into Lebanon, Syria, and Jordan so that Israel would no longer have access to them (Lowi, 1990, p. 227). The Arabs were determined "to deprive the snake of Arab blood which it has sucked" (BBC, 1965, p. A/3). Israel also demonized its enemy; it referred to the Arabs as "those who openly threaten to complete Hitler's work" (BBC, 1967, p. A/12). Acute tensions in the 1960s, accompanied by threats and counterthreats, border clashes, and retaliations, led to a frightening military buildup in the region, eventually culminating in yet another Arab-Israeli war.

This type of outward adversarial focus, in which disputants see "the other" as the main problem, is the norm in intense conflicts, and culture militates parties against one another by promoting ethnocentric and exclusionary perceptions (White, 1977). This pattern can be found wherever ethnic groups are engaged in deep, identity-related conflict, outwardly articulated and expressed in terms of rivalry for control of tangible territorial, economic, and/or military resources and for a monopoly over international support to which the less tangible "cultural" issues of identity and recognition are intimately connected. Such an approach perpetuates fruitless negotiation, at best, and promotes repeated outbursts of violence, at worst.

How Culture Might Be Employed
to Facilitate Solutions:
The Reflexive Approach

Suggest to parties engaged in exploratory dialogue that adversarial definitions and solution strategies are the norm and may well be, in significant measure, why so little progress toward a lasting solution has been made. Then ask the parties to articulate their underlying motivations, hopes, and fears in the conflict. Having done so and having heard similar concerns expressed by the other side, parties could begin to acknowledge the serious limitations of adversarial and coercive approaches.

To break the cycle of adversarial conflict framing and solution seeking, a reflexive telling of self can serve as a powerful transition. In other words, changing the way parties define their conflict—from an outward view of it to an inward-looking analysis—can broaden significantly their analyses of the conflict. This telling of self, in the presence of adversaries when possible or filtered through the mind of a third party, can engender a range of possibilities for creative problem framing and solution generation.

Lewin (1948) spoke of the need for parties in intense intergroup conflict to unfreeze their analyses and attitudes about the situation and each other. One method for doing this is by getting parties to talk about their national values. Parties are asked to articulate cultural concerns that motivate them: the underlying grammar (Cohen, 1990) or the hidden dimension (Hall,

1966) of the conflict. Moreover, they are asked to express them such that the other side can truly understand, if not believe, that these concerns are indeed primary motivating forces.

The reflexive approach to conflict framing provides a vehicle for conflict resolution evaluation and prescription. For a solution to be mutually acceptable, it must address the variety of deeply felt concerns. Thus, for instance, each side may articulate solutions that will further their own separate, though not necessarily exclusive, needs for identity, safety, recognition, justice, participation, and so forth. The extent to which past or future proposals for water use in the Middle East address these sorts of existential concerns may play an important role in determining whether they will be accepted and implemented. If solutions threaten or frustrate these cultural concerns further, it is likely that they will be rejected.

The reflexive approach serves to unfreeze parties from total reliance on the adversarial "us versus them" mode and provides room for a more integrative mode. The underlying concerns for identity and cultural integrity have been ignored far too long in diplomatic efforts in the Middle East. Bringing such issues into focus—within the context of concrete, practical issues, such as access to water resources—may have a constructive effect on an overall peace process. If encouraged to articulate underlying concerns that are at stake in the conflict, parties would make more progress in spelling out what must be addressed for a mutually acceptable solution to be forged. As Zartman and Berman (1982, p. 84) write, "Issues of recognition, of dignity, of acceptance, of rights and justice may be more important than the actual disposition of a material good, and taking them into account may facilitate a solution." They go on to cite master negotiator Averell Harriman: "Instead of people going to extremes of trying to explain what 'nefarious plans' the other side has, we ought to spend our time trying to understand what motivates these other people" (p. 84).

By shifting emphasis to common cultural concerns and relating them, where appropriate, to technical issues within the larger political conflict, the possibility of a new agenda for joint problem solving may be launched. It is at the integrative mode of problem framing and solution generation that this agenda is built.

Toward Resolving the Water Dispute:
The Integrative Approach

After parties have described their reflexive analyses of the situation, they are asked to find the intersections of their underlying concerns. This discovery then leads to an attempt at integrative bargaining, in which they are asked to invent creative and largely "win-win" (positive-sum) solutions to their common problems. Such an approach may foster mutual aid between the parties in solution implementation.

Some theorists argue that because significant elements of the Arab-Israeli conflict, in particular the Israeli-Palestinian conflict, are identity based and existential, the conflict is zero-sum by definition (Benvenisti, 1986). Although this gloomy description may indeed be valid empirically, it need be neither prescriptive nor predictive.[17] Instead it may motivate us to seek new ways to harness, in a constructive manner, the values, motivations, hopes, and fears that make this conflict so intense.

One may suggest, for example, that because conflicts such as that between the Arabs and the Israelis are so deeply rooted in the participants' sense of self and, hence, they are not willing to compromise on virtually any issue, one of the parties must be vanquished or both must cooperate for the sake of enlightened self-interest.[18] Because neither the Arabs nor the Israelis can vanquish the other, yet both continue to frustrate the other's social and economic development and sense of security, cooperation is necessary.

Integrative solutions are those that all parties to a conflict are committed to, instead of being coerced into by external forces, because they all gain from them and, perhaps more important, because it can be demonstrated that such solutions are best suited to fulfilling their needs (Albin, 1991; Litterer & Lewicki, 1985; Metcalf & Urwick, 1940; Pruitt & Rubin, 1986). Disputing parties become motivated to "help" the other side achieve certain goals because of the gains they can envision for themselves through such cooperation. For instance, the insecurity of either side is viewed as a concrete problem for both. In feeling insecure, each side often will act in ways that will lead the other side to feel insecure as well (Jervis, 1976). By articulating common frustrations and perceived threats, an agenda for joint problem solving is set. This agenda can be both incremental and holistic at the same time. It can be designed to work on "pieces of peace" in ways that symbolically and practically are part of a total fabric of peace.

Integrative solutions cannot be imposed from the outside; they must be motivated internally and derived from the parties themselves. Nonetheless third parties may inspire and support them. The following ideas for integrative solutions are provided for illustrative purposes only.

Keeping the various cultural concerns at the forefront of their minds as they seek to craft solutions by which all parties may gain, the disputants would be encouraged to brainstorm on a whole range of cooperative arrangements. For instance, they may seek to present a "peace bill" to the world community for $35 billion in water development aid. With this money they could draw up and begin to implement elaborate formulas for sharing the water of the various river basins of the region among the concerned states in a mutually satisfactory fashion and according to need. They could draw up and implement plans to "import" water from water-rich to water-poor areas of the region. In the short term, the disputants could establish research and policy-implementation teams. Among their various tasks, they could investigate conservation techniques that would stop highly wasteful water consumption practices. They could explore ways in which capital and technology could be shared such that irrigation techniques, recycling wastewater, and perhaps even the desalination of seawater could be implemented wherever appropriate. The international community could be called on to lend its vast knowledge and expertise, in addition to financial resources.

Meeting in the Middle:
Coordinating Functional and Political Approaches

As noted above, efforts have been made to resolve the protracted conflict in the Middle East by promoting functional cooperation, most notably in water resource development in the Jordan basin. In the cases of both the Johnston mission in the 1950s and the Maqarin/Unity Dam schemes more recently, mediation efforts were inspired by the belief that functional cooperation would provide the foundation for broadly based peace. The outcomes of these two episodes, however, call into question the effectiveness of political functionalism as a dispute resolution technique in protracted, culture-based conflict settings (Lowi, 1993).

Political functionalists argue that the combination of large sacrifices in national sovereignty, ongoing functional cooperation among adversaries, and the creation of supranational, task-related organizations is the most promising avenue toward peace. According to Mitrany (1986, pp. 97-98), the architect of political functionalism, "Every activity organized in that way would be a layer of peaceful life," insofar as "economic unification would build up the foundation for political agreement." The development among states of an ever-widening range of interdependencies in economic, technical, and welfare areas would not only enmesh governments but also encourage actors to set aside their political differences. Functional integration eventually would spill over into more broadly based regional peace. Politics would have to be bypassed and value- and culture-laden issues neutralized.

On two occasions over the course of the history of the Jordan water conflict, the United States government did what the functionalists suggest: It treated the highly charged psychocultural environment in the Middle

East as an abstraction in its attempts to resolve some of the tensions in the region. Because parties' values, perceptions, and sentiments were viewed as obstacles to cooperation, U.S. mediation efforts, rather than address them, paid them insufficient attention. The Arabs and Israelis could not do likewise, however, for cognitive elements and conflicting organizing principles— both of which had originated in a particular historical experience—influence considerably their assumptions and interactions.

Indeed the absence of ideological consensus and agreement of any sort served as a deterrent to cooperation. As some of the "cognitive" approaches to the study of cooperation rightly point out, "historically situated" states respond to their environment in light of their very particular normative and ideological constraints (Haggard & Simmons, 1987; Lipschutz, 1989). In the Jordan basin, cooperation in water resource development could not be realized because of the "cognitive" variables at play in the larger political conflict. Cooperation does not materialize when political rivalry engages underlying visceral concerns, as elaborated in the Arab-Israeli conflict, that would necessarily be ignored by functional arrangements. Besides, when a dispute over water resources is embedded in a larger political rivalry, it can neither be conceived of as a discrete conflict over a resource nor be resolved as such. The possibility of sharing water cannot be treated as a straightforward, unambiguous issue, unlinked to the political conflict, especially because implicit in water-use arrangements is formal acceptance of the other and its rights as a political entity. Efforts at resolving the Jordan water conflict demonstrate that the riparian dispute in a protracted conflict setting is not simply about water; it takes on many of the attributes of the larger conflict. Stated differently, the parties involved view the riparian dispute as a manifestation, or microcosm, of the political rivalry. To wit, between Arabs and Israelis, politics cannot be bypassed, nor can value- and culture-laden issues be neutralized. Rather they must be articulated and accommodated.

Given the experiences in resolving riparian dispute in the Jordan basin, the realist critics of functionalism are correct: States that are adversaries in the "high politics" of war and diplomacy do not allow extensive cooperation in the sphere of "low politics," centered on economic and welfare issues. In fact, the spillover effect runs in the opposite direction of that suggested by Mitrany: Economics and welfare collaboration are retarded by "high politics" conflicts between states.

Although functional cooperation may not be operational as long as political conflicts are so intense, the latter perhaps could be made more tractable if adversaries see some benefit to be had from peace or, at least, stability. Thus illustrating the benefits of sharing water, for instance, could have a salutary effect on the effort (and the will) to promote political peace between Arabs and Israelis. Although functionalists clearly have over-stated the panacea of cooperation in technical matters, there may well be an important iterative process by which progress beginning at the political level—that is, the Arab-Israeli peace process—requires concrete progress at the "practical" level—for example, sharing water resources for both con-solidation and fruition.

Functional solutions to water disputes would be tied back into a com-prehensive peace process, giving momentum to it by providing incentives for successful outcomes and demonstrating the relative gains that parties could achieve by working together. For example, water resources would be distributed more appropriately, and regional market forces would function to promote the comparative advantages of states to the benefit of all.

One of the main obstacles to successful negotiation and conflict manage-ment in protracted social conflicts is that compromise is unacceptable to the parties. Although often expressed in terms of instruments of state, such as territory and political control, these conflicts are essentially about existential human concerns. Thus compromise of any kind seems highly threatening. To build a willingness to make concessions, and indeed at some point parties do have to give a little in terms of the institutional dimensions of their conflicts, parties first must perceive the benefits that may be derived from cooperation and joint problem solving. Integrative and positive-sum solutions to shared problems, which can build confidence, enhance mutual safety, and protect identities, are likely to be necessary preconditions for successful distributive bargaining and compromise in intense ethnic conflicts.

Notes

1. The historical overview of the Jordan water conflict is drawn from Lowi (1993).

2. Memorandum from the legal adviser of the State Department on Development of Water Resources of the Jordan River Valley, 6 Oct. 1953, *United States National Archives* (USNA) 684a.85322/10-653.

3. Memorandum of Agreement between United States Department of State and the Ten-nessee Valley Authority, 18 Sept. 1952, *United States National Archives* 684a.85322/9-1852.

4. Secretary of State John Foster Dulles to Eric Johnston, *Foreign Relations of the United States, 1952-1954* (FRUS), Vol. 9, Part 1, (Washington, DC: Government Printing Office, 1986), 13 October 1953, no. 686, pp. 1348-1352. The plan was drawn up by the Charles T. Main engineering firm and published under the title *The Unified Development of the Water Resources of the Jordan Valley Region* (Boston, 1953).

5. The only remaining northern source outside Israel's command was the Hasbani tributary, rising in southeastern Lebanon. By 1978, however, Israel had gained much in-fluence in that region. Since the 1982 invasion of Lebanon, Israeli forces have maintained effective control over a part of the south and, hence, of the Hasbani as well.

6. The Unified Plan allocated a minimum of 70 mcm of Yarmouk water to the West Bank then under Jordanian jurisdiction through a feeder canal from the river to the "West Ghor."

7. The U.S. government was not prepared to mediate discussions that included Syria because of its tense diplomatic relations with that state.

8. An aquifer is a subterranean water-bearing rock formation. Underground basins can contain several aquifers.

9. Chaim Nahman Bialik, from a speech at the inauguration of the University of Jerusalem, January 4, 1925, in Hertzberg (1959, p. 284).

10. We put quotation marks around the word *acquired* because the issue of land acquisition is ideologically loaded. Zionists perceive that in the early years, land was purchased legally, while Palestinian nationalists perceive that it was usurped.

11. Interview by author with Israeli scholar, Jerusalem, April 30, 1986.

12. Interview by author with a Palestinian sociologist, Amman, February 4, 1986; with an Israeli historian of Palestine, Jerusalem, April 16, 1986.

13. We put *denied* in quotation marks for the same reason as *acquired,* see footnote 10.

14. From the statement by Ambassador Abba Eban before the Security Council, October 30, 1953, *National Archives of the State of Israel* (INA), Foreign Ministry documents (record group 93), box 360, file 6.

15. Report of a conversation with Mahmoud Riad, January 15, 1954, *United States National Archives* 683.84a322/1-1554.

16. Minutes of the opening session: talks between Ambassador Johnston and his party and members of the Israeli government, Thursday p.m. session, January 27, 1955, *INA* (box 3688, file 10).

17. By the former, we mean that because the conflict is zero-sum, let the good fight continue and may the strongest win. The latter refers to the sentiment that the conflict is hopeless and more bloodshed inevitable.

18. As the history of the Jordan water dispute illustrates, states engaged in an identity-related conflict tend to perceive all matters of mutual concern as subthemes of the larger adversarial context. All issues are considered vital; superimposed on all is the crippling political conflict.

12

China:
The Three Gorges Dam Project

KENNETH LIEBERTHAL

The idea of building a high dam in the Three Gorges section of the Yangtze (in Chinese, *Changjiang*) River has been under discussion for more than 70 years. During those decades, numerous feasibility studies have been done, before 1949 under the Nationalists and then by the Communists. These studies have received assistance from *inter alia*, Soviet, American, Canadian, and European advisers (for details, see Lieberthal & Oksenberg, 1988, pp. 290-327; Hong Qingyu, 1988). China's national legislature, the National People's Congress (NPC), in early April 1992 adopted a resolution proposed by Premier Li Peng to build the dam. The debate over this resolution proved rancorous, however, and fully one-third of the delegates either abstained or voted no on the final ballot. Because of the NPC's usual practice of unanimous balloting, this "affirmative" vote, in fact, served to highlight the deep, ongoing divisions over this project. Despite the affirmative NPC vote, therefore, the dam may yet not be built. Inability to reach final closure on this important issue has, moreover, exacted high opportunity costs on China's energy development. The difficulty in reaching a definitive decision regarding this dam can be understood better against the background of China's bureaucratic culture.

Bureaucratic culture meets the general test of culture used in this volume. It involves a "set of shared and enduring meanings, values, and beliefs that characterize . . . groups and their behavior." But the cultural nexus here is not an ethnic group or a national population. Rather it is the participants in a bureaucratic system. Arguably the deep origins of the cultural patterns characteristic of this bureaucratic system are to be found in basic cultural proclivities of the Han Chinese. They would, it seems, only organize a bureaucratic system that is compatible with their fundamental cultural values. But at a more immediate level, the specific "cultural" characteristics of China's bureaucratic culture identified below can be ascribed almost wholly to two factors: the prescriptive values articulated by national leaders, and the specific structures and histories of the bureaucracies themselves. The origins of the values of the top leaders is a question of intellectual history that extends beyond the scope of this chapter. With regard to the bureaucratic structures themselves, because these very structures consist of a broad admixture of traditional Chinese and imported Stalinist features, it is impossible to determine in more than an arbitrary fashion what within this is "Chinese."

Chinese bureaucratic behavior nevertheless exhibits specific enduring meanings, values, and beliefs that are identifiable and consequential for understanding the fate of the proposal to build the world's largest multipurpose dam on the Yangtze River. Perhaps this bureaucratic culture is especially important in China because government bureaucracies so totally dominate life in that country. Elsewhere, differing professional ethics and other factors that provide diversity in people's lives and alternative sources of influence on policy mitigate the development of specific, powerful, inclusive bureaucratic cultures. Perhaps in the United States, for example, the only real approximation to the power of China's bureaucratic culture exists within the uniformed military establishment, where there is a basic convergence of lifetime career opportunities and comprehensive social norms.

My argument of this chapter is quite simple. After introducing the proposed Three Gorges Dam project, I articulate six key components of China's bureaucratic culture and indicate how these affect decision making regarding that proposed effort. To highlight the cultural factors that are discussed, I indicate the types of basic misunderstandings that are likely to occur if foreigners become deeply involved in eventual construction of this dam. The chapter's basic theme is that it is important to determine core "cultural" characteristics of large bureaucracies involved in water projects.

These bureaucratic cultural traits may strongly affect the ability of people in the bureaucracies of different countries (and/or international organizations) to work effectively with each other in water project efforts. To the extent that bureaucratic culture traits are not understood, potentially serious problems of ineffective signaling, poor communications, and misunderstanding will affect project implementation. It is thus crucial to recognize the potential importance of the bureaucratic cultural elements and to focus attention on them accordingly. These bureaucratic cultures may or may not differ substantially from the broader national or ethnic cultural traits usually discussed by analysts.

The Three Gorges Dam: An Overview

If built, the Three Gorges Dam (TGD) will be a very large multipurpose project, with major effects on flood control downriver, on availability of electricity throughout central China, and on navigation of the key Yangtze waterway.[1] Each area—flood control, power generation, and navigation— is under the aegis of a separate nationwide bureaucracy.

The TGD would be built at Sandouping, an area just to the west of where the Yangtze spills out of the gorges into the densely populated flatlands of central China. From the eastern edge of the gorges to the large municipality of Wuhan, the Yangtze is held in its course by an extensive series of levies, called the Jingjiang dikes. Wuhan and the surrounding countryside are threatened both by Yangtze floodwater cascading through the three gorges and by other water that comes into the Yangtze by means of the Hanshui River just to the west of the city (see Figure 12.1).

The Jingjiang dikes have been fortified in recent decades, but it is not possible to heighten them to the point where they can fully contain the waters from a major flood on the Yangtze. Heavy silting, moreover, has raised the river bed above the level of the surrounding countryside. When the river overflows its banks, therefore, it waterlogs the flooded areas. A catastrophic flood causing a major failure in the dike system could, it is believed, kill between a half million and a million citizens.

One critical function of the TGD would be to reduce the chances that floodwater would breach the Jingjiang dike system. If the dam meets its promise, it should be able to provide substantial relief for the frequent flooding to which the Yangtze is subject, with minimal use of flood diversion catchments downstream of the dam. This relief would benefit enormously the people of Wuhan and of the surrounding areas, and it potentially could bring large economic payoffs in the form of avoidance of catastrophic flood losses.[2] The TGD would become part of a more

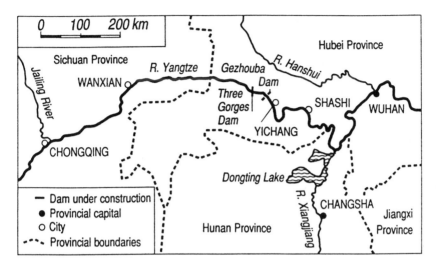

Figure 12.1. The Three Gorges Dam Project

extensive system of smaller dams on tributary rivers in Sichuan province, and one of the controversies over the TGD is whether to build it before the smaller dams or afterward. The flood control function of the TGD has been viewed as being so important that the bureaucracy that has been given primary responsibility for the dam is the water resources organization, which takes flood control and irrigation as its primary tasks.

Hydropower generation is another key function of the TGD. The central China area that would receive the primary benefit from TGD hydropower generation is a rapidly industrializing region that already experiences severe power shortages that constrain economic growth and output. The main alternative source of power for this region is thermal power generation based on burning coal. This alternative has two very serious drawbacks, however. First, the coal would have to come from Shanxi province and would place substantial additional burdens on the country's overextended rail transport system. Second, coal-based energy would exacerbate the severe air pollution from which this region already suffers. Although a part of the region's power demands can be met from smaller hydropower stations, the Gezhouba Dam (to the east of the proposed TGD), and new nuclear facilities being brought on-line near Shanghai, no combination of these sources can alleviate to a great extent the critical power shortage the region already faces.

In considering the hydropower dimension of the TGD, time line opportunity costs also loom large. The power shortage in central China is already severe. If the central government starts construction of the TGD, however, this will absorb a large percentage of the investment funds that otherwise could be used to bring coal-fired power stations on-line quickly in the area. But under even the most optimistic scenarios, the Three Gorges Dam would not generate its first kilowatt-hour of electricity until its 10th year of construction and would not come fully up to power until 18 years after full-scale construction begins. Each year of delay before dam construction begins, moreover, simply puts off the day when the dam will become a substantial contributor to power in the region.

Navigation on the Yangtze River is of crucial importance for the economy of central China. Currently, though, the river to the west of Wuhan presents treacherous navigational conditions, with many hidden shoals, shifting sand bars, and rapidly changing water levels. To the west of the gorges themselves, only small ships and barges can penetrate. The TGD might provide substantial relief for these conditions. It could create a reservoir deep enough to submerge the dangerous shoals and sand bars, and it would provide for much greater predictability in the depth of the river. In addition, the reservoir would reduce the eastward water flow rate between Chongqing, a major city to the west of the gorges, and the dam, thus providing for significant economies in navigational costs going upstream. If the proposed dam with a normal water level of 175 m is built, Chongqing could become a major port that would link southwest China with the rich central China economy.

With navigation, too, there are problems. First, the 18-year period of construction of the dam is so long that there are serious concerns about the effect of dam construction on traffic on the Yangtze. The bureaucracy in charge of river transport thus is demanding extensive and expensive efforts to prevent interruptions in this important traffic. In addition, Yangtze silting dynamics are sufficiently complex that specialists have argued for decades over the potential effects of the dam on silt deposits throughout the river. Dam opponents have argued *inter alia* that the reservoir backwater will create silt deposits that, over a period of years, will render the port of Chongqing virtually useless. Opponents also have expressed concerns over the effects of the dam on silting downstream, arguing that the results could make the stretch between the Gezhouba Dam and the Wuhan municipality more treacherous and might even weaken the Jingjiang dike system (by scouring out some of its base) (Fang Zongdai, 1988b).

Each of the three principal tasks of the TGD, therefore, is very important to the welfare of central China, and each also raises questions of priorities, opportunity costs, and potential new problems. In addition, each task would require somewhat different operation of the dam, and thus it will be impossible to have the dam meet its full potential simultaneously in all three areas. Flood control, for example, requires reducing the water level behind the dam just before the high water season and at flood tides, discharging water at a faster rate than can be wholly captured for power generation, but hydropower generation calls for maintaining consistently high water levels. Both flood control and hydropower can, at times, demand rapid releases of large amounts of water through the dam, but these releases upset navigation below the dam.

Models for achieving optimization among these various tasks are becoming more sophisticated.[3] The technical unknowns in constructing and operating the TGD remain large, however. Many of these unknowns, moreover, concern environmental issues. Dam critics have argued that the TGD could ruin the habitat for the Yangtze sturgeon, dolphin, and other species. Some have contended that the dam's reservoir will produce changes in local temperatures and weather patterns that could severely affect vegetation and agriculture. A few point to the possibility that the dam will increase earthquake potential in the area. Others worry about the long-term effects of new silting patterns. And obviously, if the dam should ever give way (or if the cofferdam were to collapse during construction, as occurred on the Tianshengqiao Dam), the resulting environmental catastrophe would be immense. Dam supporters argue, in turn, that if the TGD is not built, central China will have to rely overwhelmingly on coal-fired power plants and will remain vulnerable to the danger of disastrous flooding, both of which are extremely harmful to the environment.

There are, moreover, inherent conflicts of interest that cannot be eliminated, even through sophisticated management of the project. Geographically, the biggest conflict of interest concerns management of the refugee problem. In brief, provinces downstream of the dam—especially Hubei and Hunan—receive the main benefits of this project, but Sichuan province, just upstream of the dam, will have to pay a major price in terms of resettlement of refugees whose homes and workplaces are flooded by the reservoir. The number of refugees will reach approximately 1.30 million people, most of whom live in Sichuan province.[4] Even though the central government would make substantial contributions toward funding the refugee resettlement program, a major burden of this effort—politically, organizationally, and financially—would fall on the province, and Sichuan is, naturally, chary of the dam as a consequence.

In sum, the Three Gorges Dam is a very large project that recently has been approved only after decades of debate and that remains very controversial. This project is potentially highly consequential in various ways for both central and southwest China—overall, a vast stretch of territory with a population well up in the tens of millions. It is, moreover, a multipurpose project whose various key functions fall under the aegis of different Chinese bureaucracies.

China's Bureaucratic Culture

All of the key participants in the TGD deliberations are Han Chinese, and thus no major cultural differences among these people have affected the dynamics of the decision-making process. Rather, the process has been affected deeply by the culture that is common to all participants—the People's Republic of China's bureaucratic culture.

All major dam projects are affected by the stresses and strains inherent in matrix problems in large-scale organizations. Dams are by their nature both functional and territorial entities. Large-scale, multipurpose dams inevitably exacerbate the tensions characteristic of bureaucratic bodies that must coordinate work both vertically (functionally) and horizontally (territorially).

Although such tensions are inevitable, it is imperative to understand the bureaucratic culture of the organizations concerned to fathom how these tensions will "play out" in the course of project deliberation and implementation. *Bureaucratic culture* refers to the fundamental, enduring meanings, values, and beliefs bureaucrats harbor about the considerations that should affect decisions. In the Chinese case, these considerations, in turn, apparently emerge from two sources: the structural allocation of authority within the political system, and the prescriptive values articulated by the country's top leaders. Some important changes have occurred in these spheres over time; they are examined later in the chapter.

Certain dimensions of China's bureaucratic culture have affected significantly in a number of ways the deliberations concerning the Three Gorges Dam project. Six dimensions of this culture have been particularly salient to the history of consideration of the TGD. These six facets do not in themselves provide a complete picture of China's bureaucratic culture. Rather they are the particular elements in that culture that seem to have had the greatest effect on deliberations concerning this project over the decades. They are put forward here to illustrate the types of information about pertinent bureaucracies beyond that conveyed in organizational charts that are important for understanding bureaucratic outcomes.

Nonrepresentation of Interests and
Bureaucratic Core Missions

First, dams always adversely affect the interests of some citizens (typically those whose land will be flooded by the reservoir) and promote the interests of others (e.g., those threatened by floods, those who need additional electricity). A key consideration in most dam planning, therefore, is the issue of how citizens' interests are represented in the decision-making process.

China does not recognize that citizens should seek objective representation of their interests in the political system. The Chinese concept is, rather, that the state decides what core missions, or tasks, should be performed and then assigns particular bureaucracies to carry out those tasks. Thus, for example, peasants who live along the Jingjiang dikes have a very strong interest in flood control along the Yangtze. The state would crush quickly any relatively autonomous effort by those peasants to organize themselves to exert pressure "from the bottom up" to influence state policy regarding this issue. Rather these peasants are "represented" only insofar as the bureaucracy entrusted with the task of flood control focuses its efforts on this particular locale (Lieberthal & Oksenberg, 1988, pp. 396-401).[5]

This distinction between representation of interests and assignment of tasks is a subtle but important one. It means, effectively, that the only legitimate players in the decision-making game are bureaucratic units whose assigned tasks may be affected by the project, plus the top political leadership. The independent views of the people most affected by the dam are not relevant—except insofar as these views may affect the ability of the bureaucrats to implement the decisions that have been made.

The array of bureaucracies whose tasks are affected by the TGD is very large, and thus decision making on this project has involved an unwieldy melange of bureaucratic units. The Yangtze Valley Planning Office (YVPO), situated in Wuhan, is one of the key bureaucratic players. This office, created in the mid-1950s,[6] is responsible for planning for the development of the entire Yangtze watershed. The main tasks of this office, like that for comparable offices on China's other major rivers, are planning for flood control and for irrigation. The YVPO is under the national ministry in charge of flood control and irrigation[7] and, recognizing the tremendous flood danger that faces the peasants to the east of the gorges, it has been the strongest champion of building a high dam at the Three Gorges. The YVPO also has been in charge of designing the dam and coordinating most of the pertinent feasibility studies.

The Yangtze Navigational Bureau of the Ministry of Communications is another key player. This bureau's task is to maintain navigation along the river, and it has viewed from the start the risks to navigation in construction of the dam as far outweighing the possible benefits that the dam's promoters promise two decades hence. This bureau thus consistently has challenged the analyses of the YVPO-sponsored studies.

The Ministry of Power[8] would like to solve the power shortage as quickly as possible, but it also has concerns about coal transport and other problems.

This ministry thus has been somewhat ambivalent about the dam. It worries that dam construction will absorb for a long period the funds needed for thermal power expansion, and it is very concerned that, once built, the dam will not be used to maximize the benefits in terms of power generation.

Important territorial actors are also in China's bureaucratic landscape. For purposes of the TGD project, the most important of these are the provincial leaders of Sichuan (above the dam), Hubei and Hunan (below the dam), and the municipalities of Chongqing (above the dam) and Wuhan (below the dam). For reasons explained below, Sichuan strongly prefers that first priority be given to building smaller dams on the tributaries to the Yangtze in Sichuan province. Chongqing is somewhat ambivalent but on balance supports the dam because it will have an average water level of about 175 m, which will enable Chongqing to become the key port linking southwest China with central China. Wuhan, Hubei, and Hunan strongly support the dam, primarily for flood control reasons.

The sense of mission of Chinese bureaucracies is very strong, and each bureaucracy develops its own kind of spirit around its core mission (see Lieberthal & Oksenberg, 1988, chap. 3). Some people in the Yangtze Valley Planning Office, for example, decades ago became engineers solely to participate in designing and building the Three Gorges Dam. Personnel continuities, especially at the level of the key bureaus within the provinces and national ministries that deal with this project, are also very impressive. Thus a type of community of bureaucrats has gelled over the years and has struggled among themselves for decades over whether to commence construction of this mammoth dam. Almost all of these individuals see the dam through the lenses of their own bureaucratic core missions, and they act and argue accordingly.

Bureaucratic Ranks Are Important

The second pertinent aspect of China's bureaucratic culture is the tremendous importance it attaches to ranks. China is a thoroughly bureaucratized society, and every bureaucratic unit is assigned a formal rank in an integrated nationwide scale of ranks. Even economic corporations and schools have assigned bureaucratic ranks that determine how they fit into the overall bureaucratic framework that governs the country.

One key feature of the ranking system is that units of the same rank cannot issue binding orders to each other. In this context it is important to note that ministries and provinces have the same bureaucratic rank, as the bureaus under ministries and provinces share one rank. Because all ministries and provinces share the same rank, no ministry or province can issue binding orders to any other ministry or province. The Three Gorges Dam project, as noted above, encroaches on the assigned tasks of a wide array of ministries and provinces (and their subordinate units), but none of these is in a position simply to command the obedience or acquiescence of any other one (Lieberthal & Oksenberg, 1988, chaps. 2 and 4).

There are two operational consequences to this structural dimension of China's allocation of authority. The first is a natural tendency to push things up to a higher level in the system to obtain a decision from some body that does have command authority over all of the involved units. At the stage of deciding whether to build the TGD, this body is the State Council (the Chinese equivalent of the cabinet or council of ministers) and the National People's Congress. Once construction actually begins, the State Council will become the highest governmental organ of appeal.

Because higher level bodies tend to become overloaded in the Chinese system, over time a second response has become a core part of the country's bureaucratic culture—that is, to seek consensus among all affected units before a project is presented for final decision making. This proclivity to engage in consensus building produces very extensive efforts at consultation and bargaining among affected units (see Lampton, 1987). Inevitably one unit has the lead responsibility for any given project (for the TGD, it is the water resource people), but this unit then spends a great deal of effort in working with other affected units to secure their input and their general support for the project. As reflected in the sharp division in the NPC over whether to build the TGD, even after decades of effort no consensus has been reached on this project.

The drive for consensus can produce a phenomenon known in the United States as "gold plating" of a project.[9] Essentially the lead organization may add significant enhancements to the project in order to win over other participants. In the Three Gorges Dam proposal, for example, it appears that the YVPO made extraordinary efforts to garner support from the navigation people through promises of building the world's largest ship lift and other measures to keep the dam from interfering with transport along the Yangtze. Gold plating is not the only result of the consensus-building effort. Other priorities in China's bureaucratic culture that affect the bargaining to produce a consensus are discussed below.

Territorial Units Must Be Won Over

The third pertinent characteristic of China's bureaucratic culture is the importance attached to winning over the pertinent territorial units. This operational perspective results from a very practical matter: Although territorial units cannot outright refuse to cooperate with orders from the top leadership, the territorial leaders can, nevertheless, effectively sabotage a major project over a period of years.

Inevitably a project such as the TGD requires very active and effective cooperation of the key provincial authorities. Most of the resettlement issue, for example, must be handled operationally by the territorial political apparatus. Many supplies, such as those needed to support the large construction force required by the project, are provided by the provincial and local authorities. Some land must be redistributed, and that again becomes the responsibility of the territorial leadership. In myriad additional ways, the territorial leadership can sabotage a project simply by dragging its feet on support efforts (and, of course, pointing to "objective difficulties" that explain its worse-than-expected performance).

The central leaders well understand the need to gain the enthusiastic support of the provincial leadership. Typically, therefore, they cut deals with the provincial leaders that can be very wide ranging, complex, and subtle. The province may receive in return some combination of additional investment funds, a reduced tax burden, greater access to interprovincial rail transport, additional electricity for its factories, more favorable regulations governing foreign direct investment and retention of foreign exchange, and so forth. Typically the province's own workers will be employed in undertaking the construction project, and the province will be promised some direct benefit once the project is completed (Lieberthal & Oksenberg, 1988, chap. 7). Provinces, in turn, cut similar deals with their subordinate municipalities and counties.

The Three Gorges Dam project, overall, seriously disadvantages Sichuan province in a number of ways. It creates a huge reservoir that partially submerges prime tourist areas. It engenders a monumental refugee problem that will require tremendous efforts to handle without producing social unrest (Fang Zongdai & Wang Shouzhong, 1988). The reservoir will require the reassignment of numerous local officials from the areas that will be flooded—always a very sensitive political issue. The dam project soaks up investment funds that otherwise might have been used for flood control and hydropower generation on smaller tributaries to the Yangtze in Sichuan. It will provide its key benefits—flood control and most of the electricity it generates—to the downstream provinces (Lieberthal & Oksenberg, 1988, pp. 278-279). And—a subtle matter—it will potentially greatly strengthen Chongqing municipality, but the capital of the province is in Chengdu City, whose officials are jealous of Chongqing's rising stature.

Given these and other concerns, the YVPO and its allies in favor of constructing the dam have not been able to find a formula that Sichuan supports for dam construction. Sichuan's strongest objection has been to the resettlement burden it must assume. As a consequence, in the mid-1980s (when it seemed that a positive decision to begin dam construction was imminent) the central government offered to carve out a new "Three Gorges province" that would encompass the area bearing the main resettlement burden. Beijing would provide an array of special investment, tax, and foreign trade advantages to this new province to help it develop. The central government went so far as to appoint a shadow government for this new province before the idea eventually faded as the project again ran into obstacles on other grounds (Lieberthal & Oksenberg, 1988, chap. 6). The April 1992 decision to build the dam makes no mention of a new Three Gorges province.

Even the fact that the authorities at one point floated the idea of carving out a new province demonstrates the importance of territorial sensitivities in China's bureaucratic culture. Because by almost any measure Sichuan province (with a population of more than 100 million people) will be a major loser from construction of the TGD, this bureaucratic norm effectively makes it important for the center to continue to find ways to encourage Sichuan's enthusiasm throughout project implementation.

Employment Must Be Maximized

Fourth, maximizing employment is a highly prized goal of each Chinese bureaucracy. In crude terms, one might argue that this norm derives simply from the population pressure in a country with more than 1.1 billion citizens. In fact, however, it appears that a major contributing factor is that bureaucratic units are social welfare bodies deeply involved in many aspects of their employees' lives. The heads of major bureaucratic units (including government offices, research institutes, and enterprises), for example, spend much of the time arranging for employee housing and health benefits, adjudicating marriage disputes, managing the birth control effort, and so forth. Chinese employees need permission from their unit head to marry, to obtain a divorce, or to have a child. Major units, in addition, provide housing, schooling, transportation, sanitary and health facilities, pensions, death benefits, and much more. Running a major unit in China is more like being the mayor of a small city in the United States than it is like being an American bureaucrat or entrepreneur.

A large number of employees is also a sign of power in China's bureaucratic culture. This norm prevails despite repeated efforts by the top leadership over the years to streamline the country's burgeoning bureaucracy. Thus it is frequently the case that bureaucratic units will seek to expand their employment rolls even when they already have a surfeit of people for the work they must perform. In addition it violates most norms of China's bureaucratic practice to fire someone from his or her job. Better to keep the person on reduced wages with no real work to perform than to let him or her go in the name of greater efficiency.[10]

This approach directly affects the pressures and constraints in the Three Gorges Dam decision making. In the early 1970s, the advocates of the dam nearly succeeded in obtaining a decision to build the project, but in the final analysis the central leadership stepped back from this commitment. The top leaders—Premier Zhou Enlai and Party Chairman Mao Zedong— decided instead to construct the Gezhouba Dam about 40 km to the east of the TGD site. They sought, by this decision, to gain experience (especially in large lock construction) from building an ambitious but smaller structure. The decision also had other advantages: Gezhouba eventually would serve as a regulator dam to help dampen and control the water surges from the TGD; Gezhouba would be less expensive to construct, and at the time China faced severe financial pressures in the later stages of the disruptive Cultural Revolution; and Gezhouba posed fewer risks of catastrophic results should the pertinent modeling of silting and other controversial aspects prove faulty. The idea was to build the Gezhouba dam in about 4 years and then to transfer the labor force to construct the more ambitious TGD (Hong Qingyu, 1988; Lieberthal & Oksenberg, 1988, chap. 6).

Gezhouba took nearly 20 years to complete, rather than the original much shorter anticipated time. It also ran substantially over the initial budget. But for purposes of the present inquiry, the most important aspect of Gezhouba is that it brought together a construction force of nearly 50,000 people. The YVPO and the other units involved in this dam's development oversaw the construction of a new city, located to the west of the Gezhouba Dam site itself, to house these workers and their families (Ludlow, 1980).

With the completion of the Gezhouba Dam in the late 1980s, one of the main pressures to forge ahead with the TGD is precisely the existence of this very large labor force. The force basically is being kept in place to work on the TGD, and none of the units that control these workers would like to reduce their personnel roster through reassignment or force reductions. But as of spring 1992, there is little for these workers to do. In addition the TGD has very different construction requirements from those of Gezhouba. The TGD configuration and location are such that it will require far greater use of sophisticated heavy equipment and, ideally, far fewer construction workers. But the construction teams will exert tremendous pressures to adopt an approach that will enable them to bring the whole Gezhouba construction force into play, and this idea will be seen by other officials in China as fair and appropriate, given the high employment bureaucratic norm (based on interviews with Chinese officials).

Because the units that actually will build the dam have the same bureaucratic rank as the YVPO, essentially the TGD designers (the YVPO) will have no line authority over the actual builders. Compromises, therefore, will be necessary to increase the size of the labor force that can be employed to construct this important dam. China's bureaucratic culture, thus, will affect seriously the approach taken to actual dam construction.

Neglect of Economic Cost-Benefit Analysis

Fifth, the bureaucratic culture of Beijing seriously undervalues the notion of cost-effectiveness. This norm of neglecting economic analysis probably stems from several sources. In part, it reflects the fact that China during the 1950s adopted a Soviet model of economic organization, replete with administratively fixed prices for all major industrial items. As a result of this adoption of administrative prices plus very little use of foreign trade from the late 1950s until the late 1970s, it became virtually impossible to conduct an economic analysis of domestic projects based on realistic shadow prices. Such analyses, therefore, received little weight.

Beyond the difficulty of obtaining real price data, another factor also encouraged neglect of serious cost-benefit analysis; that is, the key decision-makers were officials who had joined the revolution before 1949 and who, in most cases, were either illiterate or semiliterate individuals from China's rural areas. Major tensions arose between this politically dominant cohort and China's relatively small group of technically trained personnel, especially those personnel who had received Western education before 1949. As a result, those who held political power tended to view with disdain and actual hostility the more sophisticated Western tools of economic analysis that only a few foreign-trained intellectuals knew how to apply. To the victors in the revolutionary wars, what counted were real results—jobs, products, budgets, prestige, and power—rather than the sophisticated formulas and obscure concepts of technical economists.[11]

The result of this view is that, until the 1980s, the planning for the TGD took place with a remarkable lack of serious economic analysis of the costs and benefits of the project. The first serious attention to this dimension of the project came in the wake of a study mission by the United States Bureau of Reclamation, which recommended that the YVPO undertake the type of cost-benefit analysis routinely done on American water resource projects (Lieberthal & Oksenberg, 1988, chap. 6).

Although efforts have been made to carry out pertinent economic analyses of the TGD during the 1980s, these efforts remain, overall, remarkably thin (Lieberthal & Oksenberg, 1988, pp. 279-281; Wang Jiazhu, 1988). China's bureaucratic culture regarding this dimension is changing (as explained below), but such deeply embedded cultural norms evolve very slowly. This is, in part, a matter requiring considerable time to master the tools necessary to carry out a sophisticated economic analysis. Beyond matters of methodology, though, is an issue of mindset. At an operational level in the Chinese bureaucratic world, few officials, even in 1992, placed priority on economic efficiency over such other values as high employment, larger budgets, enhanced prestige, and so forth. Put differently, high prestige flows far more easily from a demonstrated ability to increase one's personnel roster and to take on new projects than it does from effecting major cost savings or eliminating a project that would have been very wasteful.

Bureaucratic Departmentalism

Finally, China's bureaucratic culture establishes important barriers to effective communication and cooperation across bureaucratic boundaries. The most important "great walls" in China are actually the divisions between the bureaucratic organizations that govern the country. This fact is true, notwithstanding the strong incentives toward consensus building noted above.

The Chinese have a term for this difficulty in achieving cooperation: *departmentalism*. This phenomenon evidently stems from a number of factors. Beijing stresses secrecy regarding almost all matters taken up by the governing bureaucracies; therefore there is a generalized reluctance to share information across boundaries within the government. In addition, the vast majority of officials spend their entire careers within one functional bureaucratic system. They therefore tend strongly to view projects from the point of view of the potential effect of the undertaking on the resources and prestige of their own bureaucratic niche. One of the most powerful resources in a society as closed as is China is information itself, and thus information tends to be hoarded with a vengeance (Harding, 1982). The reformers of the 1980s, as explained below, have tried hard to modify this situation, but the results to date have been very limited.

This information hoarding and difficulty in cooperation has hampered decision making on the TGD project throughout its history. Each bureaucracy has tended to present the others with only the results of its analysis without providing the underlying data and methodologies. Not surprisingly the debate over construction of the dam has been informed by widely differing estimates of key parameters (such as the size and cost of the refugee resettlement problem) arrived at by different relevant bureaucratic units.

One of the more visible repercussions of this phenomenon has been in the use of foreign expertise in the 1980s to improve decision making on the dam. During that decade foreigners began to become involved in various types of pertinent studies. It became apparent, though, that each foreign advisory unit was employed by just one of the key actors in the TGD deliberations and was kept largely or wholly ignorant of the actual overall state of play on decision making about the project (based on interviews with foreign advisers to the TGD). Thus, for example, those American consultants brought in by the YVPO consistently received advice to the effect that the TGD was about to be approved, and they remained remarkably ill-informed about the actual meetings and concerns that were shaping the TGD prospects.

The Reforms Since 1978

The reformers that seized the initiative in Chinese politics in the late 1970s took many measures during the ensuing decade to change some of the characteristics of China's bureaucratic culture. They, in general, viewed this culture as standing in the way of the country's achieving the type of technologically dynamic, economically efficient growth that would prove critical to long-term prosperity and security.

In several areas the reformers took particularly strong initiatives. First, they sought to increase the transparency of the economic decision-making system and to rationalize the terms on which such decisions were reached. These broad goals involved a number of concrete efforts.

Beginning in the early 1980s, the reformers stressed the importance of performing economic feasibility studies on major projects. These studies were to go beyond testing merely the physical possibilities of doing the project and were to address the costs and future economic benefits of the undertaking. This change of heart was sparked concretely by the very poor quality of decision making regarding the Baoshan steel plant near Shanghai at the end of the 1970s.[12] Subsequently China received a great deal of advice from the World Bank and the IMF regarding both feasibility studies and economic transparency, and the reformers used this foreign advice as a tool to pry open their own bureaucracies (Jacobson & Oksenberg, 1990).

In addition, the reformers' overall desire to increase the use of market forces and to invite foreign participation in the country's economic development created strong incentives to rationalize China's price structure. Actual changes in prices were constrained by the fear of rampant inflation, should controlled prices be allowed to float freely.[13] The reformers, therefore, undertook a series of partial measures to adjust particular prices and to allow the prices for portions of output to float within defined levels (Harding, 1987, pp. 110-112, 285). The result proved far less effective in producing market-oriented behavior—or true prices—than the reformers had hoped, but some progress was made. The enhanced role of foreign firms in the economy also began to make it easier for the Chinese to determine shadow prices for their goods that better approximated real international competitive prices.

The reformers also developed new staff organizations to overcome some of the bureaucratic problems noted above. In particular, Zhao Ziyang, the premier and/or general-secretary of the Communist Party for most of the 1980s, worked hard to develop a set of "research institutes" in the State Council to assist in policy formulation through overcoming bureaucratic boundaries and analyzing more effectively externalities in policy decision. The staff members of these institutes developed ties throughout the country's bureaucratic leviathan to obtain information for policy analysis (Halpern, 1992, pp. 125-149).

Finally, the reformers made a concentrated effort after 1983 to retire the older officials who had joined the revolution before 1949 and to replace them with more technically competent younger people (Manion, 1992, pp. 216-244). These incoming officials, presumably, would be less wedded to old notions of maximizing employment and minimizing economic analysis, and this would impact on the bureaucratic culture described above.[14]

All of these reform initiatives have had an impact, but in virtually every case the impact has been limited and the results sometimes very different from what had been intended. Overall, prices have not been rationalized to the extent that economic results outweigh other factors in China's decision making (Huang Yasheng, 1990; Lieberthal & Oksenberg, 1988, chap. 4; Walder, 1989, 1991, pp. 308-333). Even younger officials act according to many of the same considerations that shaped the behavior of their predecessors because cultural norms have not changed sufficiently to provide distinctly different incentives to ambitious cadres (Lieberthal & Prahalad, 1989).

In addition, the emphasis in the 1980s on greater use of feasibility studies and on greater freedom to raise objections has made it increasingly legitimate for dissenting bureaucratic units to pursue their own positions more tenaciously in the decision-making process. No longer do these units run as high a risk of being castigated for being obstreperous in the face of a desire by upper levels to move a project along. Now new arguments based on additional detailed studies have a kind of inherent legitimacy that enables disgruntled participants effectively to tie up the decision-making process on major projects. The top leaders, anxious to demonstrate their support for rational decision making, are now far more reluctant simply to ride roughshod over bureaucratic dissenters in order to launch a major effort.

Conclusion: The Three Gorges Dam
and China's Bureaucratic Culture

This analysis provides only a partial picture of the complex issues that swirl around the decision making on the Three Gorges Dam project. It by no means exhausts the range of ways bureaucratic culture has affected the process of decision making on this dam. Rather, its goal has been more modest.

This analysis has sought to demonstrate a simple, powerful observation: that bureaucratic norms have played and continue to play a very important role in decision making on the TGD and that they will affect implementation of this project, too. Many of the norms described are found also, to a greater or lesser extent, in other bureaucracies—they are not uniquely "Chinese." But the particular combination of traits and the extent to which they characterize China's bureaucratic behavior are noteworthy and warrant referring to this combination of norms as indicative of China's "bureaucratic culture." The characteristics of this "culture" have the potential to change more rapidly than the types of traits that often are subsumed under the notion of national culture, but they are, nevertheless, of long-term duration and change only over protracted periods of time.

The bureaucratic culture described above made it, on balance, very difficult to reach agreement to construct the TGD. As noted, moreover, even with the formal NPC approval in April 1992, it remains possible that the dam will never, in fact, be built. If dam construction should commence, however, it is almost certain that foreigners will play a substantial role as advisers and financial supporters and in other capacities. In the mid-1980s an American-based consortium formed to propose a bid to build the Three Gorges Dam. The details of their initial proposal never became public, but enough information leaked to provide a sense of the approach being advocated. This approach sought to minimize the use of labor and to use sophisticated machinery to the full extent warranted by the dam construction conditions at the Three Gorges. It posited a situation in which the foreigners could carry out their part of the overall effort largely without interference from territorial authorities in China. The key basis of calculation was that of a rigorous cost-benefit analysis, wherein the consortium sought to provide the final product in the shortest possible time and with the least cost.

This American-led effort did not bear fruit. Had Beijing's leaders agreed to this approach, however, it would almost certainly have encountered a very significant amount of trouble during implementation. Put simply, the bureaucratic culture of the American consortium—stressing discipline, technical sophistication, cost control, a lean work force, and top speed—clashed in too many respects with the equally strong bureaucratic culture of the Chinese officials with whom they would have to cooperate. Given this situation, even if the consortium were able to deliver fully on its promises (a prospect made less likely by the clash of bureaucratic cultures), many on the Chinese side would view the American-led effort as mean-spirited, misguided, and, at best, only partially successful. Throughout project implementation, moreover, the Americans would view actions by their Chinese counterparts—actions that reflect China's own bureaucratic culture—as amounting to little more than outright Chinese obstructionism.

Thus foreigners will find that they fare badly in working on this project unless they have some understanding of the consequences of the six characteristics of China's bureaucratic culture enumerated above: (a) the nonrepresentation of interests and the importance of bureaucratic missions, (b) the relationship-structuring ranking system, (c) the importance of territorial actors, (d) the high value attached to maximizing employment, (e) the continuing discomfort with economic cost-benefit analysis, and (f) the great reluctance to cooperate fully with other bureaucracies. Foreign firms hired to work with the YVPO, the design organ for the TGD, must understand, for example that this body cannot exercise control over the people who are actually building the dam. Many of the activities of the YVPO, therefore, will be aimed at reaching compromises with those independent construction units but, in accordance with the general norm of keeping secrets, the YVPO is extremely unlikely to inform its foreign advisers of the reasons for its behavior and decisions. The foreign advisers, in turn, may easily make the mistake of assuming that all of the details built into the design actually will guide the activities of those who are constructing the dam structure.

This phenomenon of bureaucratic culture is not, of course, limited to either the Three Gorges Dam or to China itself. Because Chinese society is bureaucratized to an unusual degree and the Chinese bureaucracies themselves are of uniquely large scale, these phenomena may be more important in China than they would be in other countries. The fact that the TGD impacts in such major fashion on the core missions of so many functional and territorial bureaucratic actors, moreover, probably makes it an unusually powerful example of the effect of bureaucratic culture on decision making. But these "cultural" matters are, overall, more general problems, and they warrant careful examination with respect to all major projects that require international cooperation around the globe.

Notes

1. This section draws heavily from Lieberthal & Oksenberg, 1988, chapter 6.

2. The actual benefits realized will also depend on the dam's effects on silting and downstream scouring (the latter due to a method of proposed operation called "detaining the clear water and discharging turbid water"), and thus debate continues to take place on this issue. For a basically pessimistic assessment, see Fang Zongdai (1988a).

3. See, overall, the contributions to *Chinese Geography and Environment, 1*(3-4), (Fall and Winter 1988): Fang Zongdai 1988a, 1988b; Fang Zongdai & Wang Shouzhong, 1988; Hong Quingyu, 1988; Wang Jiazhu, 1988.

4. Some flavor of the dispute over the number of refugees is provided in Fang Zongdai and Wang Shouzhong (1988).

5. For a discussion of the concept of *interests* in Chinese culture, see Nathan (1985). Also pertinent is Strand (1990).

6. The Yangtze Valley Planning Office (YVPO) actually was resurrected from a comparable office that the Kuomintang had established before 1949.

7. This ministry sometimes has existed as a separate Ministry of Water Resources and at other times has been merged to form a Ministry of Water Resources and Electric Power.

8. This Ministry of Power, too, has gone through a number of changes in its name and in its associations with related ministries.

9. Gold plating in the United States typically does not result from consensus building, though.

10. For the peculiar results of reforms on the behavior of officials and enterprise managers, see Huang Yasheng (1990); Lieberthal & Oksenberg (1988, chap. 4); and Walder (1989).

11. Lord (1990, pp. 70-93) conveys a flavor of this. See also Hong Yung Lee (1991).

12. The decision-making shortcomings of this project became public because the project involved large-scale cooperation with Japanese firms. See Ryosei Kokubun (1986).

13. China's basically monopoly-dominated economy, in any case, would have made full market conversion produce the problems of monopoly capitalism, rather than the advantages of unfettered competition.

14. For an analysis of cadre change and its potential impact, see Li Cheng & White (1990).

PART III

ANALYSIS

13

Implications for Practitioners

JESWALD W. SALACUSE

Conventional wisdom holds that differences in culture among negotiators are almost always an obstacle to agreement. But culture in a
negotiation can be much more than an obstacle: It can be a weapon, a fortress,
or a bridge.

For the most part, the cases in this book support the traditional view, for
they illustrate in many ways that when the two sides at the negotiating table
come from different cultures, this fact invariably complicates a negotiation.
Culture is a powerful factor shaping how people think, communicate, and
behave. It therefore affects how they negotiate. The process of negotiating a
purely domestic relationship and negotiating an international relationship
have much in common. But surely the factor that is almost always present in
international negotiations and generally absent from domestic negotiations is a difference in culture.

In talking about their experiences, practitioners of international negotiation invariably point to differences in culture as among the more difficult,
yet intriguing, elements they have faced. The practitioner's fascination
with culture in negotiation has spawned what amounts to a distinct literary

genre: the "Negotiating With . . ." literature. Numerous books and articles, bearing such titles as "Negotiating With the Japanese," "Negotiating With the Arabs," and "Negotiating With the Chinese," purport to lead the novice through the intricacies of negotiating in specific foreign cultures. (For a bibliography of such literature, see Salacuse, 1991, pp. 174-183.)

This literature is concerned primarily with culture's effect on negotiating style—the way persons from different cultures conduct themselves in negotiating sessions. Thus these books and articles tell us that the Japanese seek to avoid conflict and therefore use the words "it is difficult" to mean "no"; that the French first seek agreement on basic principles before talking about details; and that Arabs and Thais are offended by the sight of the soles of their counterparts' shoes during a negotiating session. Failure to understand these stylistic differences can impede the two sides reaching agreement. Culture, then, is a barrier to understanding. The case studies in this book also illustrate differences in style and how they may complicate negotiations. For example, the Israeli preference for direct forms of communication and the Egyptian preference for indirect forms served to exacerbate relations between the two sides. The Egyptians interpreted Israeli directness as aggression and, therefore, were insulted. The Israelis viewed Egyptian indirectness with impatience and suspected them of insincerity and of not saying what they meant.

Although style is important, it is only one element in a negotiation—only one way in which culture can create an obstacle to agreement. Unlike the "Negotiating With . . ." literature, what all the case studies show is that culture also can have a profound impact on the very substance of the negotiation itself. For one thing, the rivers that were the subject of the negotiations were given different meanings by the negotiators because of their individual cultures. For another, in most of the cases, differing cultural values were at the heart of the conflict that the negotiating sides were seeking to resolve. In a sense the disputes in each of the case studies were profoundly cultural in nature.

Most experienced international practitioners know that the most difficult cultural problems in a negotiation are not about style—about when to shake hands and when not to show the sole of your shoe. The most difficult cultural problems are those that center around differences in values—particularly when those values concern national identity, as they do in many of the cases in this book. The fundamental cultural differences between northern and southern Sudanese, between Arabs and Turks, between Israelis and Arabs are not matters of negotiating style. Rather they are matters of deeply held beliefs by each of the communities who sent those negotiators to the table.

Although culture has a profound effect on negotiation, it is well to remember that no negotiator is a cultural robot. Behavior at the negotiating table can be affected by numerous other factors as well—the personality of the negotiator, the organization that the negotiator represents, the specific context in which a particular negotiation is taking place. In short, negotiators who enter a foreign culture should be careful not to allow cultural stereotypes to determine their relationship with the parties on the other side of the table. The "Negotiating With . . ." literature has a tendency to create cultural stereotypes, and these stereotypes, if accepted, may distort reality. For example, a person negotiating with a culture stereotyped as "hard and shrewd bargainers" might wrongly treat the other side's concessions with great skepticism but would tend to view the very same concessions from a culture characterized as "open and honest" as a good faith effort to reach agreement.

A fundamental question for any negotiator is: What is the culture I am dealing with, and how does it affect the negotiation I am engaged in? The definition of culture used in this book is "a set of shared and enduring meanings, values, and beliefs that characterize national, ethnic, or other groups and orient their behavior." Does this mean that everything that is foreign and unfamiliar to a negotiator should be considered as "culture"? Certainly not.

In determining which phenomena are cultural, one should emphasize the words *"shared* and *enduring* meanings, values, and beliefs"—particularly those meanings, values, and beliefs associated with a particular ethnic group or community. Although the bureaucracies of each negotiator definitely affect the negotiating process, as the case study on China's Three Gorges Dam project clearly demonstrates, one wonders whether bureaucratic values should be classed as culture or whether they should not be recognized in a separate category as "bureaucracy." Certainly it is difficult to label particular bureaucratic behavior in China or elsewhere as "enduring." Experienced negotiators know that the other side's bureaucracy affects the negotiating process, but they do not ordinarily consider it to be "culture." Bureaucracy can be as important as culture in a negotiation; consequently it may be better to recognize it as a distinct variable in a negotiation and not subsume it with the many other factors that go to make up culture.

If differences in culture are a distinguishing characteristic of international negotiations, as opposed to purely domestic negotiations, what precise impact does culture have on the process of negotiation? In short, what is the problem with culture? Culture is always present in any negotiation, domestic or international, because negotiators always belong to or represent a culture of one sort or another. Culture becomes a problem in negotiation when the negotiators belong to or represent *different* cultures. The problem of culture in negotiation is one of *cultural differences*. And cultural differences complicated each of the case studies in this book.

But to point to cultural differences is not sufficient. Cultural differences existed in the negotiations over the Rhine, yet the parties were able to achieve agreement, while the cultural differences in the negotiations over the Nile, Jordan, and Euphrates contributed to failure. Beyond noting the existence of cultural differences, one must seek to determine the nature of those differences.

Culture: A Weapon and a Fortress

The obstacle created by cultural differences in a negotiation can often be dismantled with patient dialogue between the parties. Thus the experienced American business executive in Japan, through observation and study, can come to understand the nuances of the Japanese negotiating style, and the Japanese diplomat in Washington, through diligence and patient inquiry, will arrive at an understanding of how U.S. government officials think and communicate. But some kinds of cultural differences are more than simple barriers; they create seemingly unbridgeable divisions that appear to separate the parties irrevocably and permanently.

The case studies indicate that cultural differences become the greatest obstacles to a negotiated agreement when one party fears that the other side will seek to impose its culture or to use it to dominate. In the negotiations between northerners and southerners in the Sudan, the southern Sudanese clearly perceived the northerners as intending to impose their culture on the south. In the negotiations over the Euphrates, the Arabs seemed obsessed with memories of the Ottoman Turk domination of Arab lands and, moreover, felt that the Turks believed themselves to be culturally superior to the Arabs. In the negotiations between Arabs and Israelis over the Jordan River basin, each side viewed the other's culture as potentially a threat. Thus cultural differences became equated with differences in power between the two sides. If one side represents a dominant culture, the weaker side may view the dominant culture as a weapon that will damage the weaker side's interests—one of the greatest of which is cultural cohesion. For example, in the civil rights movement in the United States in the 1960s and 1970s, black power advocates opposed the kind of racial integration that would require African Americans to adopt the symbols of white culture and to give up traditionally black culture. To the extent that African

Americans became integrated into white culture, black power groups would lose influence with the African-American community.

Similarly, in France, ultranationalist political leaders, such as Le Pen, claim to see the presence of large numbers of Arab immigrants as a weapon aimed at traditional French culture. Emphasizing the threat of a cultural weapon allows Le Pen to mobilize followers and to increase his political power.

When does culture become a weapon in negotiation? It becomes a weapon when one party perceives the other side's culture as presenting the risk of forcibly changing the "shared and enduring meanings, values, and beliefs that characterize" *the first party's ethnic group*. Thus the southern Sudanese clearly saw in northern Sudanese culture the threat that southern Sudanese culture would be changed by the north—for example, through the imposition on the south of Islamic law. And the Arabs and Israelis saw in each other's culture the threat of forcible change to their own respective cultures.

Faced with a culture that it perceives as a weapon aimed against it, a party to negotiation becomes defensive and uses its own culture as a fortress to protect itself from a cultural onslaught. In the Jordan River basin negotiations, for example, Israelis and Arabs stressed their individual cultures to defend their respective national identities. In the Sudan, the southerners, threatened by northern culture, reasserted their cultural identity to protect themselves. One method of using your culture to defend yourself is to demonize the other side on the basis of alleged negative cultural traits—a phenomenon that clearly was present in the negotiations over the Nile, Jordan, and Euphrates rivers. The more one side appears to assert its culture in a negotiation, the more the other side retreats within its cultural fortress. As a result the distance dividing the two sides at the table increases.

One of the lessons of this weapon-and-fortress phenomenon is that negotiators should try to understand how their culture is perceived by the other side. Persons from dominant cultures, such as the northern Sudanese in their relationship with southerners or Europeans in their negotiations with poor developing countries, may assume that the other side admires, envies, or even desires to adopt some or all of the dominant culture; consequently the dominant side might feel that demonstrating cultural superiority will influence the other side to come to agreement. In reality, of course, the weaker side often fears the dominant culture and views any signs of cultural superiority as aggressiveness and a potential threat.

A second lesson for negotiators is to avoid all actions and statements that the other side might interpret as cultural arrogance and aggressiveness. Insisting on structuring a transaction the "way it is done in America" may not convince the other side of the superiority of the technique proposed. Rather that statement may seem a manifestation of a cultural arrogance that will be met with the defensive response "that's not the way we do things here" or "when in Rome. . . . " Insisting on negotiating in a particular language may, under certain conditions, be interpreted as an assertion of cultural superiority—because one of the most salient manifestations of any culture is language.

It is important to recognize when the other side in a negotiation has raised its own culture against you as a defensive fortress. Such behavior may be a clear signal that it feels threatened by your culture, and, therefore, you need to look at your own behavior. Other symptoms of fortress behavior are a rigid insistence by the other side on respect for its cultural formalities or assertions that "outsiders" could never understand its culture. The Japanese sometimes adopt this stance in their negotiations with Westerners.

Culture as a Bridge

Instead of serving as a weapon or a fortress, culture also can become a bridge between the two sides in an international negotiation. More precisely, one side can try to use the other side's culture to build that bridge. Skilled negotiators understand that they must find some common basis with the other side on which to build a relationship. One might call this a "bridging" technique in negotiation. When President Sadat, in his meetings with the Sudanese, emphasized that his mother had been born in the Sudan, he was seeking to use a common cultural thread to build that connection. Sadat was engaged in bridging. In effect, he was saying: "Like you, I am Sudanese; therefore we have some common cultural links. I understand you and I value your culture. Therefore you can have confidence in me." Of course, when the precise area of his mother's birth—west, north, or south Sudan—kept changing with his Sudanese interlocutor's own region of origin, the genuineness of Sadat's cultural links to the Sudan came into question. The essence of this technique is for one side to create community with the other side. An African American negotiating a business transaction in Nigeria or Ghana stresses his or her African heritage as a way of building a relationship with the negotiating counterparts. An Italian American in Rome will seek to do the same thing.

In only one of the cases was any attempt made to use culture to build bridges. In the negotiations over the Rhine, mutual respect for the parties' cultures contributed to success. Although the author suggests that an "international culture" was at work, it is also possible that the parties understood and appreciated each others' culture—a factor that is a necessary first step in fostering confidence and trust among those at the negotiating table. Unlike the negotiations between northern and southern Sudanese concerning the Jonglei project, negotiations among Europeans over the Rhine did not demonstrate evidence of cultural aggression or cultural defensiveness. In the Rhine case, the parties negotiated as cultural equals. In the Sudan they clearly did not. Indeed the Rhine negotiators seemed to emphasize their common cultural identity—that of being Europeans—rather than their individual nationalistic identities. What the cases suggest is that a negotiator faced with a counterpart from another culture should seek to use that other culture as a bridge—as a means for creating a relationship with that counterpart.

Faced with a different culture, a negotiator should ask how he or she may use that culture to build a link or relationship with the other side. If some common historical element exists, such as the fact that Sadat's mother was born in Sudan, a negotiator should seek to establish that element and to make it known to the other side. But in many cases, such common cultural trait is lacking. How, for example, can a U.S. negotiator, whose parents came from Sweden, use culture as a bridge in conducting negotiations in China or in Thailand. One way is to demonstrate interest in, knowledge of, respect for, and appreciation of Chinese or Thai culture. Failure to demonstrate interest in the culture of the other side can be interpreted easily as an act of cultural superiority and arrogance—a statement that the other side's culture is not significant or important. As the chapter on the Jordan River basin negotiations suggests, one can begin to break down the wall of cultural differences, not by ignoring those differences, but rather by encouraging the other side to talk about its culture. Thus the negotiator should develop ways of inquiring about the other side's culture and of encouraging the other side to talk about its culture. Questions about culture, when framed in an uncritical way, are messages that state, "Your culture (and therefore you and your people) is interesting, important, and worth learning about." Invariably, sincere questions about culture will elicit sincere answers. People like to talk about themselves, and one's culture is very much a part of one's identity.

A second implication is that negotiators should be tolerant and respectful of cultural differences. Once differences are understood, negotiators should seek ways of accommodating them. One technique is to find parallels or similarities in cultural practices and beliefs between the two sides. Through this approach a negotiator is saying to his or her counterpart that they both share a common humanity and that shared human values underlie their two cultures. An example of this common humanity was the shared sense of European cultural traits among the participants in the Rhine negotiations.

In the midst of a particularly tense negotiation between Americans and Israelis, Golda Meir expressed sincere sympathy to one of the U.S. negotiators whose wife recently had died, and she alluded to her own recent loss of a loved one. That interaction between the two negotiators changed the atmosphere dramatically. Meir's expression of sympathy and her reference to a shared tragic experience served to build a relationship—a bridge—that led to more productive negotiations between Israelis and Americans in the talks. This incident suggests yet another way to bridge the cultural divide: to find some common experience—often a cultural experience—that the two negotiators share and to use that common experience to begin building a bridge. Thus the fact that an American diplomat and a Swedish diplomat both attended the London School of Economics can serve as one pillar on which to begin building a needed bridge. To accomplish bridging effectively, one must, of course, seek to know and understand one's counterpart. In one case, for example, conversation between a London-trained Nigerian lawyer and French-trained Benin judge was stiff and halting for over an hour, until they discovered by accident that they were both Yoruba and could converse in a common mother tongue. A further implication is that, in preparation for an international negotiation, a practitioner should try to learn as much as possible about the other side's culture. How do you learn a culture? Certainly a study of the other party's history is a good beginning. Consultation with persons who know or have negotiated with that culture is also useful. One of the functions of consultants in many international business negotiations is to advise on the cultural problems related to the talks. But as indicated above, the richest sources of cultural knowledge may be your counterpart on the other side of the negotiation table.

And finally, sometimes a basis for a bridge can be found in a third culture, a foreign culture that both negotiators admire or appreciate. For example, trade negotiations between a Thai diplomat and an American official improved measurably when they realized that they both had a deep love of Italian opera.

Knowledge of the other side alone is not enough to allow successful bridging. Cultural bridging, like bridge construction, requires the cooperation of the parties at both ends of the divide, and no negotiator will permit a bridge to be built if he or she feels threatened or sees the bridge as a long-term danger to security. Consequently negotiators who want to build a bridge to their counterpart must be concerned to strengthen the other side's sense of security, not weaken it, as occasionally happens in an international negotiation.

The Cross-Cultural Negotiator

A related question, but one not considered by the cases, is: What kinds of persons are best able to conduct cross-cultural negotiations? That is a supremely practical question, for no negotiation can begin until the respective sides have chosen their negotiators. Persons having the same culture of the other side may or may not be an effective choice. On the one hand, such persons are certainly knowledgeable about the culture and its potential impact on the negotiation. On the other hand, the other side may consider them to be "turncoats" or "traitors" because they are not representing their culture of origin, but rather that of an adversary. For example, a Syrian-born Jew who had immigrated to Israel might not be an effective member of an Israeli negotiating team in talks with Syria.

Anecdotal evidence suggests that bicultural persons—individuals born in one culture but living and working in another—may be highly effective international negotiators, not because they have substantive knowledge of a relevant culture, but because through experience they have learned to communicate and relate effectively to persons from other cultures. Similarly persons from minority or subordinate groups within a given society, who have learned to relate to members of a dominant group, also may have developed the skills useful in cross-cultural communication and negotiation. They have learned to interpret correctly the cultural messages and signals from the dominant group and to communicate to that group in its own language. For example, African American or women executives and diplomats who have worked successfully in predominantly white male corporate bureaucracies probably have mastered many of the same skills that an effective cross-cultural negotiator needs in an international negotiation.

The case study on the Rhine asserts that experienced negotiators may develop an "international culture," which allows them to overcome the barriers caused by national cultural differences. This proposition has yet to be established by empirical evidence and is open to question. An individual's culture is pervasive, something that is very much a part of one's identity and personality. It is not changed as easily as a suit of clothes. A Western businessperson who meets a highly skilled negotiator from another country, such as former oil minister Sheik Zaki Yamani of Saudi Arabia or Sony president Akio Morita of Japan, may be tempted to conclude that because of their sophistication, the two men are somehow less attached to their own cultures or that they have become "Western" or "international." Such conclusions are not only culturally arrogant but also greatly deceptive. Yamani remains thoroughly Saudi, and Morita is still very Japanese. What both have gained through years of experience in international life is the knowledge of how to communicate with persons from other cultures. To the Western businessperson, Yamani and Morita seem "Westernized" because they are communicating with Westerners in a way that Westerners readily understand. Both Yamani and Morita, through experience, have become skilled at cultural bridging.

Similarly, in the Rhine negotiations, the various European negotiators appeared to have an international culture, but what they really had developed was a way of communicating with one another that could be readily understood. That method of communication, though useful, does not qualify as a culture in the sense of an "enduring set of values of a particular ethnic group."

Moreover, although some negotiators may like to believe that they have "risen above" their own cultures and have become culturally international, that assertion is, in most cases, a self-deception and, if really true in a few instances, may actually limit their effectiveness as negotiators. If negotiators are perceived by the persons they represent as not attached to their common culture, their principals may repudiate them. For example, the negotiators of the Maastricht Treaty to advance European political unity probably saw themselves culturally as Europeans, a factor that facilitated agreement on the treaty's text. But their failure to represent national interests contributed to the contested response that the treaty received in the individual nations of Europe.

As is well known, any international negotiation is accompanied by internal negotiations within the respective sides represented at the table. Negotiators who have lost touch with their culture may find that their effectiveness in those internal negotiations is reduced substantially as a result. In the Sudan case, for example, Abel Alier, the head of the regional government in the south, was accused of not representing southern culture and of having his interests too aligned with those of the northern government in Khartoum. Sometimes nationalist elements in a country suspect that their country's diplomatic service is guilty of the same tendencies. Thus the challenge for effective international negotiators is to remain linked to their own culture, while at the same time finding ways to build bridges to the culture with whose representatives they are negotiating.

14

Lessons for Theory and Research

GUY OLIVIER FAURE

JEFFREY Z. RUBIN

A ny international negotiation is an encounter between cultures and a confrontation among values. Understanding the consequences of such chemistry, let alone predicting these consequences, may seem to require mysterious acts of divination, whether it be reading poultry entrails, examining the shoulder blades of mammals, or inspecting the footprints of a fox in a patch of sand.

In this final chapter, we build on two preliminary and straightforward observations. First, culture provides significance to objects and gives meaning to action. A river is more than a moving body of water: It is a divine being, a foster mother, or the symbolic basis for ancestral hate. Second, negotiator action builds on meaning, informing the negotiator how, according to the implicit rules and norms of one's culture, it makes sense to act and what underlying meanings to ascribe.

Memory, Freud's "magic slate," establishes the diachronic aspects of cultural activity, resulting not only in the fixation of past experience but also in its integration, interpretation, and transformation. The fact that historical memory, like mythology, has no authors, only narrators, makes it easy to appreciate the importance of culture's effects. In short, the impact of culture, in negotiation and beyond, is vast.

This book has tried to look beyond the fuzzy question of whether culture has an influence on international negotiation to more precise and potentially answerable questions. First, under what conditions and according to which circumstances do cultural aspects of negotiation play a role? Second, how do these cultural elements have the impact they do—what are the variables involved, and what are the affected components of the negotiation? Third, what are the observed consequences of these variables, with what induced effects, on which outcomes?

In the first section of this chapter we address these questions; the answers suggested have been based on the case analyses. Methodological issues are the focus of the following section, while in the third section we address several important scientific issues and questions for the researcher with an interest in the study of culture. In the final section we return to the four analytic chapters on culture and address the question of whether and when culture matters.

Lessons From the Cases

When Does Culture Play a Role: Limiting Conditions

This book deliberately has introduced a common link among the different cases in order to facilitate comparative analysis. That link is *water.* In making this choice (see Chapter 6), we are aware that the possible effects of culture may have been "diluted." Each case concerns neighboring populations, cultures living in the vicinity of a common watercourse. Such geographical proximity may reduce or mask cultural differences. Moreover, the fact that the neighboring cultures in the cases chosen are interdependent in a variety of ways suggests that interaction, exchange, and the phenomenon of diffusion draw them closer. In the conclusions that follow, therefore, bear in mind that the cases may have fostered conditions of relatively low intercultural salience. Hence any conclusions regarding culture are *in spite of* forces toward assimilation induced by common interests.

On the other side of this issue is the fact that, with one exception (the Black Sea), all of the cases involve rivers. This factor necessarily implies that some countries or parties are upstream, while others are down, and, as argued earlier (Chapter 6), such asymmetry might bring cultural considerations to the fore. On the basis of the data that emerged from the case studies, it appears that power asymmetry may actually *dampen* the effects of culture by focusing attention on the structural constraints imposed by location along a river, at the expense of the more subtle effects of cultural variables.

A third common characteristic among the cases is the small number of parties involved. For purposes of conceptual simplicity, we deliberately have chosen cases involving two, three, or four parties, drawn from different cultures. Conceivably the influence of culture is greater in cases with fewer parties than in negotiation bringing together a large number of parties as in a major international conference. Lang (Chapter 4) advances the hypothesis that "multilateral negotiations . . . are likely to be less affected by national cultures," and Pisarev (Chapter 9) observes about the Black Sea case that "the multilateral nature of negotiations has played an important part in 'diluting the impact of national culture.' " It thus appears that in those cases involving only two parties (Nile, Jordan), culture may have assumed a more prominent role (because of the small number of parties involved) than in the other cases, involving three or more nations (Rhine, Euphrates, Black Sea) or bureaucratic elements (Yangtze).

The number of negotiating parties to a conflict is but one of a number of variables influencing the impact of culture. Another extremely powerful factor is "history" or, more precisely, "historical memory." Witness the almost millennial religious antagonism between Christians and Muslims around the Black Sea (Chapter 9), the bitter history of relations between Jews and Arabs along the Jordan River (Chapter 11), the Euphrates-induced litigation between Arabs and Turks (Chapter 10), or the tradition of subordination between Arabs and the Nilotic populations of southern Sudan (Chapter 7). Such visions of the past not only govern the choices made by the actors but also overdetermine the emotions with which negotiating problems are perceived and treated.

When structural elements exert an overpowering effect (witness the Rhine case, Chapter 8, where shared concerns about riparian pollution have overshadowed many other considerations), institutional organization, negotiator background, and decision-making mode become fundamental mechanisms that govern negotiation. Indeed the culture that has made a difference along the Rhine is an overweening global "European culture," which has found in the negotiation process an especially favorable medium for expression. Political systems also may be considered as cultural products and, as in the Black Sea case, may contribute to existing or potential difficulties. The learning process through which each side gradually modifies its vision during negotiation then becomes an essential mechanism of cultural management.

The Euphrates case (Chapter 10) offers evidence of a situation that seems to lack any possibility of integrative potential. The conflict is so deeply rooted in culture and ideology that the fact that all three countries (Turkey, Syria, Iraq) are Islamic appears insufficient as an overarching value to enable the parties to move toward settlement. Moreover, both the zero-sum conception of relations between Turkey and its two Arab neighbors and the Syrian-Iraqi conception of their own relationship imply the existence of two exclusive cognitive maps.

Nor has the shared history of life along the Nile (Chapter 7) brought together the different peoples who reside along its banks. Rather it has proved to be a bone of contention, resulting in the political expression of deep religious antagonism that bears on the actors' very identity. The northern part of Sudan has been shaped by the forces of Islam, whereas the Nilotic populations of the south have been influenced deeply by a very different religious system that is key to their identity.

The Jordan River case (Chapter 11) describes human groups caught in a broader conflict, with deeply antagonistic representations of the other side and replete with "demonization of the enemy." Each side tends to interpret the other's every move or gesture as inherently hostile and malevolent. The parties' very conception of the conflict is zero-sum, where *one* side controls the water of the Jordan to the exclusion of the other. By extension, each side believes that it can continue to exist only if the other does not.

In the Yangtze case (Chapter 12), one can see people belonging to the same culture, that of the Chinese bureaucracy, divided against themselves. At the origin of this conflict is the bureaucratic organization itself as a cultural product of the society. The six main characteristics of Chinese bureaucracy (and perhaps other bureaucracies as well), as advanced by Lieberthal, may be helpful in understanding why the process of internal negotiation leads finally to no solution.

The conclusion we reach is not that culture is the *only* explanation of outcome, nor necessarily the *determining* element of the process. Rather the diverse cases invite the observation that any reasonable explanation of what happens in international negotiation must include the cultural aspects of the negotiation relationship.

Ways Cultural Elements Play a Role

Contrary to a widespread view, the cases demonstrate that conflict arises not merely because parties ignore cultural differences or carry distorted interpretations of their respective behavior—that is, because of communication difficulties. Culture has a number of profound effects in its own right. Culture may affect the range of strategies that negotiators develop, as well as the many ways they are implemented through tactical action. The Euphrates and Nile cases (Chapter 10 and 7, respectively) illustrate historical disputes that lead to the introduction of highly distributive strategies. Contacts between neighbors may serve to strengthen negative perceptions, assumptions, and hypotheses. In these two cases, one can see illustrations of what Kremenyuk (Chapter 5) describes as an "introversive negotiating culture"—that is, the culture of a closed society characterized by inflexible negotiating positions that are difficult to change.

The Jordan River case (Chapter 11) provides the canvas against which the moves of an exacerbated and highly symbolic conflict are depicted. The negative dispositional attributions of one's neighbors are heightened by enormous surplus meaning: Jews suspect Arabs of "wanting to complete Hitler's plan of annihilation," while Arabs accuse Jews of "wishing to suck dry their very lifeblood."

The Black Sea (Chapter 9) offers a case in which a learning process has combined with an external threat—that of irreversible pollution—to lead a distributive situation to shift toward a more integrative state. One of the deciding factors in such an evolution seems to be the general regression of ideologically based values, a former major component of the overall culture of the countries involved.

The Rhine case (Chapter 8) illustrates a homogeneous and converging cooperative strategy, from the initial negotiations to their successful conclusion. The parties' shared conception of how to approach the problem of pollution, combined with the emergence of a transnational European culture of resolving conflict by discussion and concession, helps explain this cooperative orientation. In this case one can see something typical of what Kremenyuk calls an "extraversive negotiating culture"—that is, a culture characterized by flexibility and joint problem solving.

On the other hand, the Yangtze (Chapter 12) offers a case in which conflicting bureaucratic strategies lead to the immobilization of a complex system. Each department, each territorial unit, tends to promote its own interests. The result is a process a bit like the immense rivers of Central Asia losing themselves in the sands—going nowhere. Such activity is in itself again archetypal of bureaucratic culture.

Consequences of Culture for Negotiation Outcomes

Culture, expressed through behavior (strategic choices and related tactical action) and reinforced by structural elements, led to pure and simple deadlock on the Euphrates, to a protracted process without the slightest outcome on the Yangtze, to an agreement signed with no intention of implementation along the Nile, and to a mutually satisfactory agreement on the Rhine.

The deadlock in the Euphrates case can be explained by the parties' adoption of different norms of justice and fairness, leading to conflicting conclusions over such issues as the sovereignty principle and the needs rule. The protracted, fruitless negotiations over the Three Gorges Project have their roots in a bureaucratic culture favoring inaction to the taking of even minimal risk. In the case of the Nile, the failure to implement an agreement can be explained in terms of identity problems that an opponent neglected to take into account; ignoring these problems to reach agreement more easily did nothing more than shift the difficulty instead of solving it. The Black Sea case is an advertisement for the beneficial effects of a constructive orientation; starting from the possibility of a litigation procedure that was likely to prevent any progress, the negotiators were able to establish and develop new norms and values that led to more cooperative activity. Last but not least, the Rhine case offers an example of how an emergent common culture can facilitate the resolution of significant difficulties initially arising from the symbolic meaning of the very object of negotiation—namely, the Rhine. At the same time, it shows that culture made of enduring values is not a sluggish or immutable component but is subject to evolution within its own rationale and dynamics.

General Lessons Drawn From the Cases

Each negotiation presents a very specific set of lessons that can be drawn from the influence of culture. One general conclusion is that *culture is multi-faceted: It finds more than one way to have an impact on negotiation process and outcome.* Through such diversity a rich set of options can be thrown into relief, creating a far more complex tapestry than would emerge from some more uniform or mechanistic formulation.

The Nile case (Chapter 7) adds a new question to a very old matter— negotiation as a means of managing identity. It is typically when one of the parties does not take identity into consideration that difficulties arise. Culture *is* identity, because it is culture that ultimately enables human beings to exist and to carry the meanings that allow them to know who and what they are. In the absence of such a requirement, negotiation would be reduced to an encounter between empty forms.

The case of southern Nilotic populations working with their northern counterparts in the Sudan illustrates the importance of what could be called a "cultural mediator." This individual needs to be able to communicate with the cultures involved and, therefore, be in a good position to facilitate the search for an agreement, even to manipulate the parties by playing the role of a communicator or formulator.

The Jordan case (Chapter 11) raises the problem of the management of meaning. In the technical sphere, water appears to Israelis to be an integral part of an ideology of agriculture; to Palestinians it is nothing less than an extension of the land. In the broader sphere, the interactive management of symbols has led to mutual demonization. Negotiation has remained in an embryonic state along the Jordan for as long as it has precisely because the conflict has been defined, not in terms of interests, but as the very core of group identity. Negotiation faces the formidable task of reconciling identities, far more difficult than reconciling interests.

The Euphrates case (Chapter 10) is typical of a competitive situation where cultural norms feed suspicion. The main problem concerns the management of conflicting norms regarding the valuation of a potential agreement's fairness. Such a problem leads to one of the core questions posed in international negotiation theory: Can one conceive of an agreement on substance that does not take into account the principles of fairness that govern the definition of this agreement? In other words, can one speak of two nations reaching efficient solutions without invoking notions of fairness, and doing so by referring to a selected set of values rooted in the cultures of these nations? What occasionally can be observed, though not in this case, is the capacity of culture to integrate former conflicting values into a new set and so to bridge two different concepts of fairness.

The Black Sea case (Chapter 9) offers evidence of the role played by a major cultural component in the life of people—historical memory. If historical memory can be an obstacle to reaching agreement, it also can be the object of attention in its own right—subject to evolution and the negotiation becoming a new means toward this end. Of course, the matter is no longer the social memory of the group, but its impact on the negotiators' memory. In the process of creating new values and gradually modifying old images, the parties were able to evolve a new, more effective way of managing through negotiation.

The Yangtze case (Chapter 12) demonstrates the effects of an organizational culture left to follow its own internal logic. Bureaucratic norms, it seems, invariably lead to decision avoidance, if the alternative is taking decisions that fail to satisfy the departmental interests involved. Here again the field observation can be extrapolated, because its significance goes beyond Chinese culture. Any internal negotiation in which one party is preparing for an upcoming external negotiation is a similar candidate for such dysfunctional behavior.

Finally, the Rhine (Chapter 8) offers an example of what can happen in a situation that allows the integration of common values. Here culture makes a difference by introducing common norms (e.g., those belonging to the professional culture analyzed by Lang, in Chapter 4) and superordinate goals that serve as facilitating factors. If cultural homogeneity is not sufficient to achieve agreement (as underscored by Zartman in Chapter 2), heterogeneity is far from being an insurmountable obstacle. The negotiations over the Rhine introduced an example of true cultural management despite conditions of heterogeneity; values were chosen, developed, and reinforced as a result of the learning afforded by the negotiation process itself.

Taken together, the cases point to the broad set of circumstances in which culture is likely to assume greater or lesser importance in international negotiation. Thus culture may have been a particularly important consideration in the Nile case precisely because factors such as group size or pollution were *not* very prominent. In contrast, the reason culture appears not to have been a very central consideration in the Rhine case is because a particular structural constraint (the demands of addressing a growing pollution problem) had an overpowering effect.

Closer inspection of the other cases lends general support to this observation. Of the six cases in the book, it is the Yangtze (with its preoccupation over matters of bureaucratic functioning in the construction of the Three Gorges Dam), the Black Sea (with its overwhelming concern with pollution), and the Rhine that seem to have been least influenced by cultural considerations. At the other extreme lie the three cases least constrained by structural concerns and most affected by culture: the Jordan, the Nile (with the conflict driven by central identity concerns), and the Euphrates (driven by long-standing historic dissension between Turkey and its two neighbors to the south, as well as the identity struggles between Syria and Iraq). In summary, it appears that *culture's effects on international negotiation are least prominent when structural factors are strong; and culture exerts its most powerful effects when structural factors are in remission.*

Yet another general conclusion that appears justifiable, based on the cases reviewed, is that (other things, such as structural constraints, being equal) *as conflict increases, so does the role of culture in international negotiation.* In our judgment it is the Nile, Jordan, and Euphrates cases that appear to contain conflict of a markedly greater intensity than the other three cases (Rhine, Yangtze, and Black Sea), and it is the former set of cases that most clearly show the signature of culture.

Methodological Issues

Any researcher on negotiation dealing with cultural issues is confronted with the question of method. How can one capture culture? How, more precisely, can one identify and express what is cultural in a negotiation? Techniques used to collect data concerning real-world negotiations must be adapted to the type of information sought and to the conditions of access. Borrowing from research methods used in various social science disciplines, one can identify at least five distinct approaches to the study of culture. These approaches, described briefly below, are ordered in terms of the control they allow the researcher over the object of study.

Approaches to the Study of Culture and Negotiation

First, one can make use of *archival research techniques*. One can examine the firsthand accounts of negotiators from different cultures or of mediators who have intervened in different cultural conflicts and then have written about their experiences. Or one even can examine newspaper accounts of a single negotiation, albeit written by journalists working in different cultures. Each approach makes use of written documents, allowing the researcher to test hypotheses against the backdrop of real, ongoing, and important events. No doubt this was the research approach taken by a number of the case contributors to this book, where it was necessary to rely on eyewitness accounts rather than on one's own testimony as a participant or observer.

Second, researchers interested in the study of culture and negotiation can use a technique borrowed from sociology—the *field survey*. By deliberately selecting a sample of negotiators in different cultures, all of whom are about to negotiate a particular kind of conflict (or who already have had experience doing so), then posing questions to these negotiators concerning their assumptions about the nature of the process, the other negotiator, the measure of a successful outcome, and so on, researchers can test hypotheses about the effects of culture and cultural variables on negotiation. By properly selecting a sample for investigation, it should be possible, at least in principle, to generalize from one's findings to a larger population.

Third, researchers can make use of the *field study* methodology to study the relationship between culture and negotiation. This approach, borrowed from anthropology, requires researchers to position themselves at the margins of a group and then to observe its dynamics. It is this method that probably corresponds most closely to the approach taken by most of the scholars in this book. From their knowledge of the particular water dispute in question, the researchers, though not becoming part of the groups they were observing, did the best job they could of observing the process details of the exchange in question. Some of the case authors, of course, were unable to get quite as close to the unfolding process as others, and their approach, therefore, resembles a bit more the archival method.

Participant observation is a variation on this approach, where researchers, to gather the data of interest, actually become part of the group in question. An important question bears on these observer-analysts: Should they belong to the same culture as one of the parties, or should they be cultural outsiders? Both arrangements have advantages and disadvantages. The first runs the risk of a kind of cultural blindness about one's own culture and selective attention to the other side often to the latter's detriment. The second formula does not really better ensure against these dysfunctionings; moreover, it excludes by definition the possibility of using participant observation techniques. An answer to the difficulties underlined here lies in the capacity of researchers to distance themselves from their object with the help of methodological tools. At the same time, one must continue to acknowledge, as observed earlier, that we are always prisoners of our culture—whatever that culture may happen to be.

Fourth, researchers can attempt to create a *field experiment* of sorts. This approach, unlike the three previous ones (but akin to the fifth and final approach), attempts to introduce independent variables in some systematic way, to manipulate or control them in some fashion, and then to measure certain outcomes that are used to test a set of hypotheses. For example, researchers who wish to examine the effect of communication channels and time limits on negotiation across cultural-national boundaries might elect to approach Americans and Japanese about to undertake business or trade negotiations and then persuade them to negotiate under certain conditions that the researchers would be allowed to control. Some of the negotiations between Americans and Japanese thus might take place by fax, others by phone, still others in a face-to-face exchange. Or negotiations might be structured to take place in the shadow of an impending deadline, while others might require no time limit at all. By systematically introducing the variables whose effects researchers wish to evaluate in the natural setting of a real and ongoing negotiation, they could test a set of hypotheses and work toward the establishment of causal relations.

Fifth and finally is the possibility of designing some sort of *laboratory experiment*. It is experimental social psychologists who have best developed this highly controlled, albeit arguably artificial, approach to conducting research. Artificial though the environment may be, the laboratory experiment allows researchers to systematically introduce variables under highly controlled conditions and then to examine their effects on a carefully chosen set of measures. Clearly many aspects of the relationship between culture and negotiation will *not* lend themselves to study through this approach. Rather than ignore this approach altogether, however, we would encourage researchers interested in culture to consider some of the many ways laboratory experimentation could be conducted. For example, given an interest in understanding the effects of perceptions of negotiators from different cultures on the negotiation process, researchers might wish to systematically introduce labels into a laboratory environment and then study the effect of such labels on attitudes toward, as well as actual, negotiation.

The larger point, then, is this: Although a great many approaches exist for the study of culture and negotiation, researchers—including those whose case analyses are reported here—have largely limited themselves to one or a few of these avenues. We urge future researchers to consider applying as many methods as possible, including the comparison of written with spoken language, and then to examine the extent to which the results that emerge provide convergent evidence that the findings observed truly are robust.

Possible Units of Analysis

Each of the above approaches to study is only as valuable as the researcher's ability to pick the appropriate unit of analysis. Who and what are to be studied? Possibilities include the individual actor, the cultural relationship, the larger system or subsystem, and the very conceptual framework the theorist/researcher uses. Let us consider each of these in turn.

The Individual Actor

Perhaps the most obvious unit of analysis is the individual actor in a cross-cultural conflict. The way an actor sees the game that is going on, as well as the other actors, widely concerns cultural determinations. In some societies a negotiation is first of all a social encounter; in others it is a cultural exchange; in others it is ritualized celebration; in others it is an opportunity to cross swords; and so on (Faure, 1991). The negotiator's behavior will depend narrowly on the first conception he or she has about the nature of the game. Here again it is essential to add to the works concerning these quite fundamental points, as has been done, for instance, by Weiss and Stripp (1985a) in their six national profiles of negotiators.

Actors themselves, crystallizing and expressing the combination of the various elements making a culture, should as negotiators be subjected to studies similar to those done on personality variables. Among the things perceived by the actor are which elements will influence his reactions and what are the attitudes that culturally organize the actions of people in the face of any particular event. For instance, a Swede confronted with a threat probably would not react in the same way as an Indonesian. These predispositions toward action have to be scrutinized in depth.

In focusing on the actor, it is also important to remember that the actor's spontaneous evaluation at the end of a negotiation cannot avoid being culturalized. This fact will influence, sometimes decisively, the negotiations to come. It is important, therefore, that research clarify what culturally appears as a successful negotiation: What, in the mind of the actor, is the meaning of such notions as gain and loss, the relative importance of short-term versus long-term objectives, or the relative importance of relationship versus substance.

The Cross-Cultural Relationship

A second viable unit of analysis for theorists and researchers is the cross-cultural relationship itself. Work in this area has been conducted over the years primarily by those interested in intercultural communication. The studies are rarely systematic, tending to rely on collections of more or less significant anecdotes, often tinged with subjectivity, and, in many cases, aimed at merely producing simplified recipes for action. Fortunately qualitative or quantitative studies by scholars such as Hall (1959) and Hofstede (1980) have achieved a major breakthrough in this domain, although this work does not directly address international negotiation. Here it would be quite necessary to engage research now focusing on intercultural communication between negotiators.[1]

The very phrase "cultural differences," which is the term used most often by scholars, fails to capture the reality of cultural phenomena in a satisfactory way. What bears on the outcome of a negotiation is not the "differences," but the relations between cultures. "Cultural interactions" more accurately expresses what really occurs during this type of encounter. Bicultural negotiations, in particular, may result in a unique combination of both cultures—where the whole is different from the sum of its parts. Then a new and quite intriguing question has to be posed: How does each party understand and evaluate the various events (e.g., demands, concessions) that occur during the process? Will it be done according to criteria belonging to each culture, or will it be done with reference to values stemming from the combination itself? If the second assumption plays some part in the appraisal, such an achievement can be seen as the outcome of a learning process. Thus another important question would concern the way such a process operates. Developing some knowledge on these issues would not only be of great interest but also of major utility for practitioners such as the cultural mediator.

Cultures and Subcultures

If a first unit of analysis is the actor and a second is the culturally defined negotiating relationship, then a third is the subculture(s) and cultures themselves. Traditionally, patterns of culture are linked to individual nations and lead to the definition of national negotiating styles (e.g., Binnendijk, 1987). Chapters 1 and 3 have reviewed some of the work that has examined culture as a whole. But, as observed by Faure and Sjöstedt (Chapter 1) and by Zartman (Chapter 2), a national geographical dimension is not the only one that may make sense. In some circumstances national subcultures are far more relevant, whereas in other situations the aggregation of several countries is the level corresponding to a geographical unit of cultural relevance. In this respect it would be highly desirable to develop research that aims at identifying culturally homogeneous geographical areas and relating it, among other things, to perceptions and attitudes concerning negotiation.

Theoretical Perspectives

Finally, we would argue that theoretical perspectives themselves, as they refer to a homogeneous level, constitute an appropriate unit of analysis in research on culture and negotiation. We believe it is important to frame thinking on negotiation within multiple problematiques that are likely to complement one another. For instance, the perspective adopted by Weiss and Stripp (1985a) is of a descriptive and comparative nature. It relies on a framework organized around 12 variables as foci for cross-cultural comparisons. The approach advocated in this book is of an explanatory and comprehensive nature. It aims at providing an understanding of the different ways culture influences the negotiation process. Clearly it is useful to carry on with existing approaches, even as it is necessary to elaborate new approaches both to theory and to methodology.

Ting-Toomey (1985), borrowing from Hall (1976), develops an approach focusing on the cultural context to explain variation in conflict resolution styles. Members of low versus high context cultures (the former implementing preferably implicit communication, affective rhetoric, and indirect strategies, but the latter eliciting explicit messages, rational-factorial rhetoric, and open strategies) use different logic to deal with the conflict. Such a model contrasts cultures in a dichotomous way to illuminate each one through its opposition to the other. The ultimate purpose is no longer to achieve some kind of empirical classification but to suggest a universalist instrumental typology.

From the "mental programs" distinguished by Hofstede (1980), one could derive, with the help of some adequately selected variables, some rule valid under more specific conditions than organizational behavior—such as negotiation. A productive stance would be to shift from studying dimensions of culture to scrutinizing cultural variables expressed by negotiation practitioners. Focusing on differences could allow meaningful and coherent profiles. As a further step, this stance could be developed into a structural approach by way of relating the main cultural variables to one another.

Scientific Issues and Questions
for the Researcher

We believe that the chapters in this book have served to sharpen a research focus on the relationship between culture and the issues of structure, perception, and identity.

Culture and Structure

The debate over the role of culture in international negotiation has pivoted on the confrontation between two very different approaches: one emphasizing *structural* aspects as the key ingredient in defining negotiation and its context as a coherent system, and the other focusing on the essential influence of *cultural* aspects of interaction on observed behavior, where the objective is to use culture to grasp the causal elements that explain negotiation outcomes. In our cases reviewed, we already have presented our empirical understanding of the relationship between culture and structure. Let us now look more closely at their complex conceptual relations.

Structural and cultural approaches oppose each other on the precise point of their causal link. The borderline cases often selected to illustrate culture's overarching influence on the negotiation process are too often tautological: They allow researchers to find, at the end of their demonstration, exactly what they established at the outset as their premise. For instance, if researchers choose to examine a negotiation in which the different parties come from a single culture, the effects of culture are likely to be neutralized, while the effects of structural considerations surely will be accentuated. Similarly, researchers who choose a bilateral negotiation over a single issue within a slightly structured context, where people from strikingly different cultures have been brought together, likely will find support for the very cultural hypothesis with which they began. Thus it is easy enough to find support for one's pet structural or cultural hypotheses by selectively choosing the object of study. The cases presented here constitute a more complex mixture of all of these elements and hence pose a challenge to the researcher.

The reach and use of these two theoretical approaches differ appreciably. A cultural approach is mainly descriptive and interprets events a posteriori, whereas a structural approach allows the formulation of prescriptive aspects within an a priori perspective. These two approaches appear to be complementary because each takes charge of what could appear as an inherent weakness of the other. In fact, the two approaches are in some ways narrowly interconnected, for most of the constitutive elements of structure—for example, organizational modes of functioning, as well as the decision-making system—have some cultural origin. In the same way, cultural elements never unfold in a vacuum, but always according to the possibilities of expression provided by the existing structures.

The problem of which one comes first, which has initially produced the other, is a chicken-and-egg debate without definitive answer. Cultural and structural approaches vie over the important issue of determinism. Structural theory emphasizes a rationale borne of the interdependence among the different constitutive elements of a whole system—whatever its organizational, social, or economic nature. In turn, a cultural approach presupposes a kind of behavioral and cognitive programming of the individual. Building on the metaphor of a computer, this approach sees culture as software that frames and restricts opportunities for action. At the same time, if it is in the role of culture to provide the means of interpreting reality, to give meaning to one's own behavior and to understand that of others, each individual participant must be seen as belonging to several cultural subsystems—national/ethnic, professional, organizational, familial, and so on. Such multiculturality conveyed by a negotiator denies its deterministic aspects to the extent that each of the cultural subsystems can be proven to carry its own distinct or even diverging rationale.

Cultural and structural approaches also differ in their estimates of instrumentality. To the extent that individual agents are presumed to be the authors of their own choices, they are defined as free, defying the determinism mentioned above. This, of course, is an ideal-type model in the Weberian sense, for reality shows that the number of possible options is limited considerably by structural constraints and cultural imperatives. Negotiators can never totally free themselves from the structural particulars within which they have to act; to claim to do so is to risk falling into a world of fantasy that is subject to its own rules. Similarly, actors cannot reject the culture and values that give them the *raison d'être* and justification for their action. Thus, confronted with a structural theory or a theory of the autonomous actor, the cultural approach occupies a strong position and in no way could just refer to an overdetermined theory of subsidiarity.

Culture and Perception

One of the main effects of culture on negotiation concerns the actor's perception of the situation itself. Definition of the problem governs all of the actions to come. It allows or makes impossible any related solution. The reflexive approach suggested by Lowi and Rothman (Chapter 11) implies a common perception of the problem, and precisely such a perception makes it possible (at least in theory) to design a solution. Starting with actors carrying conflicting definitions of reality, it may be possible to reframe issues and underlying concerns in ways that help initiate a problem-solving process. One of the difficulties of such a task is that all logically possible reframings are not necessarily culturally acceptable.

Perception organizes itself from cultural lenses that cannot be modified at leisure. For instance, a study of the Japanese (Van Zandt, 1970) shows that they consider the French and the British to be the most polite, while Americans are the least polite. On the one hand, considered from an acultural viewpoint, politeness does not mean anything by itself. On the other hand, referring to national cultural norms, what offends a Japanese is not necessarily what displeases an American. What can be drawn from such an observation is that, in terms of problem-solving action, it is neither useful nor advisable to try to get each of the actors moving toward a common understanding of what constitutes polite behavior; rather each should try to help the other understand the meaning of their acts on a politeness dimension. Below we illustrate how failure to understand one's own cultural biases and stereotypes can create serous difficulties in negotiation.

At a minimum, one lesson to be drawn from the cases is that perceptions are an important determinant of the kinds of work that transpires in multicultural negotiations. The perceptual "baggage" that each of two or more sides brings with them to the table—in the form of stereotypic expectations about how negotiators from particular cultures are likely to behave—may overdetermine the very things that one sees. As the cases make clear, the very questions we are likely to pose—indeed, our very frame of reference—is influenced heavily by cultural perspective. Deng's rich analysis of the conflict between northern and southern Sudan (Chapter 7), imbued as it is with poetic images of the Nile and the symbolic meaning of the land—images central to the Dinka perspective of southern Sudan—surely would not have been written in the same way by a resident of the Muslim north. And when Slim (Chapter 10) writes, "The Turks deliberately fomented hatred between the ethnic groups that co-existed in the provinces they ruled," it is fair to wonder whether a Turkish analyst would have seen things in the same way as the author, who is Lebanese. In short, *we are each prisoners of our culture. The questions we ask, the things we notice, even our capacity as analysts to examine certain features while overlooking others are determined in large part by the forces of culture.*

Layered on top of our own respective cultural origins and biases is a tendency to carry different expectations with us as we enter into negotiation with people from other cultures. These expectations, in turn, can set in play powerful psychological forces that may, via the phenomenon of self-fulfilling prophecy, bring about confirmation of our expectations.

All decision makers, whether they are negotiators or not, probably find it useful to fall back on stereotypic perceptions in their dealings with others. Such stereotypes help simplify an otherwise overwhelmingly complex environment, to sort a continuum of colors into more easily understood blacks and whites. Stereotypes, however, also deprive perceivers of the true richness and diversity of the social world, while depriving the objects of stereotyping of their individuality. As perceivers, we remain aware of our own individuality, while the objects of our stereotypes are regarded as "exemplars" of some broader culture, rather than as individuals.

The cases in this book document the fact that we enter into negotiation with stereotypic perceptions and expectations of people from different cultures. To illustrate the consequences of such stereotypic perceptions, consider a simple illustration. Suppose negotiators begin with the view that people from Culture A tend to be fair-minded in their approach to the settlement of conflict, while negotiators from Culture B are rather sneaky, manipulative, and untrustworthy. Notice how differently we are likely to perceive and react to identical behavior by a Culture A negotiator and a Culture B negotiator. Suppose that, in the course of a negotiation, our counterpart makes a concession and asks us to do likewise. Issuing from the mouth of the Culture A negotiator, such a request is likely to lead us to conclude that it is only fair that we reciprocate the other's concession with one of our own; fairness begets fairness. The same concession, however, when advanced by the Culture B negotiator, almost certainly will lead us to conclude that he or she is trying to deceive us, to soften us up, to lead us to behave in some weak or foolish way, and that therefore we should respond, not with a concession of our own, but with stiffening resolve (intransigence).

Suppose instead that our counterpart digs in at some point and refuses to budge. This is precisely what we would expect the Culture B negotiator to do, and, given such behavior, we are likely to dig in ourselves and avoid the possibility of being bullied by the other. The same intransigence, however, when displayed by the Culture A negotiator, may cause us to think that our fair and trustworthy counterpart simply has gone as far as he or she can go and that the other's intransigence must mean that a bottom line has been reached; hence, if agreement is to be concluded, we likely will have to be the ones to make further concessions.

The other negotiator's behavior is identical in this illustration. It is the perceiver's own expectations that are strikingly different. Such differentiating perceptions, in turn, may create the very behavior we anticipate. If I believe you are untrustworthy, I am likely to respond both to your concessions and to your intransigence with intransigence of my own, leading you to dig in and creating the very enemy I hypothesize to exist. If I believe you to be fundamentally fair-minded and therefore respond to both your concessions and your intransigence with concessions of my own, then you are likely to behave in more cordial ways, confirming my "prophecy" (see Breslin, 1989; Pruitt & Rubin, 1986; Rubin & Sander, 1991).

Culture and Identity

Cultural difficulties involving group identity can present almost insurmountable obstacles to negotiators, as shown by some of the cases analyzed in Part II. Witness the conflict over the Jonglei Canal project on the Nile (Chapter 7). This project, "associated with the problems of North-South dualistic, Arab-African, Muslim-Christian-Animist Sudan," led the parties to the conflict to fight an "identity war" over the very survival of two very different cultures. Similarly, in the Euphrates case (Chapter 10), Slim describes the identity struggle between the secular culture of modern-day Turkey and the Muslim-Arab culture of Syria and Iraq, as well as the intense struggle for supremacy (again, largely organized around issues of culture) between the very similar cultures of Syria and Iraq. Finally the Jordan case (Chapter 11) points to the symbolic importance of both the Jordan and "the land" for both Arabs and Jews and, underlying that, the deeply held and shared concerns of both cultures about security and legitimacy—indeed, the very essence of survival.

Identity in these three cases, more than in the three others, is the crucial element; negotiators who go against the values of their own culture see themselves as disqualified and cannot lay themselves open to such consequences. Betraying the elements that comprise one's identity is a denial of oneself and denies one's existence at a symbolic level. When identity is built not only by difference but also through opposition to one or another social group, any change likely to improve the conditions for a real negotiation appears especially difficult to implement. Identity management is probably the most difficult challenge to meet among the main tasks concerning international negotiation.

Any social process contributes to the making of an identity. Paul Valery, French poet, wrote: "Born as several, I die as one," expressing the idea that life had transformed potentiality into a unique identity. Thus what is involved in any social process is the produced identity, which can be supported, challenged, or denied during negotiation. Difficult to grasp, even more difficult to manipulate, identity aspects are an essential stake within the dynamics of negotiations, particularly those fraught with conflict.

Closing the Circle

Early in this book, four analysts were asked to respond to the question: Does culture make a difference in international negotiation? Now, at the book's conclusion, and informed by the six case analyses, let us return to these four chapters and place them in context.

Easily the most provocative of these chapters is the one by Zartman (Chapter 2). It is Zartman, after all, who has issued this challenge: "Culture is . . . every bit as relevant . . . [to an understanding of the negotiation process] . . . as breakfast." He goes on to assert that culture is tautological, vaguely measured, epiphenomenal, and ultimately known only for its negative effects. We respond to each of these charges, in turn, relying whenever possible on the words of the other authors.

In arguing that culture is a tautological concept, Zartman offers the following illustration: "Social structure is claimed to determine culture, but social structure is a cultural trait and hence determined by culture, of which it is a part." Like other critics of cultural formulations, Zartman is confusing tautology with complexity and dynamism. If nothing else, the chapters in this book demonstrate that culture is a concept whose interactions with other concepts (e.g., structure) invariably are intertwined and often very difficult to unravel. As Faure and Sjöstedt point out in Chapter 1, "culture . . . is both a product and a source." It is both a dependent variable, reflecting the impact of diverse considerations, and an independent variable, with determining effects on negotiating behavior and outcomes. For the researcher who wishes to embark on a research enterprise that leads along a straight and narrow conceptual line from start to finish, culture is clearly an area to avoid. But for the researcher who is willing to seek out continua rather than dichotomies, circles rather than lines, multiple sources of conceptual interconnection rather than single causal arrows, then the domain of culture is rich indeed. Culture is a woefully complex, maddeningly dynamic phenomenon that does not lend itself easily to causal analysis. But it is also a richly rewarding area to pursue.

The assertion that culture is a tautological concept, we believe, pivots on the consideration of culture's causal role in relation to other types of causation. One of the contributions of this book is to show that cultural issues relate to problems of different kinds: communication, perception, identity. As long as the cultural aspects influencing negotiation only concern communication, the resulting difficulties can be reasonably overcome; that has been shown in the very many studies made in the domain of intercultural communication. On the other hand, when what is at stake are perceptions, concerning either the nature of the negotiation or the actors, these perceptions produce distortions that are harder to correct, and classical techniques to classify and improve communication have only a minor effect. When the stakes involve the very identity of the actor, the cases presented here tend to prove that such an issue belongs to a very specific domain that cannot be subsumed under communication approaches, but refers to the structure of the subject within the very process of negotiation.

Such a classification according to the scope of the cultural intervention allows the formulation of hypotheses on its role importance compared to other types of causation. When it is a matter of communication, what is provided is a combination among culture, structure, and actors' interests. When it is a matter of perception, cultural aspects may, under specific circumstances, overdetermine other aspects; they are part of the very definition of the problem and of the action that is supposed to lead to its solution. When it is a matter of identity, it tends to become the unique problem in the sense that it overshadows all of the others and erects itself as the prerequisite. Future research might continue profitably along this track.

Zartman's second assertion is that culture is a vague concept, "drawing very little agreement among analysts" (see chapter 2, p. 19). We quite agree. There *has* been shockingly little consistency in cultural formulations over the years, and even less agreement among those few analysts who have bothered to examine the relationship between culture and negotiation. All the more reason, we would argue, to develop projects such as the present one, for scientific examination of the complex interconnections among the many facets of culture and the domain of international negotiation. That culture is a vague concept is not a reason to abandon it, but to improve it.

If, as Edouard Herriot observed (cited by Faure & Sjöstedt in Chapter 1), "culture . . . is what remains when one has forgotten everything," the task of understanding and/or measuring culture is incredibly difficult. This is not a reason to give up the quest, but to pursue the understanding of culture with more vigor than ever. To do so requires framing questions in ways that can be answered (e.g., not does culture matter, but how and under what special conditions). It also requires, not confounding the inquiry, as when Zartman writes: "African culture is what Africans (or whoever) do, and they do it because they are Africans (or whoever)." African culture is considerably more than what Africans *do* (as the cases in this book have made abundantly clear); moreover, the things Africans do result from causes other than merely being African.

Zartman's third charge is that of "epiphenomenology," the idea that culture's contribution to the understanding of negotiation is derivative of other, more basic processes. He argues persuasively that negotiation outcomes are heavily determined by considerations other than culture, notably a host of structural and process variables. Again we entirely agree. Culture's effect on negotiation is subtle and easily explained away in terms of other, more prominent and noisy considerations. This subtlety, however, does not eliminate the importance of culture, nor does it relegate the concept to secondary or derivative status. Zartman's assertion that "culture is to negotiation what birds flying into engines are to flying airplanes . . . practical impediments that need to be taken into account (and avoided) once the basic process is fully understood and implemented" trivializes as a nuisance variable a broad and worthy area of study. Negotiating outcomes are influenced not only by a rich array of structural and process considerations but also by individual differences in personality and style and by broader cultural variations. Moroccans *are* different from the French, Thais *are* different from Malaysians, and these differences should not be minimized or ignored. Rather they should become the object of intellectual inquiry, deepening knowledge, and eventual action.

Finally, like other critics of culture's conceptual importance, Zartman argues that culture is known exclusively for its negative effects; that is, culture is used to explain negotiation failures, but rarely, if ever, finds use as an explanation for negotiation success. He is partially right, we believe, for culture too often *has* been used to explain away negotiating failures. As other contributors to the book have observed, however, culture also can be used to explain negotiation successes. Moreover, culture can be used to make such negotiation successes more likely.

In Chapter 3, Cohen provides a good illustration of the ways cultural similarity or dissimilarity can make compatible interaction (and, by extension, successful negotiation) more likely. The negotiations over Rhine pollution (Chapter 8) provide an example of largely similar cultures that have succeeded in working well together. Illustrations of largely dissimilar cultures that have succeeded in working well together can be found in the Black Sea case (Chapter 9), also in Strazar's (1981) analysis of negotiations between Japan and the United States at the San Francisco Conference of 1951. To be sure, culture can be used to explain negotiation failures, but as these illustrations are meant to document, it can also help account for negotiation success.[2]

Other contributors to the book have pointed to some of the other ways culture can assist in reaching negotiated agreements. Both Lang (Chapter 4) and Kremenyuk (Chapter 5), as well as Zartman and Berman (1982), point to the emergence of a cadre of professional negotiators who are developing a special culture of their own. As characterized by Lang, the professional negotiator's culture embodies a sense of accommodation, awareness of the importance of good communication, flexibility and creativity, willingness to transcend issues of national character, and the prioritizing of issues of dispute prevention. Kremenyuk, similarly, calls for the importance of developing a "universal" negotiating culture, to include a universal code of conduct. Both of these analysts point correctly to the importance, in a world of growing interdependence, of developing a special culture of negotiation and of using the norms of this professional culture as a lever to make negotiation success more likely.

Cohen (Chapter 3) develops a somewhat different, but compatible, perspective on culture's positive contribution to negotiation. He points to the desirability of developing a cadre of what he calls Model C negotiators, a group of culturally sensitive actors who "do not naively assume that underneath we are all the same." These are negotiators who have been socialized to understand the importance of cultural dimensions, to be sensitive to conflict nuances, and to be able to read between the lines.

But it is left to Lowi and Rothman (Chapter 11), in their analysis of the chronic conflict between Palestinians and Israelis over the Jordan River, to provide the sharpest retort to the criticism that culture is only of value in explaining and predicting negotiation failure. Culture, they observe "is a highly reflexive phenomenon . . . where one stands and who one is— one's context, identity, cultural norms, values, priorities—influences what one sees, how one perceives and interprets events and invests them with meaning." Such reflexivity, in turn, can lead to constructive dialogue. The fact that both Palestinians and Israelis share a political and ideological culture that lays claim to the same land, leading to shared feelings of disenfranchisement, can, paradoxically, provide a bridge for meta-level understanding. Hearing that one's counterpart has similar identity concerns may, at least in theory, lead to a superordinate understanding and willingness to help. Viewed this way, the very forces that divide cultures (e.g., a shared focus on identity concerns) actually can offer a lever for conflict resolution by introducing the possibility of shared concern at a transcendent level.

The world, we are convinced, will continue to become a smaller, more interdependent place. In such a climate, the role of culture in the management of conflict through negotiation and other means should become and, we believe, *will* become an increasingly important part of the researcher's agenda. It is our hope that this book has helped give impetus to the development of this research and ideological agenda. The "solution" to the so-called "problem" posed by culture is neither to ignore nor to derogate it, but to understand it better. And in so doing, it is our conviction that the efficacy of negotiation as an instrument of international relations can be greatly enhanced.

Notes

1. We note in passing that too much of the research and writing on intercultural communication has regarded communication as an obstacle to effective exchange. On the basis of several of the chapters in this book, we believe communication also should be studied as a facilitator in framing the negotiation process. Witness the Rhine (Chapter 8) in this regard, as well as the ideology espoused on the Jordan (Chapter 11).

2. Provoked by Cohen's useful distinction between the effects on negotiation of similar versus dissimilar cultures, we note that this book provides no evidence in support of any clear causal relationship. Sometimes (witness the Rhine) cultural similarity contributes to negotiation success, but at other times (witness the Euphrates) similarity seems to get in the way. Cultural dissimilarity certainly can contribute to negotiation failure (witness the historical discord between Israelis and Egyptians, as described by Cohen in Chapter 4), but dissimilarity also can contribute to negotiation success (e.g., the U.S.-Japan negotiations).

References

Abu-Nimer, M. (1993). *Can Western conflict resolution approaches be adopted in a Middle Eastern context?* Unpublished manuscript, SAIS-WIN Group.

Adler, N. (1986). *International dimensions of organizational behavior.* Boston: Kent.

Akoun, A. (1989). *L'illusion sociale.* Paris: PUF.

Albin, C. (1991). Negotiating indivisible goods: The case of Jerusalem. *Jerusalem Journal of International Relations, 13*(1), 45-76.

Alier, A. (1990). *The southern Sudan: Too many agreements dishonored.* Exeter, UK: Ithaca.

Ali Mohamed, O. M. (1984). Conflict and cooperation in the Nile basin. In M. O. Beshir (Ed.), *The Nile valley countries: Continuity and change* (Vol. 2, pp. 2-3). Khartoum: Khartoum University Press.

Anand, R. P. (Ed.). (1981). *Cultural factors in international relations.* New Delhi: Abinhav.

Armstrong, R., Beseat, K., & Karanja-Diefomach, B. W. M., et al. (1979). *Socio-political aspects of the palaver in some African countries.* Paris: UNESCO.

Avruch, K., & Black, P. W. (1991). The culture question and conflict resolution. *Peace and Change, 16,* 22-45.

Axelrod, R. (1976). *Structure of decisions: The cognitive maps of political elites.* Princeton, NJ: Princeton University Press.

Azar, E. E. (1990). *The management of protracted social conflicts: Theory and cases.* Aldershot, UK: Dartmouth.

233

Babbitt, E., & McDonald, A. (1986). *Negotiations analysis as a tool in the management of international rivers.* Paper presented at the IIASA Workshop on the Management of International River Basin Conflicts, Laxenburg, Austria.

Barth, F. (Ed.). (1969). *Ethnic groups and boundaries: The social organization of culture difference.* Boston: Little, Brown.

Benedict, R. (1934). *Patterns of culture.* Boston: Houghton Mifflin.

Benvenisti, M. (1986). *Conflicts and contradictions.* New York: Random House.

Beshir, M. O. (1968). *The southern Sudan: Background to conflict.* London: C. Hurst.

Beshir, M. O. (1974). *The southern Sudan: From conflict to peace.* New York: Barnes & Noble.

Beshir, M. O. (Ed.). (1984). *The Nile valley countries: Continuity and change* (Sudanese Library Series, No. 12, Vol. 2). Khartoum: Khartoum University PRess.

Binnendijk, H. (Ed.). (1987). *National negotiating styles.* Washington, DC: Center for the Study of Foreign Affairs, Foreign Service Institute, U.S. Department of State.

Black, P. W., & Avruch, K. (1989). Some issues in thinking about culture and the resolution of conflict. *Humanity and Society, 13,* 187-194.

Blake, R., & Mouton, J. (1962). The intergroup dynamics of win-lose conflict and problem-solving collaboration in union-management relations. In M. Sherif (Ed.), *Intergroup relations and leadership* (pp. 94-140). New York: John Wiley.

Blaker, M. K. (1977a). *Japanese international negotiating style.* New York: Columbia University Press.

Blaker, M. K. (1977b). Probe, push, and panic: The Japanese tactical style in international negotiations. In R. A. Scalapino (Ed.), *The foreign policy of modern Japan* (pp. 55-101). Berkeley: University of California Press.

Bochner, S. (Ed.). (1981). *The mediating person: Bridges between cultures.* Boston: G. K. Hall.

Bokova, J. (1991). Bulgaria and ethnic tensions in the Balkans. *Mediterranean Quarterly, 2,* 88-98.

Braudel, F. (1969). *Ecrits sur l'Histoire.* Paris: Flammarion.

Brehmer, B., & Hammond, K. (1977). Cognitive factors in interpersonal conflict. In D. Druckman (Ed.), *Negotiations* (pp. 79-103). Beverly Hills, CA: Sage.

Breslin, J. W. (1989). Breaking away from subtle biases. *Negotiation Journal, 5,* 219-222.

British Broadcasting Corporation (BBC). (1964a, January 15). Arab press comment on the Arab summit conference. In *BBC: Summary of World Broadcasts: Part 4. The Middle East* (No. 1453, p. A/3). United Kingdom: Monitoring Service of the BBC.

British Broadcasting Corporation (BBC). (1964b, January 18). Statement on the Arab summit conference. In *BBC: Summary of World Broadcasts: Part 4. The Middle East* (No. 1456, p. A/1). United Kingdom: Monitoring Service of the BBC.

British Broadcasting Corporation (BBC). (1965, January 18). Egyptian comment on Israeli reactions. In *BBC: Summary of World Broadcasts: Part 4. The Middle East* (No. 1761, p. A/3). United Kingdom: Monitoring Service of the BBC.

British Broadcasting Corporation (BBC). (1967, May 27). Israeli comment on the crisis. In *BBC: Summary of World Broadcasts: Part 4. The Middle East* (No. 2476, p. A/12). United Kingdom: Monitoring Service of the BBC.

Burton, J. (1986). The history of international conflict resolution. In E. Azar & J. Burton (Eds.), *International conflict resolution: Theory and practice* (pp. 40-55). Boulder, CO: Lynne Reinner.

Carter, J. (1983). *Keeping faith: Memoirs of a president.* New York: Bantam.

Casse, P., & Deol, S. (1985). *Managing intercultural negotiations.* Yarmouth, ME: Intercultural Press.

Cohen, R. (1990). *Culture and conflict in Egyptian-Israeli relations: A dialogue of the deaf.* Bloomington: Indiana University Press.

Cohen, R. (1991). *Negotiating across cultures: Communication obstacles in international diplomacy.* Washington, DC: U.S. Institute of Peace Press.

Collins, R. O. (1985). The big ditch: The Jonglei Canal scheme. In M. W. Doly (Ed.), *Modernization in the Sudan* (pp. 136-137). New York: Lilian Barber.

Collins, R. O. (1990). *The waters of the Nile: Hydropolitics and the Jonglei Canal, 1900-1988.* Oxford, UK: Clarendon.

Deng, F. M. (1973). *Dynamics of identification: A basis for national integration in the Sudan.* Khartoum: Khartoum University Press.

Deng, F. M. (1978). *Africans of two worlds: The Dinka in the Afro-Arab Sudan.* New Haven, CT: Yale University Press.

Deng, F. M. (1980). *Dinka cosmology.* London: Ithaca.

Dennet, R., & Johnson, J. (Eds.). (1951). *Negotiating with the Russians.* New York: World Peace Foundation.

De-Reuck, A. (1990). A theory of conflict resolution by problem solving. In J. Burton & F. Dukes (Eds.), *Conflict: Readings in management and resolution.* New York: St. Martin's.

Destler, I. M., Sato, H., Clapp, P., & Fukuri, H. (1976). *Managing an alliance: The politics of U.S.-Japanese relations.* Washington, DC: Brookings Institution.

Druckman, D., Benton, A. A., Ali, F., & Bagur, J. S. (1975, September). Cultural differences in bargaining behavior. *Journal of Conflict Resolution, 3,* 413-452.

Dupont, C. (1993). The Rhine: A study of inland water negotiations. In G. Sjöstedt (Ed.), *International environmental negotiation* (pp. 135-148). Newbury Park, CA: Sage.

El-Affendi, A. (1991). *Turabi's revolution: Islam and power in the Sudan.* London: Seal.

El-Sammani, M. O. (1988). The Jonglei Canal: On the evolution of the project model. In M. K. M. Arou & B. Yongo-Buro (Eds.), *Conference on north-south relations since Addis Ababa* (p. 3). Khartoum: University of Khartoum, Institute of African and Asian Studies.

El-Semmani, M. O. (1984). *Jonglei Canal dynamics of planned change in the Twic area.* Khartoum: Khartoum University Press.

Elgström, O. (1990). Norms, culture, and cognitive patterns in foreign aid negotiations. *Negotiation Journal, 6,* 147-159.

Elgström, O. (1992). *Foreign aid negotiation: The Swedish-Tanzanian aid dialogue.* Aldershot,UK: Avebury.

Fang Zongdai. (1988a). The flood prevention function of the Three Gorges project: Disadvantages outweigh the advantages. *Chinese Geography and Environment, 1*(4), 66-80.

Fang Zongdai. (1988b). Flood prevention function: Qian Ning, Zhang Ren, and Chen Zhicong. *Chinese Geography and Environment, 1*(4), 26-65.

Fang Zongdai & Wang Shouzhong. (1988). Resettlement problem of the Three Gorges project. *Chinese Geography and Environment, 1*(4), 81-89.

Faure, G. O. (1991). Negotiating in the orient: Encounters in the Peshawar Bazaar. *Negotiation Journal, 7,* 279-290.

Fisher, G. (1979). *The cross-cultural dimension in international negotiation.* Washington, DC: Foreign Service Institute. (mimeo)

Fisher, G. (1980). *International negotiation: A cross-cultural perspective.* Chicago: Intercultural Press.

Fisher, G. (1988). *Mindsets.* Yarmouth, ME: Intercultural Press.

Fisher, R. (1986). The structure of negotiation: An alternative model. *Negotiation Journal, 2,* 233-235.

Fletcher, E. R. (1988, June 15). Egyptian ties: Tapping the potential. *Jerusalem Post,* p. 5.

Foreign relations of the United States, 1952-1954 (FRUS). (1986). Washington, DC: Government Printing Office.

Franklin, S. (1990, March 8). Turkey's water projects upset neighbors. *Chicago Tribune,* p. 28.

Glenn, E. S., Witmeyer, D., & Stevenson, K. A. (1977). Cultural styles of persuasion. *International Journal of Intercultural Relations, 1*(3), 52-65.

Graham, J. L. (1985). The influence of culture on the process of business negotiations. *Journal of International Business Studies, 16,* 81-96.

Grieco, J. M. (1988). Anarchy and the limits of cooperation: A realist critique of the newest liberal institutionalism. *International Organization, 42*(3), 486-507.

Gubser, P. (1983). *Jordan: Crossroads of Middle Eastern events.* Boulder, CO: Westview.

Gudykunst, W. B., & Kim, Y. Y. (1984). *Communicating with strangers: An approach to intercultural communication.* Reading, MA: Addison-Wesley.

Gulliver, P. H. (1979). *Disputes and negotiations: A cross-cultural perspective.* New York: Academic Press.

Haggard, S., & Simmons, B. (1987). Theories of international regimes. *International Organization, 41*(3), 491-515.

Hall, E. T. (1959). *The silent language.* Greenwich, CT: Fawcett.

Hall, E. T. (1966). *The hidden dimension.* Garden City, NY: Doubleday.

Hall, E. T. (1976). *Beyond culture.* Garden City, NY: Doubleday.

Halpern, N. (1992). Information flows and policy coordination in Chinese bureaucracy. In K. Lieberthal & D. M. Lampton (Eds.), *Bureaucracy, politics, and decision making in post-Mao China* (pp. 125-148). Berkeley: University of California Press.

Harding, H. (1982, October). From China with disdain. *Asian Survey,* pp. 934-958.

Harding, H. (1987). *China's second revolution.* Washington: Brookings Institution.

Helling, G. C. (1959). *A study of Turkish values by means of nationality stereotypes.* Unpublished doctoral dissertation, University of Minnesota.

Hertzberg, A. (1959). *The Zionist idea.* Garden City, NY: Doubleday.

Hofstede, G. (1980). *Culture's consequences: International differences in work-related values.* Beverly Hills, CA: Sage.

Hofstede, G. (1989). Cultural predictors of national negotiating styles. In F. Mautner-Markhof (Ed.), *Processes of international negotiations* (pp. 193-201). Boulder, CO: Westview.

Hong Qingyu. (1988). Review of the previous period's work on the Three Gorges project. *Chinese Geography and Environment, 1*(3), 14-36.

Hong Yung Lee. (1991). *From revolutionary cadres to party technocrats in Socialist China.* Berkeley: University of California Press.

Howell, P., Lock, N., & Cobb, S. (Eds.). (1988). *The Jonglei Canal: Impact and opportunity.* Cambridge, UK: Cambridge University Press.

Huang Yasheng. (1990, September). Web of interests and patterns of behavior of Chinese local economic bureaucracies and enterprises during reforms. *China Quarterly,* pp. 431-458.

Ibrahim, S. (1980). *Itijahat al-Ra'y al-Am al-Arabi Nahwa Mas'alat al-Wuhda.* Beirut: Merkaz Dirasat al-Wuhda al-Arabiya.

Iklé, F. C. (1987). *How nations negotiate.* New York: Harper & Row.

Inbar, M., & Maos, J. (1984). Water resource planning and development in the northern Jordan valley. *Water International, 9.*

International Commission for the Protection of the Rhine. *Yearly activity report.* Koblenz, Germany: ICPR.

Iriye, A. (1979). Culture and power: International relations as intercultural relations. *Diplomatic History, 3,* 115-128.

Jacobson, H., & Oksenberg, M. (1990). *China's participation in the IMF, the World Bank, and the GATT: Toward a global economic order.* Ann Arbor: University of Michigan.

Janosik, R. J. (1986). *Japanese and American bargaining behavior.* Unpublished manuscript.

Janosik, R. J. (1987). Rethinking the culture-negotiation link. *Negotiation Journal, 3,* 385-396.

Jensen, L. (1983). Soviet-American behavior in disarmament negotiations. In I. W. Zartman (Ed.), *The 50% solution* (pp. 288-321). New Haven, CT: Yale University Press.

Jervis, R. (1976). *Perception and misperception in international politics.* Princeton, NJ: Princeton University Press.

Kasfir, N. (1990). Peacemaking and social cleavages in Sudan. In J. V. Montville (Ed.), *Conflict and peacemaking in multiethnic societies* (pp. 363-387). Lexington, MA: D. C. Heath.

Kasper, D. M. (1988). *Holding over Tokyo: US-Japan air service negotiations* (Case #104, Pew Program in Case Teaching and Writing in International Affairs). Pittsburgh: University of Pittsburgh.

Kazuo, O. (1979). How the "Inscrutables" negotiate with the "inscrutables": Chinese negotiating tactics vis-à-vis the Japanese. *China Quarterly, 79,* 529-552.

Kelman, H. (1987). The political psychology of the Israeli-Palestinian conflict: How can we overcome the barriers to a negotiated solution? *Journal of Political Psychology, 8*(3), 347-363.

Kelman, H., & Cohen, S. (1976). The problem-solving workshop: A social psychological contribution to the resolution of international conflict. *Journal of Peace Research, 13,* 79-90.

Khoury, F. J. (1964, May). The US, the UN and the Jordan River issue. *Middle East Forum.*

Khuri, F. (1968, August). The etiquette of bargaining in the Middle East. *American Anthropologist, 4,* 698-706.

Kimmerling, B. (1983). *Zionism and territory.* Berkeley: University of California, Institute of International Studies.

Kimura, H. (1980). Soviet and Japanese negotiating behavior: The spring 1977 fisheries talks. *Orbis, 24,* 43-67.

Kimura, H. (1981). Soviet and Japanese negotiating behavior: The spring 1977 fisheries talks. In R. P. Anand (Ed.), *Cultural factors in international relations.* New Delhi: Abinhav.

Kluckhohn, C. (1951a). The study of culture. In D. Lerner & H. D. Lasswell (Eds.), *The policy sciences* (pp. 86-101). Stanford, CA: Stanford University Press.

Kluckhohn, C. (1951b). Value and value-orientation in the theory of action. In T. Parsons & E. Shils (Eds.), *Toward a general theory of action* (pp. 388-433). Cambridge, MA: Harvard University Press.

Kluckhohn F., & Strodbeck, F. L. (1961). *Variations in value-orientations.* Westport, CT: Greenwood.

Kokubun, R. (1986, March). The politics of foreign economic policy-making in China: The case of plant cancellations with Japan. *China Quarterly,* pp. 19-44.

Kolars, J. (1990). The course of water in the Arab Middle East. *American-Arab Affairs, 33,* 57-68.

Konikoff, A. (1946). *Transjordan: An economic survey.* Jerusalem: Economic Research Institute of the Jewish Agency for Palestine.

Korzenny, F., & Ting-Toomey, S. (Eds.). (1990). *Communicating for peace: Diplomacy and negotiation.* Newbury Park, CA: Sage.

Kovacs, G. (1986). *Decision support systems for managing large international rivers.* Paper presented at the IIASA Workshop on the Management of International River Basin Conflicts, Laxenburg, Austria.

Kremenyuk, V. A. (Ed.). (1991). *International negotiation: Analysis, approaches, issues.* San Francisco: Jossey-Bass.

Kroeber, A., & Kluckhohn, C. (1963). *Culture: A critical review of concepts and definitions.* New York: Random House.

Kunihiro, M. (1972). U.S.-Japan communications. In H. Rosovsky (Ed.), *Discord in the Pacific: Challenges to the Japanese-American alliance* (pp. 155-172). Washington, DC: Columbia.

Lall, A. (1968). *How Communist China negotiates.* New York: Columbia University Press.

Lampton, D. M. (1987). Chinese politics: The bargaining treadmill. *Issues and Studies, 23*(3), 11-14.

Lang, W. (1989a). Multilateral negotiations: The role of presiding officers. In F. Mautner-Markhof (Ed.), *Processes of international negotiations* (pp. 23-42). Boulder, CO: Westview.

Lang, W. (1989b). The Second Review Conference of the 1972 Biological Weapons Convention. In J. Kaufmann (Ed.), *Effective negotiation, case studies in conference diplomacy* (pp. 191-203). Dordrecht: Martinus Nijhoff.

Lang, W. (1991). Negotiations on the environment. In V. A. Kremenyuk (Ed.), *International negotiation: Analysis, approaches, issues* (pp. 343-356). San Francisco: Jossey-Bass.

Laqueur, W. (1972). *A history of Zionism.* New York: Schocken.

Lewin, K. (1948). *Resolving social conflicts.* New York: Harper & Row.

Lewis, B. (1968). *The emergence of modern Turkey.* Oxford, UK: Oxford University Press.

Li Cheng & White, L. (1990, March). Elite transformation and modern change in mainland China and Taiwan: Empirical data and the theory of technocracy. *China Quarterly,* pp. 1-35.

Lieberthal, K., & Oksenberg, M. (1988). *Policy makers in China: Leaders, structures, and processes.* Princeton, NJ: Princeton University Press.

Lieberthal, K., & Prahalad, C. K. (1989, March/April). Multinational corporate investment in China. *China Business Review.*

Lienhardt, G. (1961). *Divinity and experience: The religion of the Dinka.* Oxford, UK: Clarendon.

Lienhardt, G. (1963). The Dinka of the Nile basin. *The Listener, 69,* 828.

Lipschutz, R. D. (1989). *When nations clash: Raw materials, ideology and foreign policy.* Cambridge, MA: Ballinger.

Litterer, J., & Lewicki, R. (1985). *Negotiation.* Homewood, IL: Irwin.

Lord, B. (1990). *Legacies: A Chinese mosaic.* New York: Random House.

Loucks, D. P., & Salewicz, K. A. (1986). *Interactive modeling and conflict negotiation in water resources planning.* Paper presented at the IIASA Workshop on the Management of International River Basin Conflicts, Laxenburg, Austria.

Lowi, M. R. (1990). *The politics of water under conditions of scarcity and conflict: The Jordan River and riparian states.* Unpublished doctoral dissertation, Princeton University.

Lowi, M. R. (1992, September). West Bank water resources and the resolution of conflict in the Middle East. *Environmental Change and Acute Conflict* (American Academy of Arts and Sciences) Occasional Paper No. 1).

Lowi, M. R. (1993). *Water and power: The politics of a scarce resource in the Jordan River basin.* Cambridge, UK: Cambridge University Press.

Ludlow, N. (1980, May/June). Gezhouba on the Yangzi. *China Business Review,* pp. 11-15.

Manion, M. (1992). The behavior of middlemen in the cadre retirement process. In K. Lieberthal & D. M. Lampton (Eds.), *Bureaucracy, politics, and decision making in post-Mao China* (pp. 216-244). Berkeley: University of California Press.

Markarian, E. S. (1983). *Teoria culturi i sovremennaja nauka* [The theory of culture and modern science]. Moscow: Nauka.

Mawut, L. L. (1986). *The southern Sudan: Why back to arms.* Khartoum: St. George.

McDonald Jr., J. W. (1984). *How to be a delegate.* Washington, DC: Center for the Study of Foreign Affairs, Foreign Service Institute, U.S. Department of State.

Mermet, G. (1991). *Euroscopie.* Paris: Larousse.

Metcalf, H., & Urwick, L. (Eds.). (1940). *Dynamic administration: The collected papers of Mary Parker Follett.* New York: Harper.

Ministry of Foreign Affairs. (1973). *Peace and unity in the Sudan: An African achievement.* Khartoum: Khartoum University Press.

Mitrany, D. (1986). *A working peace system.* Chicago: Quadrangle. (Original published in 1943)

Moffett, G. D. (1990, March 13). Downstream fears feed tensions. *Christian Science Monitor,* p. 4.

Moran, R., & Stripp, W. (1991). *Successful international business negotiations.* Houston: Gulf.

Murphy, I. L. (1986). *The workshop in retrospect: An interpretive viewpoint.* Paper presented at the IIASA Workshop on the Management of International River Basin Conflicts, Laxenburg, Austria.

Murphy, I. L., & Sabadell, J. E. (1986). International river basins: A policy model for conflict resolution. *Resources Policy, 12,* 133-144.

Mushakoji, K. (1968). Negotiation between the West and the non-West. *Proceedings of the International Peace Research Association* (2nd conference, Vol. 1, pp. 208-231). Assen, The Netherlands: Koninlijke van Gorcum.

Mushakoji, K. (1972). The strategies of negotiation: An American-Japanese comparison. In J. A. Laponce & P. Smoker (Eds.), *Experimentation and simulation in political science* (pp. 109-131). Toronto: University of Toronto Press.

Nader, L., & Todd, Jr., J. (1978). *The disputing process.* New York: Columbia University Press.

Naff, T., & Matson, C. (1984). *Water in the Middle East: Conflict or cooperation?* Boulder, CO: Westview.

Nathan, A. (1985). *Chinese democracy.* Berkeley: University of California Press.

National Archives of the State of Israel (INA). (1953). Foreign Ministry documents (record group 93, box 360, file 6).

National Archives of the State of Israel (INA). (1955). (box 3688, file 10).

New Encyclopedia Britannica, Ready Reference (Vol. 3). (1990). Chicago: Encyclopedia Britannica.

Nicolson, H. (1954). *The evolution of diplomatic method.* London: Constable.

Nicolson, H. (1964). *Diplomacy.* New York: Oxford University Press.

Osgood, C. E. (1962). *An alternative to war or surrender.* Urbana: University of Illinois Press.

Parsons, T., & Shils, E. (Eds.). (1951). *Toward a general theory of action.* Cambridge, MA: Harvard University Press.

Plantey, A. (1982). A cultural approach to international negotiation. *International Social Science Journal, 93,* 535-543.

Poortinga, Y. H., & Hendriks, E. C. (1989). Culture as a factor in international negotiations: A proposed research project from a psychological perspective. In F. Mautner-Markhof (Ed.), *Processes of international negotiations* (pp. 203-212). Boulder, CO: Westview.

Posses, F. (1978). *The art of international negotiation.* London: Business Press.

Pruitt, D. G. (1981). *Negotiation behavior.* New York: Academic Press.

Pruitt, D. G., & Rubin, J. Z. (1986). *Social conflict: Escalation, stalemate, and settlement.* New York: Random House.

Pye, L. (1982). *Chinese commercial negotiating style.* Cambridge, MA: Oelgeschlager, Gunn, & Hain.

Reed, C. (1987, June 25). Irrigation and power program will transpose southeastern Turkey; Plans include 15 dams and 18 hydroelectric plants. *Engineering News-Record,* p. 28.

Rhin actualité. (Sept. 90, May 1990, April 1991). Koblenz: ICPR.

Robbins, P. (1991). *Turkey and the Middle East.* New York: Council on Foreign Relations Press.

Roberts, W. D. (1948). *The Sudan government and irrigation projects on the Upper Nile.*

Rodinson, M. (1981). *The Arabs.* London: Croom Helm.

Rothman, J. (1989, July). Supplementing tradition: A theoretical and practical typology for international conflict management. *Negotiation Journal,* pp. 265-277.

Rothman, J. (1991). Conflict research and resolution: Cyprus. *Annals of American Political and Social Science, 518,* 95-108.

Rothman, J. (1992). *From confrontation to cooperation: Resolving ethnic and regional conflict.* Newbury Park, CA: Sage.

Rubin, J. Z., & Brown, B. (1975). *The social psychology of bargaining and negotiation.* New York: Academic Press.

Rubin, J. Z., & Sander, F. E. A. (1991). Culture, negotiation, and the eye of the beholder. *Negotiation Journal, 7,* 249-254.

Ruchay, D. (1990). *Inland water case study: Negotiation on the Rhine.* Laxenburg, Austria: IIASA. (mimeo)

Said, E. (1980). *The question of Palestine.* New York: Vintage.

Salacuse, J. W. (1991). *Making global deals: Negotiating in the international market place.* Boston: Houghton Mufflin.

Sanderson, L. P., & Sanderson, N. (1981). *Education, religion and politics in southern Sudan: 1899-1961.* London: Ithaca.

Sawyer, J., & Guetzkow, J. (1965). Bargaining and negotiation in international relations. In H. C. Kelman (Ed.), *International behavior: A social-psychological analysis* (pp. 466-520). New York: Holt, Rinehart & Winston.

Sayigh, R. (1979). *Palestinians: From peasants to revolutionaries.* London: Zed.

Schelling, T. C. (1960). *The strategy of conflict.* Cambridge, MA: Harvard University Press.

Scudder, T. (1990). Victims of development revisited: The political costs of river basin development. *Bulletin of the Institute for Development Anthropology, 8,* 1-5.

Scudder, T. (1991). *Culture and negotiation: An introductory chapter.* Laxenburg: IIASA. (mimeographed)

Singer, M. R. (1987). *Intercultural communication: A perceptual approach.* Englewood Cliffs, NJ: Prentice-Hall.

Smith, R. F. (1989). *Negotiating with the Soviets.* Bloomington: Indiana University Press.

Snyder, G., & Diesing, P. (1977). *Conflict among nations.* Princeton, NJ: Princeton University Press.

Solanes, M. (1986). *The United Nations role in promoting and fostering cooperation in the field of international water resources.* Paper presented at the IIASA Workshop on the Management of International River Basin Conflicts, Laxenburg, Austria.

Soviet-diplomacy and negotiating behavior: Emerging new context for US diplomacy. (1979). Study prepared by the Senior Specialists Division, Congressional Research Service, Library of Congress, Committee on Foreign Affairs, US Senate. Washington, DC: Government Printing Office.

Stening, B. W. (1979). Problems in cross-cultural contact: A literature review. *International Journal of Intercultural Relations, 3,* 269-313.

Stoetzel, J. (1983). *Les valeurs du temps présent: Une enquête européene.* [The values of the present time: A European survey]. Paris: PUF.

Strand, D. (1990, May/June). Protest in Beijing: Civil society and the public sphere. *Problems of Communism,* pp. 1-16.

Strazar, M. D. (1981). The San Francisco Peace Treaty: Cross-cultural elements in the interaction between the Americans and the Japanese. In R. P. Anand (Ed.), *Cultural factors in international relations* (pp. 63-76). New Delhi: Abinhav.

Sunshine, R. (1990). *Negotiating for international development: A practitioner's handbook.* Dordrecht: Martinus Nijhoff.

Ting-Toomey, S. (1985). Toward a theory of conflict and culture. In W. B. Gudykunst, P. Steward, & S. Ting-Toomey (Eds.), *Communication, culture, and organizational processes* (pp. 71-86). Beverly Hills, CA: Sage.

Tylor, E. H. (1958). *Primitive culture.* New York: Harper & Row. (Original work published 1871)

United States National Archives (USNA). (1952). 684a.85322/9-1852.

United States National Archives (USNA). (1953). 684a.85322/10-63.

United States National Archives (USNA). (1954). 683.84a322/1-1554.

Van Zandt, H. F. (1970). How to negotiate in Japan. *Harvard Business Review, 48,* 45-56.

Visorsky, A. F. (1979). *Chernoe more. Mejdunarodno-pravovie voprosi* [Black Sea: International and legal issues]. Kiev: Naukova Dumka.

Vlachos, E. (1986a). *The challenges of transboundary river basins.* Paper presented at the IIASA Workshop on the Management of International River Basin Conflicts, Laxenburg, Austria.

Vlachos, E. (1986b). *A selected bibliography on transboundary river basin conflicts.* Paper presented at the IIASA Workshop on the Management of International River Basin Conflicts, Laxenburg, Austria.

Vlachos, E. (1986c). *Some key findings of the workshop.* Paper presented at the IIASA Workshop on the Management of International River Basin Conflicts, Laxenburg, Austria.

Wai, D. M. (1981). *The African-Arab conflict in the Sudan.* London: African Publishing.

Walder, A. (1989, June). Factory and manager in an era of reform. *China Quarterly,* pp. 242-264.

Walder, A. (1991). Local bargaining relationships and urban industrial finance. In K. Lieberthal & D. M. Lampton (Eds.), *Bureaucracy, politics, and decision making in post-Mao China* (pp. 308-333). Berkeley: University of California Press.

Wang, J-H. (1981). Some cultural factors affecting Chinese in treaty negotiation. In R. P. Anand (Ed.), *Cultural factors in international relations* (pp. 97-112). New Delhi: Abinhav.

Wang Jiazhu. (1988). The Three Gorges project needs exactly how much investment? *Chinese Geography and Environment, 1*(4), 101-111.

Weiss, S. E., & Stripp, W. (1985a). *Negotiating with foreign business persons: An introduction for Americans with propositions on six cultures* (Working Paper No. 1). New York: New York University Faculty of Business Administration.

Weiss, S. E., & Stripp, W. (1985b). *Negotiating with foreign persons.* New York: New York University Press.

Whelan, J. (1988). *Soviet diplomacy and negotiating behavior* (Vol. 1). Washington, DC: Government Printing Office.

Whelan, J. (1991). *Soviet diplomacy and negotiating behavior* (Vol. 2.). Washington, DC: Government Printing Office.

White, R. K. (1977). Misperceptions in the Arab-Israeli conflict. *Journal of Social Issues,*
    33(1), 190-221.
Williams, N. B. (1990, January 14). Parched Iraq, Syria jittery as Turks divert Euphrates to
    power project. *The Los Angeles Times,* p. 8.
Ya'acobi, G. (1989). *On the razor's edge.* Tel Aviv: Edanim.
Young, K. (1968). *Negotiating with the Chinese communists.* New York: McGraw-Hill.
Zaman, A. (1990, January 15). Iraq concern at damming of Euphrates. *The Daily Telegraph,*
    p. 9.
Zartman, I. W., & Berman, M. (1982). *The practical negotiator.* New Haven, CT: Yale
    University Press.

Index

243

About the Contributors

Raymond Cohen, Ph.D., is Professor of International Relations in the Department of International Relations, Hebrew University of Jerusalem, Israel. His interest in the influence of intercultural factors on communication and negotiation was aroused by living in the Middle East and following the Arab-Israeli conflict over many years. His book *Culture and Conflict in Egyptian-Israeli Relations: A Dialogue of the Deaf* was a result of this observation. His general introduction to the topic, *Negotiating Across Cultures: Communication Obstacles in International Diplomacy,* was written while he was a Peace Fellow in the Jennings Randolph Program of the United States Institute of Peace, 1988-1989.

Francis M. Deng, Ph.D., is a Senior Fellow at the Brookings Institution in Washington, DC. He is a former Ambassador from the Sudan to the United States, Scandinavia, and Canada and was Sudanese Minister of State for Foreign Affairs from 1976 to 1979. His doctorate is in Juridical Science from Yale University. He has written extensively on law, anthropology, politics, oral history, and folklore in the Sudan and is also the author of two novels.

Christophe Dupont is Director of the "Negotiation Laboratory" at the Business School of Lille, France; he is also a consultant at CRC Conseils Associés, Jouy-en-Josas, France. He is the author of *La Négociation: Conduite, Théorie, Applications* and co-author of several books and articles on negotiation.

Guy Olivier Faure is Associate Professor of Sociology at the Sorbonne University, Paris, where he teaches international negotiation. His major research interests are in business negotiations, especially with China and Asian countries, focusing on strategies and cultural issues. He also is concerned with developing interdisciplinary approaches. Among his latest publications are the following co-authored books: *International Negotiation: Analysis, Approaches, Issues* (V. Kremenyuk, Ed.), *Processes of International Negotiations* (F. Mautner-Markhof, Ed.), *Evolutionary Systems Design: Policy-Making Under Complexity* (M. Shakun, Ed.), *Conflits et Negociations dans le Commerce International: L'Uruguay Round* (Messerlin and Vellas, Eds.), and *International Environmental Negotiations* (G. Sjöstedt, Ed.).

Victor A. Kremenyuk is Deputy Director at the Institute for U.S.A. and Canada Studies, Russian Academy of Sciences in Moscow. His areas of interest are international conflict resolution, crisis management, foreign policy, and the negotiation process. He has published more than 100 works in Russian and other languages and, most recently, edited a state-of-the-art compendium sponsored by IIASA entitled *International Negotiation: Analysis, Approaches, Issues.* His contributions include "Processes of International Negotiation" (F. Mautner-Markhof, Ed.), "Windows of Opportunity" (G. Allison, W. Ury, and B. Allyn, Eds.), and "Cold War as Cooperation" (R. Kanet and E. Kolodziej, Eds.). He is IIASA Research Associate.

Winfried Lang is an Austrian career diplomat and Professor of International Law and International Relations at the University of Vienna and Austria's Ambassador to International Organizations in Geneva. He chaired the OECD Transfrontier Pollution Group (1977 to 1982) and presided over UN conferences on the protection of the ozone layer (1985), on biological and bacteriological weapons (1986), and on substances that deplete the ozone layer (1987). He has published several books and articles on integration policy, protection of the environment, international negotiations, neutrality, and the law of treaties.

Kenneth Lieberthal holds a B.A. from Dartmouth College and a Ph.D. from Columbia University. He has been Professor of Political Science at the University of Michigan since 1983. His recent work concentrates on policy process in the People's Republic of China and includes the following publications: *Inter alia, Policy Making in China* (with Michel Oksenberg) and *Bureaucracy, Politics, and Policy Making in Post Mao China* (with David Lampton).

Miriam Lowi, Ph.D., ia a Visiting Fellow at the Center for Energy and Environmental Studies at Princeton University. She has taught at the Woodrow Wilson School, as well as in the Departments of Politics and of Near Eastern Studies at Princeton. She is a member of the International Peace Research Association, Commission on Peace-Building in the Middle East. Currently her book, *Water and Power: The Politics of a Scarce Resource in the Jordan River Basin,* is in press at Cambridge University Press.

Vladimir Pisarev is a Senior Research Fellow at the Institute for U.S.A. and Canada Studies, Russian Academy of Sciences in Moscow. He holds a doctorate in history and has focused research attention on analyzing the marine policies of the United States. His recent work on ecology and tourism was presented to the 1990 CSCE meeting on the Mediterranean.

Jay Rothman, Ph.D., is Director of the Conflict Resolution Program at The Leonard Davis Institute for International Relations, The Hebrew University of Jerusalem. He also spends half the year as Visiting Assistant Professor in the Department of Political Science, Haverford and Bryn Mawr Colleges. He authored *From Confrontation to Cooperation: Resolving Ethnic and Regional Conflict.*

Jeffrey Z. Rubin is Professor of Psychology at Tufts University, Senior Fellow at the Program on Negotiation at Harvard Law School, and Adjunct Professor of Diplomacy, Fletcher School of Law and Diplomacy, Tufts University. He is the author, coauthor, or editor of more than a dozen books and numerous articles on interpersonal and international conflict and negotiation, as well as on the role of third-party intervention in the dispute settlement process. His recent books include *Social Conflict: Escalation, Stalemate, and Settlement* (with D. Pruitt), *Leadership and Negotiation in the Middle East* (with B. Kellerman), *When Families Fight* (with C. Rubin), and *Negotiation Theory and Practice* (with J. W. Breslin).

Jeswald W. Salacuse is Dean and Henry J. Baker Professor of Commercial Law, The Fletcher School of Law and Diplomacy, Tufts University.

He is the author of *Making Global Deals: Negotiating in the International Market Place*, his most recent book.

Gunnar Sjöstedt is Senior Research Fellow at the Swedish Institute of International Affairs and also Associate Professor of Political Science at the University of Stockholm. His research work is concerned with processes of international cooperation and consultations in which negotiations represent an important element. He has studied the OECD as a communication system and the external role of the European community, and is currently working on a project dealing with the transformation of the international trade regime incorporated in GATT and its external relations.

Randa M. Slim, Ph.D., is a political psychologist currently serving as Program Officer at the Kettering Foundation in Dayton, Ohio. Previously she was a Visiting Adjunct Professor at the American University of Beirut. Her work focuses on the theory and practice of supplemental diplomacy, through a series of unofficial dialogues that bring American citizens together with Soviet, Chinese, and South American citizens to explore issues of common concern; the processes of conflict analysis and conflict resolution; the role of justice rules in intergroup behavior; and processes of citizen participation in political decision making.

I. William Zartman is Jacob Blaustein Professor of Conflict Resolution and International Organization at the Nitze School of Advanced International Studies (SAIS) of The John Hopkins University. He is the author of *The 50% Solution, The Negotiation Process,* and *Positive Sum,* among other books. He is organizer of the Washington Interest in Negotiations (WIN) Group and director of the Conflict Reduction in Regional Conflicts (CRIRC) Project conducted by SAIS and the Institute for U.S.A. and Canada Studies in Moscow.